Logic 301

DIL

International Library of Psychology
Philosophy and Scientific Method

LOGICAL STUDIES

International Library of Psychology
Philosophy and Scientific Method

GENERAL EDITOR—C. K. OGDEN, M.A. (*Magdalene College, Cambridge*)

*Asterisks denote that other books by the same author are included in this series.
A complete list will be found at the end of the volume.*

LOGICAL STUDIES

by

GEORG HENRIK VON WRIGHT

LONDON
ROUTLEDGE AND KEGAN PAUL

First published in 1957
© *by Routledge & Kegan Paul Ltd.*
Broadway House
68–74 Carter Lane
London, E.C.4

Printed in Great Britain
by W. & J. Mackay & Co. Ltd.
Chatham

TABLE OF CONTENTS

v

PREFACE

IN this volume eight essays are included. Five of them had been published before. None of the five, however, is reprinted without alterations or additions.

The first three essays deal with the problem of *logical truth*. Their aim is to elucidate what is meant by saying that logical truth is formal—dependent of form and independent of content—or that logical truth is tautologous. The results achieved are hardly novel. In the course of the discussion some methods (distributive normal forms) are developed, which yield a solution to some cases of the so-called decision problem of the predicate calculus.

'Form and Content in Logic', Cambridge 1949 is reprinted with the permission of the Syndics of the Cambridge University Press. Two Appendices have been added. 'On the Idea of Logical Truth (I)' was first published in *Societas Scientiarum Fennica, Commentationes Physico-Mathematicae* XIV **4**, 1948 and 'On Double Quantification' in the same series Vol. XVI **3**, 1952.

It was the study of distributive normal forms that awakened my interest in modality. The next three essays are in the field of *modal logic*. It is one of the attractions of this comparatively undeveloped branch of logical theory that it has applications in a variety of highly divergent directions. One such application is to the study of processes in nature which are in a characteristic sense additive or linear. Another application is to the logical study of norms (normative discourse). This latter study is important to ethics and the philosophy of law. But it must be pursued with much more refinement than in my first paper (here republished) on deontic logic. Philosophically, I find this paper very unsatisfactory. For one thing, because it treats of norms as a kind of proposition which may be true or false. This, I think, is a mistake. Deontic logic gets part of its philosophic significance from the fact that norms and valuations, though removed from the realm of truth, yet are subject to logical law. This shows that logic, so to speak, has a wider reach than truth.

It was always thought that modality is akin to probability.

Yet it was a surprise to me, when I first noted that a modal logic could be constructed which contains an analogue to the multiplication principle of probability theory. This 'new' modal logic differs from 'classical' modal logic in that it treats modality as a relative and not as an absolute notion—a distinction of which the germ may be found in Aristotle's distinction between modality (necessity) ἐξ ὑποθέσεως and ἁπλῶς. The logic of the relative modalities can, in a characteristic sense, be said to include the logic of the absolute modalities as a limiting case. Probability theory again may be regarded as a metric extension of this new modal logic. I believe that it has interesting applications in the fields of axiology and deontology, which I hope to be able to study in future publications.

'Deontic Logic' was published in *Mind*, Vol. 60, N.S., 1951 and 'Interpretations of Modal Logic' in *Mind*, Vol. 61, N.S., 1952. They are reprinted with the permission of the Editor. A first version of 'A New System of Modal Logic' appeared in the *Proceedings of the XIth International Congress of Philosophy*, Vol 5, Amsterdam-Louvain, 1953. The present version is different and developed much more in detail.

Related to modal logic are the problems of the conditional (the if-then) and of entailment (logical consequence). Conditionality exhibits two aspects, rather different in nature. The first is a feature of intensionality which seems to be peculiar to all hypothetical asserting, knowing, and believing, and which explains why the if-then relation cannot be 'formalized' on a level with truth-functional *or* with modal notions. The second aspect discloses the problem of natural necessity which, in its turn, is closely related to the problem of the inductive ground.

The concept of entailment too, the discussion of which with C. I. Lewis was the very point from which modern research in modal logic started, seems to be out of the reach of a definition in terms of possibility, necessity, and truth-connectives. In the last essay in this volume, I try to show that in the logic of entailment *epistemic* notions enter. The concept of entailment is closely related to the concept of demonstrability. And the demonstrable is that which, by means of logic, we *may* come to *know*.

PREFACE

The essay on conditionals was, in more than one version, read and criticized by Dr. Rogers Albritton and the essay on the new modal logic by Mr. Peter Geach. I am much indebted to their assistance and criticism. I am also grateful to Dr. Casimir Lewy for the stimulus which discussions with him has provided to the development of my views of entailment.

Cambridge,
May 1956   GEORG HENRIK VON WRIGHT

FORM AND CONTENT IN LOGIC

(1949)

ONE of the main objects of the logicians' inquiries has traditionally been various provinces of what might be called logical truth.

The most ancient and best known example is Aristotle's theory of the syllogism. Let us say a few words about it.

An Aristotelian syllogism is, e.g. 'if all Europeans are white men and some Europeans are Mohammedans, then some white men are Mohammedans.'

The syllogism is an if-then-sentence.[1] The if-sentence consists in its turn of two sentences, viz. 'all Europeans are white men' and 'some Europeans are Mohammedans', joined by the word 'and'. They are called premisses. The then-sentence is called the conclusion.

The syllogism itself obviously expresses a true proposition. It expresses a true proposition, even if one or both of the premisses and the conclusion should happen to express false propositions. It might actually be the case that some Europeans are not white and that no Europeans nor any other white men are Mohammedans. But it nevertheless remains true that *if* all Europeans are white men and some are Mohammedans, *then* some white men are Mohammedans.

The words which occur in the syllogism can be divided into two groups.

The first group consists of words for which other words can be substituted without affecting the truth of the proposition expressed by the syllogism. We shall call them variable words. It is plain that the variables in our example are the words 'Europeans', 'white men', and 'Mohammedans'. We could also have said: 'If all x are y and some x are z, then some y are z' without saying what x and y and z mean.

[1]See Appendix III at the end of this paper.

The second group consists of words for which it is impossible to substitute other words without affecting the truth of the proposition expressed by the syllogism. We shall call these words (logical) constants. The constants in our example are the words 'if-then', 'all', 'are', 'and', and 'some'.

We shall say that the variables give to the syllogism its content, and that the constants give to it its form. Since the syllogism expresses a true proposition independently of the meaning of the variables, we shall say that the syllogism expresses truth because of its form and independently of its content.

From the point of view of truth the syllogism itself behaves differently from the premisses and the conclusion. Whether it is true or not that all x are y essentially depends upon what x and y mean. The premisses and the conclusion, unlike the syllogism, thus express truth or falsehood according to their content and not for reasons of form.

Similar remarks about truth and form and content apply to all valid Aristotelian syllogisms.

We shall say that a sentence, which expresses truth because of its form and independently of its content, expresses formal or logical truth.

The Stoics started investigations into another province of logical truth, which had not been systematically studied by Aristotle, and which, because of the predominance of the Aristotelian tradition, was not very much cultivated before the renaissance of logic in the second half of the nineteenth century.

An example from this province is provided by the following sentence: 'If there is thunder, if there is lightning, then there is not lightning, if there is not thunder.'

Like our syllogism, this sentence is an if-then-sentence. It consists itself of two conditional sentences, viz. 'there is thunder, if there is lightning' and 'there is not lightning, if there is not thunder'. The first conditional sentence consists in its turn of two sentences, viz. 'there is thunder' and 'there is lightning', joined by the word 'if'. The second conditional sentence again consists of the two sentences 'there is not lightning' and 'there is not thunder', joined by the word 'if'. But the sentence 'there is not lightning' consists of the sentence 'there is lightning', into which has been inserted the word 'not', and similarly the sentence 'there is not thunder' consists of the sentence 'there is thunder', into which has been inserted the word 'not'.

Like our syllogism, the if-then-sentence now under consideration obviously expresses a true proposition.[1] This proposition is true independently of whether it is true or not that there is thunder or lightning and also of whether it is true or not that there is thunder, *if* there is lightning, and of whether it is true or not that there is not lightning, *if* there is not thunder. As a matter of fact, there can be lightning without thunder. But it nevertheless remains true that *if* there is thunder, if there is lightning, *then* there is not lightning, if there is not thunder.

As in our syllogism, we can distinguish between variables and constants in the example which we are discussing.

The variables are those parts of the sentence for which we could substitute other fragments of language without affecting the truth of the proposition expressed by the if-then-sentence. It is plain that the variables here are the sentences 'there is thunder' and 'there is lightning'. We could also have said: 'If *x*, if *y*, then not *y*, if not *x*', without saying what *x* and *y* mean. The constants are the words 'if-then' and 'not'.

We might again say that the variables give to our sentence its content, and that the constants give to it its form, and also that the sentence expresses truth because of its form and independently of its content.

It was not till the middle of the nineteenth century that logicians became systematically interested in an important province of logical truth, of which the following sentence is an example: 'If somebody is teacher of somebody, then somebody is pupil of somebody.'

This sentence also obviously expresses a true proposition. It is plain that it has variable parts, i.e. contains words for which we could substitute other words without affecting the truth of what we say. It is further plain that the existence of variables has to do with the fact that we used teachers and pupils to

[1]This is not in contradiction with the account of conditionals, given in the seventh essay of the present volume. What is here called 'if-then-sentences' are material implication sentences. (1955)

illustrate something which would also be true of, say, parents and children.

On the other hand, the words 'teacher' and 'pupil' could not be regarded as *two* variables of our sentence. For if we say 'if somebody is *x* of somebody, then somebody is *y* of somebody', then we obviously say something the truth or falsehood of which essentially depends upon the meaning of *x* and *y*. What we say is true, if *x* and *y* mean teacher and pupil, or parent and child, or master and servant respectively. But it is not true, e.g., if *x* means teacher and *y* means servant. Somebody could be somebody's teacher without anybody being somebody's servant.

The problem of discovering what is variable and what is constant in our third example is thus somewhat more difficult than in the two first examples. This is due to an insufficiency of our language.

The relations of a teacher to his pupil, or a parent to his child, or a master to his servant have a common feature, for which, however, there is no word in ordinary language. The logician must invent a word for it. He speaks about relations and their converse relations. Whenever one person is another person's teacher, the latter is without exception the former person's pupil, and for this reason we call the relation of a pupil to his teacher the converse relation of the relation of a teacher to his pupil. Instead of 'pupil' a logician might say 'teacher converse', and similarly instead of 'child' he might say 'parent converse' and instead of 'servant' he might say 'master converse'. And if he then said 'if somebody is *x* of somebody, then somebody is *x* converse of somebody', he would say something, the truth of which is independent of the meaning of *x* in the same sense in which the truth of 'if *x*, if *y*, then not *y*, if not *x*' is independent of the meaning of *x* and *y*.

Thus our third example contains one variable only, viz. the word 'teacher' (*or* 'pupil'). Its constants are the words 'if-then', 'somebody', 'is', and 'converse'. The constant 'converse', however, does not occur explicitly in the sentence, because we say 'pupil' ('teacher') when we mean what the logician calls a 'teacher converse'.

We might again say that the variable gives to our sentence its content, and that the constants give to it its form, and that the sentence expresses truth because of its form and independently of its content.

It is of some interest to observe that there are logical constants for which ordinary language has no name and for which the logician must invent a technical term. This fact probably offers a partial explanation why some branches of logic were much retarded in their development before the rise of so-called symbolic logic.

What we have said about variables and constants above is still vague. The following remarks are intended to make the distinction somewhat more precise:

In our syllogism there occurred three variables. The syllogism, we said, expresses a true proposition independently of the meaning of the variables. This, however, is subject to an important restriction. We must not substitute for the variables words which would make the whole expression void of meaning. We could not, for example, substitute numerals for the variables. We must substitute for them words *of the same kind as* 'Europeans', 'white men', and 'Mohammedans'. This means that we must substitute for them names of some properties (classes).

Similarly, it is obvious that in our second example we can only substitute for the variables sentences, i.e. linguistic expressions of propositions. In our third example again we can only substitute for the variable a name of a relation.

These restrictions on the meaning of the variables offer a suitable basis for a classification of expressions.

First, there are expressions in which the variables mean propositions. Their study belongs to a discipline known as the Logic of Propositions. Its foundations were laid by the Stoics. Its systematic study in modern times dates from Frege. It is a province of logic which is today pretty thoroughly explored.

Secondly, there are expressions in which the variables mean properties (classes). Their study belongs to a discipline which can conveniently be called the Logic of Properties (Classes). It includes, but is by no means coextensive with, the theory of the syllogism.

Thirdly, there are expressions in which the variables mean relations. The Logic of Relations was hardly studied at all before de Morgan. Important contributions to it were made by

Peirce and Schröder and the authors of *Principia Mathematica*. It still remains, however, a comparatively unexplored branch of logic.

There are other provinces of logic (and logical truth) besides the three mentioned, but we shall not discuss them here.

The three provinces mentioned are hierarchically related. This is seen from a consideration of logical constants. All the constants of the Logic of Propositions occur among the constants of the Logic of Properties, and all the constants of the Logic of Properties among the constants of the Logic of Relations. But some constants of the Logic of Properties, e.g. 'all' and 'some', do not belong to the Logic of Propositions, and some constants of the Logic of Relations, e.g. 'converse', do not belong to the Logic of Properties.

It is an old observation that truth is sometimes dependent upon 'form' and sometimes upon 'content'. This observation has obviously something to do, e.g., with Leibniz's distinction between *vérités de raison* and *vérités de faits*, and with Kant's distinction between *analytische Urteile* and *synthetische Urteile*.

The distinction between form and content, however, is far from clear. What we have said above to elucidate it does not give us any means of determining whether a given sentence expresses logical truth or not. On the contrary, in distinguishing between the form and content of expressions we presupposed an insight into the truth of the propositions which they express and how this truth may be affected by the substitution of parts in the expressions. Nor does what Leibniz or Kant said in order to elucidate their above-mentioned distinctions help us very much.

A substantial contribution to the clarification of the idea of logical truth was made by Wittgenstein in his *Tractatus logico-philosophicus*. Wittgenstein there tried to give an account of the idea of logical truth by using the idea of a tautology which in its turn is based on the idea of a truth-function.

Let us call truth and falsehood truth-values. We can then define a truth-function in the following way:

A given proposition is a truth-function of n propositions, if for every possible combination of truth-values in the n propositions there is a rule determining the truth-value of the given

6

proposition. (There are many problems attached to this definition which we shall not discuss here.)

As we know, the Logic of Propositions studies expressions the variable parts of which are sentences. It was known before Wittgenstein that these expressions could be regarded as expressing truth-functions of the propositions expressed by their variable parts. Wittgenstein's new observation could be described as follows:

Among the truth-functions of n propositions there is the proposition which has the truth-value 'true' for every possible combination of truth-values in the n propositions. We call this truth-function the tautology of the n propositions. It is plain that if an expression of propositional logic expresses the tautology of the propositions expressed by its variables, then what it expresses is true independently of the content of the variables. For whatever propositions the variables mean, the expression itself means a true proposition.

What truth-function of the propositions expressed by its variables a given expression of propositional logic itself expresses can always be found out or decided 'mechanically' in so-called truth-tables. The idea of truth-tables was developed by Wittgenstein and independently of him by Post.[1] The characterization of logical truths as tautologies gets part of its importance from this fact, that one can for any given expression of propositional logic decide whether it expresses a tautology or not.

The tautology of n propositions is a proposition which is true for every possible combination of truth-values in the n propositions. The combinations are mutually exclusive, i.e. n given propositions are never true and false in more than one of these ways. The combinations are also collectively exhaustive, i.e. n given propositions are always true and false in one of these ways. The tautology of the n propositions is the proposition which is true independently of which of these combinations of truth-values actually is the case with the n propositions. Logical truth could therefore be said to consist in agreement with every one of a number of mutually exclusive and collectively exhaustive possibilities.

---

[1]Post, 'Introduction to a General Theory of Elementary Propositions', in *Amer. Journ. of Math.* **43**, 1921.

It is the character of (mutual exclusiveness and) collective exhaustiveness of the possibilities which entitles us to speak of them as representing *every possible* combination of truth-values in the n propositions. And this character itself is a consequence of two principles which are basic in relation to the concept of a truth-function and the construction of truth-tables and thus also to the decision whether an expression of propositional logic expresses logical truth or not. These principles are (i) that every proposition has a truth-value (is true *or* false) and (ii) that no proposition has more than one truth-value (is not true *and* false). We might call the first of them the Principle of Excluded Middle and the second the Principle of Contradiction.

It is an illusion to think that these two principles could themselves be proved to be tautologies and hence logical truths in the same sense as, e.g. 'it is raining or it is not raining' expresses the tautology of the proposition that it is raining. I shall not discuss here what sort of truths the two principles in question are or might be.

The concept of a tautology works very well for the purpose of clarifying the idea of logical truth or 'independence of content' in propositional logic, i.e. in that province of logical truth where the variable parts of the expressions which we study are sentences. Can it be applied for a similar purpose in those provinces of logical truth where the variables mean properties or relations?

This question could be answered affirmatively, if it could be shown that the logical constants which occur in expressions about properties and relations can be somehow 'eliminated' and 'replaced' by logical constants of propositional logic.

Consider again our syllogism. Suppose there are only two men in the world. We call them 'Smith' and 'Jones'. Instead of saying 'all Europeans are white men' we can also say 'if Smith is a European, then Smith is a white man, and if Jones is a European, then Jones is a white man'. Instead of saying 'some Europeans are Mohammedans' we can say 'Smith is a European and Smith is a Mohammedan or Jones is a European and Jones is a Mohammedan'. And instead of saying 'some white men are Mohammedans' we can say 'Smith is a white man and Smith is

a Mohammedan or Jones is a white man and Jones is a Mohammedan'. If we substitute these equivalent sentences for the
premises and the conclusion in our syllogism, we get a new
if-then-sentence. It contains the logical constants 'if-then', 'and',
'or', 'not' and the six sentences 'Smith is a European', 'Smith
is a Mohammedan', 'Smith is a white man', 'Jones is a European', 'Jones is a Mohammedan', and 'Jones is a white man'.
The constants mentioned are constants of propositional logic.
The new expression which we get, therefore, expresses a truth-
function of the propositions expressed by the six sentences. If we
examine in a truth-table which truth-function of them it
expresses, we shall find that it expresses their tautology.

It is 'intuitively' obvious that if the number of men were,
not two, but one or three or four or five or just any number n
we should always get a tautology if we replaced, as above, the
all-sentences and the some-sentences by new sentences, consisting of the words 'if-then', 'and', 'or', and 'not', and parts
which are themselves sentences. Let us call a world with only
one man, with only two men, with only three men, etc., a
'possible world'. We can then say that the syllogism turns out
to be a tautology in all possible worlds, if we eliminate from it
the words 'all' and 'some' as described above.

Similar remarks about the elimination of constants apply to
our example from relational logic: 'If somebody is teacher of
somebody, then somebody is pupil of somebody.' The new
expression which we get after the elimination contains the
logical constants 'if-then', 'and', and 'or', and parts which are
themselves sentences. If we examine in a truth-table which
truth-function of the propositions expressed by these sentences
the expression itself expresses, we shall find that it expresses
their tautology.

It might now be suggested that the concept of a tautology in
all possible worlds gives the proper meaning to the idea of
logical truth or 'independence of content' in the Logic of
Properties and the Logic of Relations.

The concept of a tautology in all possible worlds has a certain
intuitive plausibility. But it is far from clear. There are at least
two difficulties worth observation.

For any given world of n things we can use a truth-table to decide whether any given expression of the Logic of Properties or Relations expresses a tautology in *this* world or not. But we cannot use truth-tables to show that such an expression expresses a tautology in *all* possible worlds, since the number of possible worlds is unlimited. When we said above that our syllogism expresses a tautology in all possible worlds, we referred to 'intuition'. Sometimes, however, we can refer to considerations (other than truth-tables) which amount to a 'proof' that an expression expresses a tautology in all possible worlds. This could actually have been done in the case of the syllogism and also in the case of our example about teachers and pupils. But the very nature of these proofs is far from clear, and besides one has not been able to provide a general instrument of proof which would make it possible in the case of any expression to decide whether it expresses a tautology in all possible worlds or not.

I now come to the second difficulty.

Consider the expression 'every man is shorter than some man'. Whatever be the number of men in the world, this expresses a falsehood. For among any number *n* of men, there will always be a tallest man (or several tallest men). It follows from this that the expression 'not every man is shorter than some man' expresses a truth in all possible worlds of men. But is this really a logical truth? Substitute for the word 'man' the word 'prime (number)' and for the word 'shorter' the word 'smaller'. Then we get the expressions 'every prime is smaller than some prime' and 'not every prime is smaller than some prime' respectively. The latter expresses a truth in any world of *n* numbers. Yet it expresses a false proposition.

These considerations take us to a distinction between finite and infinite worlds. Something can be true of any finite world without being true of an infinite world. Among any finite number of numbers there is a greatest number, but among all numbers there is not. Many things, on the other hand, are true of any finite world and also of infinite worlds. The syllogisms, for example, are valid for numbers as well as for men.

By an infinite world we shall here exclusively understand the world of natural numbers.

What it means for an expression to express a tautology in a

possible finite world is clear. It means to express a tautology in the sense of propositional logic of a finite number of propositions. Which these propositions are can be found out by applying to the expression in question a technique for eliminating from it logical constants like 'all' and 'some' and 'converse'. What it means for an expression to express a tautology in an infinite world, however, is so far from clear that it is probably quite senseless. For there is no technique for the elimination of logical constants which would give us a finite number of propositions, of which the expression in question expressed the tautology.

It does not seem unplausible to suggest that to express a tautology in all possible finite worlds is a necessary criterion of logical truth.[1] But, as we have seen, this will hardly do as a sufficient criterion.

A sufficient criterion might be obtained in the following way:

Take an expression which fulfils the necessary criterion, i.e. expresses a tautology in all possible finite worlds. Take the contradictory of this expression. Let it be the case that we can substitute for its variable parts names of properties and relations from the world of numbers and in this way obtain a proposition which is true for numbers. We then say that the expression from which we started does *not* express logical truth. It would have expressed logical truth, if it had not been the case that we can substitute in the contradictory of it names of arithmetical properties and relations and in this way obtain a true proposition.

About the necessary criterion we observe that no general method is known for deciding whether a given expression satisfies it or not.[2]

About the suggested sufficient criterion we only observe here that it seems to make the idea of logical truth dependent upon the idea of truth about numbers. As is well known, there is no general technique for deciding whether an expression about

---

[1] Our concept of a tautology in all possible (finite) worlds answers to that which Hilbert calls *im Endlichen identisch.*

[2] Since this was written (1949), it has been proved that no such general method is possible. See *The Journal of Symbolic Logic*, **15**, 1950, p. 229. The proof is due to a Russian logician, Trachtenbrot. (1955)

numbers expresses a true proposition or not. There are, moreover, convincing reasons for believing that such a technique is
impossible.

I shall now try to say some words about a different way of
dealing with the problem of form and content in the Logic of
Properties and Relations. This way also uses the idea of a
tautology, but not the questionable extension of it which we
have called a tautology in all possible worlds.

I shall first speak about the Logic of Properties.

Consider again our syllogism: 'If all Europeans are white
men and some Europeans are Mohammedans, then some
white men are Mohammedans'. As already observed, the
syllogism is a sentence constructed out of the three sentences
'all Europeans are white men', 'some Europeans are Mohammedans', and 'some white men are Mohammedans' by means
of the words 'if-then' and 'and'. These words are logical constants of propositional logic. For this reason the syllogism
expresses a truth-function of the propositions expressed by the
three sentences. If, however, we construct a truth-table for the
syllogism, relying only upon the technique for the construction
of such tables in propositional logic, we shall *not* find that it
expresses the tautology of the propositions expressed by the
three sentences. This is clear, for if the two first sentences
expressed true propositions and the third a false proposition,
then the syllogism itself would express a false proposition.

To say that the syllogism expresses logical truth is thus
tantamount to saying that the propositions expressed by the
premisses and the conclusion cannot be independently true
and false in any combination of truth-values, but that the
combination under which the two premisses express true propositions and the conclusion a false proposition is an impossibility. With the difficulties caused by this impossibility, however, the technique of truth-tables in propositional logic is
incapable of coping.

We raise the following question: Could the decision-technique
of propositional logic be improved or amplified so as to make
the tautological character of the proposition expressed by the
syllogism emerge from a truth-table? It is not difficult to see
that this question can be answered affirmatively.

We begin by defining a certain set of eight conditions in the following way:

The first condition is satisfied by any man who is European, white, and Mohammedan, the second by any man who is European and white but not Mohammedan, the third by any man who is European and Mohammedan but not white, the fourth by any man who is European but neither white nor Mohammedan, the fifth by any man who is not European but white and Mohammedan, the sixth by any man who is neither European nor white but Mohammedan, the seventh by any man who is neither European nor Mohammedan but white, and the eighth by any man who is neither European nor white nor Mohammedan.

These conditions are mutually exclusive, i.e. no man can satisfy two of them. They are also collectively exhaustive, i.e. any man satisfies one of them. They can be independently satisfied or not in 256 ($= 2^8$) different ways, beginning from the case when they are all satisfied and ending with the case when none of them is satisfied. (The last case would mean that there are no men at all; if we wish, we can omit it from consideration as being an 'awkward' case.)

Anything that can be said about Europeans, white men, and Mohammedans, using the logical constants of the Logic of Propositions and of Properties can also be expressed by saying something about the way in which the eight conditions are satisfied or not. To say that all Europeans are white men is to say that the third and fourth conditions are *not* satisfied. To say the some Europeans are Mohammedans is to say that the first or third conditions are satisfied. Since to say that all Europeans are white men is to exclude the third condition from being satisfied, it follows that to say that all Europeans are white men *and* some Europeans are Mohammedans is to say that the first condition is satisfied but not the third and fourth. To say that some white men are Mohammedans, finally, is to say that the first or the fifth conditions are satisfied. What the syllogism itself says is, therefore, that if the first condition is satisfied but not the third and fourth, then the first *or* the fifth conditions are also satisfied. This is a logical truth. It is further a truth-function of the proposition that the first condition is satisfied, the proposition that the third condition is satisfied, the proposition that the fourth condition is satisfied, and the proposition that the fifth condition is satisfied. If we construct a truth-table, we shall find that it is the tautology of these four propositions.

By this means it has been shown that the syllogism expresses the tautology of four propositions. These four propositions are each to the effect that there is a man who satisfies a certain condition. We shall, therefore, call them the existence-constituents of the proposition expressed by the syllogism.

The above considerations can be generalized. Take any expression in the Logic of Properties. It contains n variable parts. These variables are names of properties. By a procedure —illustrated above for 'Europeans', 'white men', and 'Mohammedans'—we can set up a number $(= 2^n)$ of conditions, which are mutually exclusive, collectively exhaustive, and independently satisfiable. By another procedure[1] we show that the given expression in the Logic of Properties expresses a truth-function of some propositions each to the effect that there is a thing which satisfies a certain one of the conditions. These propositions we call the existence-constituents of the proposition expressed by the original expression. If the original expression expresses the tautology of its existence-constituents it expresses logical truth.

The truth-value of any proposition to the effect that there is a thing which satisfies a certain one of the conditions depends upon the content of the n names of properties which occur in the expression. The (truth-value of the) tautology of some of these propositions, however, is independent of the truth-values of the propositions themselves. Hence if the expression expresses the tautology of these propositions, it expresses truth independently of the content of the property-names.

It seems to me that the concept of a tautology of existence-constituents gives a fair account of the idea of logical truth or 'independence of content' in the Logic of Properties. It is connected with a universal decision-procedure and it avoids the

[1]There is a detailed account of these procedures and of the idea of logical truth in the Logic of Properties in the next essay. Essentially similar ideas about decidability are found in Quine's paper 'On the Logic of Quantification' (*The Journal of Symbolic Logic*, **10**, 1945).

difficulties and obscurities which are attached to the concept of a tautology in all possible worlds and which arise from the attempt to eliminate the logical constants peculiar to the Logic of Properties.

I shall now say some words about the Logic of Relations.

Consider again our example 'if somebody is teacher of somebody, then somebody is pupil of somebody'. It is a sentence constructed out of the two sentences 'somebody is teacher of somebody' and 'somebody is pupil of somebody' by means of the logical constant 'if-then'. The logical constant is one of propositional logic. For this reason our example expresses a truth-function of the propositions expressed by the two sentences. If, however, we construct a truth-table, relying upon the technique for the construction of such tables in propositional logic, we shall certainly *not* find that our example expresses the tautology of the propositions expressed by the two sentences. We therefore ask whether the amplified decision-technique of the Logic of Properties can cope with the case.

One could define a set of mutually exclusive and collectively exhaustive conditions in the following way:

The first condition is satisfied by any man who is somebody's teacher and also somebody's pupil, the second by any man who is somebody's teacher but not anybody's pupil, the third by any man who is somebody's pupil but not anybody's teacher, and the fourth by any man who is neither anybody's teacher nor anybody's pupil.

To say that somebody is teacher of somebody is to say that the first or the second conditions are satisfied. To say that somebody is pupil of somebody is to say that the second or third conditions are satisfied. Hence to say that if somebody is teacher of somebody, then somebody is pupil of somebody is to say that if the first or second conditions are satisfied, then also the second or third. This is a truth-function of the proposition that the first condition is satisfied, the proposition that the second condition is satisfied, and the proposition that the third condition is satisfied. Since each of these propositions is to the effect that there is a thing (a man) satisfying a certain condition, we shall call them the existence-constituents of the proposition that if somebody is teacher of somebody, then somebody is pupil of somebody. This last proposition is thus, like the proposition expressed by our syllogism, a truth-function of its existence-constituents. If, however, we construct a truth-table, we shall *not* find that it is their tautology.

It is easy to see why the decision-technique of the Logic of Properties cannot cope with the concept of logical truth in the case now under discussion. The failure is due to the fact that the four conditions about teachers and pupils, though they resemble our eight conditions above about Europeans, white men, and Mohammedans in being mutually exclusive and collectively exhaustive, differ from them in not being independently satisfiable or left unsatisfied. This again is due to the fact that our example, as we have already observed, contains a logical constant—peculiar to the Logic of Relations—which is not explicit in ordinary language, viz. the constant which we have called 'converse'. Or to put it in a different way: our example does not contain two variable relation-names, but only one. We can regard 'teacher' as the variable name, in which case we have for 'pupil' to read 'teacher converse'. Or we can regard 'pupil' as the variable name, in which case we have for 'teacher' to substitute 'pupil converse'.

There is a feature which is characteristic of any relation and its converse relation. We will call it their existential symmetry. This means in our example that if some of the conditions for the truth of the proposition that somebody is teacher of somebody is satisfied, then some of the conditions for the truth of the proposition that somebody is pupil of somebody is also satisfied, and vice versa. From this it follows that of the sixteen different ways in which our four conditions above might be satisfied or left unsatisfied according to the Principles of Excluded Middle or Contradiction, four ways are excluded as impossible thanks to the existential symmetry of the relations called 'teacher' and 'pupil'.

According to the above, there are thus 16 — 4 or twelve combinations of truth-values in the existence-constituents, representing the 16 — 4 or twelve different ways in which the respective conditions can be satisfied or left unsatisfied. These twelve combinations of truth-values are mutually exclusive, i.e. the existence-constituents are never true and false in more than one of these twelve ways. The combinations are also collectively exhaustive, i.e. the existence-constituents are always true and false in some of these twelve ways. It is this character of (mutual exclusiveness and) collective exhaustiveness which entitles us to speak of the twelve combinations as *all possible* combinations. (Cf. above, p. 8.)

If we construct a truth-table, we shall find that our example expresses a proposition which is true of every one of the possible combinations of truth-values in its existence-constituents. It thus expresses their tautology.

(The truth-table used in this case differs from an 'ordinary' truth-table in that certain combinations of truth-values are missing in it.)[1]

The above considerations can also be generalized. Take any expression in the Logic of Relations. It contains n variable parts. These variables are names of relations. By a procedure—*not*, however, adequately illustrated by our example above for 'teacher' and 'pupil'—we can set up a number of conditions which are mutually exclusive and collectively exhaustive, though not (in general) independently satisfiable. By another procedure we show that the given expression in the Logic of Relations expresses a truth-function of some propositions each to the effect that there is a thing which satisfies a certain one of the conditions. These propositions we call the existence-constituents of the proposition expressed by the original expression. By a third procedure, the nature of which is determined by the logical constants peculiar to relational logic,[2] we exclude certain combinations of truth-values in the existence-constituents as being impossible. The remaining combinations of truth-values represent a set of mutually exclusive and collectively exhaustive possibilities. If the original expression expresses the tautology of its existence-constituents (i.e., a proposition which is true for every one of the possible combinations of

---

[1] Truth-tables of this mutilated type were, as far as I know, for the first time mentioned by Wittgenstein in 'Some Remarks on Logical Form' in *Proceedings of the Aristotelian Society*, Supp. vol. 9, 1929. (1955)

[2] There are two (primitive) logical constants of relational logic. One is the constant which we have called 'converse'. The other is usually known as 'relative product' or 'chain'. The relation called 'uncle', e.g., is the chain-relation of the relations called 'brother' and 'father', and the relation called 'grandfather' is the chain-relation of the relation called 'father' with itself.

truth-values in the existence-constituents), it expresses logical truth.

The truth-value of any proposition to the effect that there is a thing which satisfies a certain one of the conditions depends upon the content of the n names of relations which occur in the expression. The tautology of some of these propositions, however, is independent of the truth-values of the propositions themselves. Hence if the expression expresses the tautology of these propositions, it expresses truth independently of the content of the relation-names.

It would be premature to attempt to answer the question whether the concept of a tautology of existence-constituents can give a satisfactory account of the idea of logical truth or 'independence of content' in the Logic of Relations, before settling other problems which occur in this context. One such problem is whether the concept of a tautology of existence-constituents as a criterion of logical truth is equivalent to the necessary and sufficient criterion which we have previously suggested (p. 11) or to a similar criterion. I shall not discuss this problem here.

APPENDIX I

The above outline of decision-procedures for the Logic of Propositions, Properties, and Relations mentions truth-tables. There is another technique which is equivalent to the construction of truth-tables. It consists in the transformation of a given expression into a certain 'normal form'. From this normal form can immediately be seen, whether the given expression expresses logical truth or not.

It is a well-known fact that any expression of propositional logic has what might be called a perfect disjunctive normal form (*ausgezeichnete disjunktive Normalform*). This normal form enumerates those of a number of mutually exclusive and collectively exhaustive possibilities with which the given expression expresses agreement. If it enumerates all possibilities, the expression expresses logical truth.

It is not difficult to show that any expression in the Logic of Properties has an analogous disjunctive normal form. The technique by means of which we derive it can be described as a

FORM AND CONTENT IN LOGIC

twofold application of the technique for deriving the perfect disjunctive normal form of expressions of propositional logic.[1] That the application is 'twofold' is a consequence of the fact that any expression in the Logic of Properties expresses agreement with some of a number of mutually exclusive and collectively exhaustive ways of satisfying a number of conditions, which are themselves mutually exclusive and collectively exhaustive.

It can finally be shown that also any expression of relational logic has an analogous normal form. The technique by means of which we derive it is substantially the same as the technique for deriving normal forms in the Logic of Properties. The normal forms of expressions of relational logic, however, differ from the normal forms in the Logic of Properties in that they sometimes contain redundant parts, answering to impossible combinations of truth-values in the existence-constituents.

APPENDIX II (1955)

The analogues in the Logic of Properties and of Relations to the disjunctive and conjunctive normal forms known from the Logic of Propositions may be called *distributive normal forms*. For the existence of these analogues essentially depends upon the distributivity of the existential quantifier with regard to disjunctions, and of the universal quantifier with regard to conjunctions. From the technical point of view the distributive normal forms may be contrasted with the so-called prenex normal forms.

The study of distributive normal forms in the Logic of Properties can be traced back to a paper by H. Behmann, 'Beiträge zur Algebra der Logik, insbesondere zur Entscheidungsproblem' in *Mathematische Annalen*, **86**, 1922. In Hilbert-Bernays's *Grundlagen der Mathematik* (Vol. i, pp. 146–8) the technique of these normal form derivations is described under the name of 'Zerlegung in Primärformeln'. Essentially the same technique is also described by Quine in his paper 'On the Logic of Quantification'. (Cf. above p. 14.)

That the theory of distributive normal forms can be extended

---

[1]A description of this technique of transformation into normal forms is found in the next essay.

to the Logic of Relations has been shown in detail by J. Hintikka in 'Distributive Normal Forms in the Calculus of Predicates (*Acta Philosophica Fennica*, **6**, 1953). Hintikka's thesis is the most comprehensive study of these normal forms that exists. Hintikka has also shown that the notion of a tautology of existence-constituents as a criterion of logical truth in the predicate calculus is in effect equivalent to the traditional criterion using the notion of satisfiability. His findings may be said to constitute an affirmative answer to the question, raised in the essay (p. 18), whether the idea of the tautology can give a satisfactory account of formal truth and 'independence of content' in the Logic of Relations.

Applications of the theory of distributive normal forms to Modal Logic are found in my book *An Essay in Modal Logic* (Amsterdam 1951) and in the paper 'Deontic Logic' of the present collection.

APPENDIX III (1955)

Traditionally, syllogisms are formulated as inferences of this type: 'All Europeans are white men. Some Europeans are Mohammedans. *Therefore* some white men are Mohammedans.' The formulation of syllogisms as if-then-sentences is unusual. It is found, for example, in Łukasiewicz's work on *Aristotle's Syllogistic* (1951). Łukasiewicz strongly insists that this formulation is true to Aristotle's view of the syllogism. 'All Aristotelian syllogisms', he says (p. 20), 'are implications of the type "If α and β, then γ", where α and β are the two premisses and γ is the conclusion.' Łukasiewicz also points out (p. 73 and *passim*) that 'no Aristotelian syllogism is formulated as a rule of inference with the word "therefore", as is done in the traditional logic'. 'The difference', he says (p. 21), 'between the Aristotelian and the traditional syllogism is fundamental.'

Much as these opinions of one of the finest authorities on the history of logic support the correctness of presenting Aristotelian syllogisms as done in this paper, I must own that I feel doubts about their *historical* truth. For all I can see, no conclusive support can be found in the original text, as we have it, *either* for the view that the formulation with 'therefore' *or* for the view that the formulation with 'if-then' and 'and' is *the* (historically) correct one. The use which Aristotle himself makes of 'if-then'-formulations in the context does not, in my opinion, establish Łukasiewicz's point. When, for example, Aristotle says (*Analytica Posteriora* 96ᵃ 12–14) that 'if *A* is predicated universally of *B* and *B* of *C*, then *A* too must be predicated always and in every instance of *C*', he is not *formulating* a syllogism, but *speaking about* one. And the same seems to me to hold for the only example (98ᵇ 5–10) quoted by Łukasiewicz (p. 2).

I should myself attach significance to the fact that Aristotle, as far as I have been able to find, nowhere speaks of the syllogism as a *truth* (true proposition), nor of the *proof* of a syllogism. (Cf. Łukasiewicz, op. cit., p. 44). To say with Łukasiewicz (p. 44 and p. 73) that Aristotle's own syllogistics is an 'axiomatized deductive system' is certainly a very bold 'modernization' of Aristotle. It seems to me much more to the point to say that *the notion of logical truth is unknown to Aristotle*. This is not necessarily to blame Aristotle of ignorance. It is an interesting question, to what extent logic can be developed independently of the idea of logical truth. The importance of this problem, however, was not alive to me, when I wrote the essay on form and content in logic.

ON THE IDEA OF LOGICAL TRUTH (I)

(1948)

THE aim of the present paper is to show that the idea of tautology has a wider range of application in logic than is sometimes thought.

I. THE LOGIC OF PROPOSITIONS

There are propositions.

Propositions are expressed by sentences.

The Logic of Propositions studies propositions as 'unanalysed wholes' and sentences as symbols of such unanalysed propositions.

The study will here begin by co-ordinating truth-values to propositions. We shall deal with two truth-values only. They are called truth and falsehood.

For the co-ordination of truth-values to propositions we adopt the following two principles:

i. Every proposition is true or false. We call this the Principle of Excluded Middle (in the Logic of Propositions).

ii. No proposition is true and false. We call this the Principle of Contradiction (in the Logic of Propositions).

After the adoption of i and ii we can introduce the idea of a truth-function.

A proposition is called a truth-function of n propositions, if the truth-value of the former is uniquely determined by the truth-values of the latter.

(The meaning of 'uniquely determined' will not be discussed here.)

The following seven truth-functions are defined separately:

By the negation (-proposition) of a given proposition we understand that proposition which is true, if and only if the given proposition is false. If p expresses a proposition, then $\sim p$ expresses its negation.

By the conjunction (-proposition) of two propositions we understand that proposition which is true, if and only if both the propositions are true. If p and q express propositions, then p & q expresses their conjunction.

By the disjunction (-proposition) of two propositions we understand that proposition which is true, if and only if at least one of the propositions is true. If p and q express propositions, then $p \vee q$ expresses their disjunction.

By the implication(-proposition) of a first proposition, called the antecedent(-proposition), and a second proposition, called the consequent (-proposition), we understand that proposition which is true, if and only if it is not the case that the antecedent is true and the consequent false. If p expresses the antecedent and q the consequent, then $p \rightarrow q$ expresses their implication.

(Henceforth, in talking about implications, explicit reference to the order of propositions will not be made. The order is assumed to be clear to the reader from the context.)

By the equivalence(-proposition) of two propositions we understand that proposition which is true, if and only if both the propositions are true or both are false. If p and q express propositions, then $p \longleftrightarrow q$ expresses their equivalence.

By the tautology(-proposition) of n propositions we understand that proposition which is true, whatever be the truth-values of the n propositions.

By the contradiction(-proposition) of n propositions we understand that proposition which is false, whatever be the truth-values of the n propositions.

It should be observed that, on our definition, a truth-function of any number of propositions is also a truth-function of any greater number of propositions, provided the former are included among the latter.

If a proposition is a truth-function of certain propositions and if these propositions are truth-functions of still further propositions, then the first proposition is a truth-function of the last propositions also. We call this the Principle of Transitivity (in the Logic of Propositions).

Truth-values can be co-ordinated to sentences also. We call a sentence true, if it expresses a true proposition, and false if it expresses a false proposition.

(It should be observed that actual usage of the words 'true' and 'false' applies both to propositions and to sentences. We say, e.g., that it is true *that* it is raining, but also that the sentence 'it is raining' is true.)

Similarly we call a sentence a truth-function of other sentences, if the proposition expressed by the first sentence is a truth-function of the propositions expressed by the other sentences.

Further we call $\sim p$ the negation-sentence of p, and $p \,\&\, q$ the conjunction-, $p \vee q$ the disjunction-, $p \to q$ the implication-, and $p \longleftrightarrow q$ the equivalence-sentence of p and q.

A sentence which is neither the negation-sentence of another sentence, nor the conjunction-, disjunction-, implication-, or equivalence-sentence of two other sentences is called an atomic sentence.

By a molecular complex of n sentences we understand:

i. Any one of the n sentences themselves.

ii. The negation-sentence of any molecular complex of the n sentences, and the conjunction-, disjunction-, implication-, and equivalence-sentence of any two molecular complexes of the n sentences.

The n sentences are called the constituents of their molecular complexes. If the sentences are atomic, they are called atomic constituents.

A molecular complex of n sentences is called a negation-, conjunction-, disjunction-, implication-, or equivalence-complex according to whether it is the negation-sentence of a molecular complex of the n sentences, or the conjunction-, disjunction-, implication-, or equivalence-sentence of two molecular complexes of the n sentences.

It should be observed that, on our definition, a molecular complex of any number of sentences is also a molecular complex of any greater number of sentences, provided the former are included among the latter.

As to the use of brackets we adopt the convention that the symbol $\&$ has a stronger combining force than $\vee$, $\to$, and $\longleftrightarrow$; the symbol $\vee$ than $\to$ and $\longleftrightarrow$; and the symbol $\to$ than $\longleftrightarrow$. Thus, e.g., if p, q, r, s, and t are sentences, we can instead of $([(p \,\&\, q) \vee r] \to s) \longleftrightarrow t$ write simply $p \,\&\, q \vee r \to s \longleftrightarrow t$.

In virtue of the Principle of Transitivity any molecular complex of n sentences expresses a truth-function of the propositions expressed by the n sentences themselves.

Which truth-function of the propositions expressed by its constituents a molecular complex expresses can be investigated and decided in truth-tables. This fact constitutes a solution of the so-called problem of decision (*Entscheidungsproblem*) in the Logic of Propositions. The technique of constructing truth-tables is supposed to be familiar to the reader.

If there are n propositions (sentences), there are 2^n possible combinations of truth-values in them and $2^{(2^n)}$ possible truth-functions. A combination of truth-values for which a certain truth-function is true is called a truth-condition of the truth-function.

If two truth-functions (of the same n propositions/sentences) have the same truth-conditions, they are called identical (in the realm of the n propositions/sentences).

If all truth-conditions of one truth-function are also truth-conditions of another truth-function, the first truth-function is said to entail the second.

If two molecular complexes of the same n sentences are identical, then their equivalence-sentence expresses the tautology of the propositions expressed by the n sentences themselves. The converse of this holds also.

If one molecular complex of n sentences entails another molecular complex of the same n sentences, then their implication-sentence expresses the tautology of the propositions expressed by the n sentences themselves. The converse of this holds also.

Entailment is reducible to identity. If a molecular complex of n sentences is identical with the conjunction-sentence of itself and another molecular complex of the same n sentences, then the first molecular complex entails the second. The converse of this holds also.

Be it observed that identity and entailment here mean identity and entailment in the Logic of Propositions.[1]

By a Truth of Logic (a logically true sentence) in the Logic of

---

[1] This account of entailment (and identity) can be challenged on the ground of the so-called Paradoxes of Implication. The challenge, however, is not serious for the restricted aims of the present essay. (1955)

Propositions we understand any molecular complex which expresses the tautology of the propositions expressed by its atomic constituents.

By a Law of Logic in the Logic of Propositions we understand any proposition to the effect that a certain sentence is a Truth of Logic in the Logic of Propositions.

We mention the following well-known Laws of Logic in the Logic of Propositions:

i. If p is a sentence, p v $\sim p$ is a Truth of Logic. We call this the Law of Excluded Middle (not to be confused with the Principle of Excluded Middle) in the Logic of Propositions.

ii. If p is a sentence, $\sim(p$ & $\sim p)$ is a Truth of Logic. We call this the Law of Contradiction (not to be confused with the Principle of Contradiction) in the Logic of Propositions.

iii. If p is a sentence, p is identical with $\sim\sim p$, i.e., $p \longleftrightarrow \sim\sim p$ is a Truth of Logic. We call this the Law of Double Negation.

iv. If p and q are sentences, $p \to q$ is identical with $\sim q \to \sim p$. We call this the Law of Contraposition.

v. If p and q are sentences, p & q is identical with $\sim(\sim p$ v $\sim q)$ and p v q with $\sim(\sim p$ & $\sim q)$. We call these the Laws of de Morgan.

vi. If p and q are sentences, p & q is identical with q & p and p v q with q v p. We call these the Laws of Commutation.

vii. If p, q, and r are sentences, $(p$ & $q)$ & r is identical with p & $(q$ & $r)$ and $(p$ v $q)$ v r with p v $(q$ v $r)$. We call these the Laws of Association.

viii. If p, q, and r are sentences, p & $(q$ v $r)$ is identical with p & q v p & r and p v$(q$ & $r)$ with $(p$ v $q)$ & $(p$ v $r)$. We call these the Laws of Distribution.

ix. If p and q are sentences, p & $(p \to q)$ entails q, i.e. p & $(p \to q) \to q$ is a Truth of Logic. We call this the Law of the Modus Ponens.

x. If p and q are sentences $\sim q$ & $(p \to q)$ entails $\sim p$. We call this the Law of the Modus Tollens.

In virtue of the Laws of Association we can omit brackets from conjunctions of conjunction-complexes and from disjunctions of disjunction-complexes. Thus, e.g., we write p & q & r for $(p$ & $q)$ & r or p & $(q$ & $r)$ and p v q v r for $(p$ v $q)$v r or p v $(q$ v $r)$. We can henceforth talk of conjunctions and disjunctions of n propositions or sentences (n-termed conjunctions and disjunctions).

In virtue of the above and the Law of Excluded Middle and Contradiction we call a n-termed disjunction-complex tautologous and a n-termed conjunction-complex contradictory, if at least one of its terms is the negation-sentence of another of its terms.

Any molecular complex of n sentences can be transformed into certain so-called normal forms, meaning that any such complex is identical with another molecular complex of the same n sentences which conforms to certain criteria. The conjunctive normal form is a conjunction-complex of disjunction-complexes of some of the n sentences and/or their negation-sentences, and the disjunctive normal form is a disjunction-complex of conjunction-complexes of some of the n sentences and/or their negation-sentences. If all the disjunction-complexes of the conjunctive normal form are n-termed and none of them tautologous, the normal form is called perfect (*die ausgezeichnete Normalform*). Similarly if all the conjunction-complexes of the disjunctive normal form are n-termed and none of them contradictory, the normal form is called perfect.

Let there be two sentences p and q. The perfect disjunctive normal form of a molecular complex of p and q is a disjunction-complex of some of four ($= 2^2$) conjunction-complexes p & q, p & $\sim q$, $\sim p$ & q, and $\sim p$ & $\sim q$. If there are n sentences, the perfect disjunctive normal form of a molecular complex of them is a disjunction-complex of some of 2^n conjunction-complexes.

If the two extreme cases of 0- and 1-termed disjunction-complexes are included, all molecular complexes of n sentences have a perfect disjunctive normal form.

The perfect disjunctive normal form of a molecular complex of n sentences, which expresses the tautology of the propositions expressed by the n sentences themselves, is a disjunction-complex of *all* the above 2^n conjunction-complexes.

The perfect disjunctive normal form of a molecular complex of n sentences, which expresses the conjunction of the propositions expressed by the n sentences themselves or by m of them and the negation-sentences of the remaining $n-m$ ones, is (a disjunction-complex of) *one* of the above 2^n conjunction-complexes.

The perfect disjunctive normal form of a molecular complex of n sentences, which expresses the contradiction of the propositions expressed by the n sentences themselves, is (a disjunction-complex of) *none* of the above 2^n conjunction-complexes.

It should be observed that a perfect disjunctive normal form is always 'in terms of' n sentences, of which the sentence transformed is a molecular complex. Thus, e.g. the perfect disjunctive normal form of $p \text{ v} \sim p$ in terms of p is $p \text{ v} \sim p$ but in terms of p and q (of which, according to our definition, $p \text{ v} \sim p$ is also a molecular complex) it is $p \ \& \ q \text{ v} p \ \& \ \sim q \text{ v} \sim p \ \& \ q \text{ v} \sim p \ \& \ \sim q$.

Be it remarked that the perfect disjunctive normal form of a molecular complex can be directly 'read off' from its truth-table.

The perfect disjunctive normal form of a molecular complex of n sentences, one might say, shows with which ones of the possible combinations of truth-values in the n sentences the complex expresses agreement and with which ones it expresses disagreement. If it agrees with all possibilities it is a Truth of Logic.

2. THE NON-QUANTIFIED LOGIC OF PROPERTIES

Propositions can be analysed into parts which are not themselves propositions. There are two principal ways of analysis. The first way we call the Aristotelian view of propositions. According to it, the proposition attributes a property to a thing (an object, an individual). The second we call the relational view of propositions. According to it, the proposition establishes a relation between a number of things.

(It seems that every proposition can be analysed both in the Aristotelian and in the relational way. The two ways, one might say, represent universal but not unique views of propositions.)

Let there be a proposition which is analysed in the Aristotelian way. If the proposition is true, we say that the property is present in the thing and call the thing a positive instance of the property. If the proposition is false, we say that the property is absent in the thing and call the thing a negative instance of the property. Presence and absence (of a property in a thing) are called presence-values (of the property in the thing).

It will be convenient to adopt some rudimentary form of a Theory of Logical Types. The reasons and the justification for this will not be discussed here.

All things, which are (positive or negative) instances of a given property, are of the same logical type or belong to the same Universe of Things. All properties, of which a given thing is a (positive or negative) instance, are also of the same logical type or belong to the same Universe of Properties. The Universe of Things is said to correspond to the given property, and the Universe of Properties to the given thing. It is assumed that the Universes of Things, which correspond respectively to the several members of a certain Universe of Properties, are identical, and so also the Universes of Properties, which correspond respectively to the several members of a certain Universe of Things. This will enable us to speak of a Universe of Properties and the corresponding Universe of Things, and vice versa.

The Non-Quantified Logic of Properties, as developed here, is a branch of logic 'isomorphous' to the Logic of Propositions.

The study begins by co-ordinating presence-values to properties. The co-ordination is ruled by the following two principles which follow from the corresponding principles in the Logic of Propositions:

i. Every property in a corresponding universe is present or absent in a thing. We call this the Principle of Excluded Middle (in the Non-Quantified Logic of Properties).

ii. No property in a corresponding universe is present and absent in a thing. We call this the Principle of Contradiction (in the Non-Quantified Logic of Properties).

We can now introduce the idea of a presence-function.

A property is called a presence-function of n properties, if the presence-value of the former in a thing is uniquely determined by the presence-values of the latter in the same thing.

The following seven presence-functions are defined separately:

By the negation(-property) of a given property we understand that property which is present in a thing, if and only if the given property is absent in the same thing. If P denotes, i.e., is the name of, a property, then $\sim P$ denotes its negation.

Similarly we define the conjunction-, disjunction-, implication-, and equivalence-property of two properties. If P and Q denote properties, then $P \& Q$ denotes their conjunction, $P \vee Q$ their disjunction, $P \rightarrow Q$ their implication, and $P \longleftrightarrow Q$ their equivalence.

Finally, we define the tautology(-property) of n properties as that property which is present, and the contradiction(-property) of n properties as that which is absent, in a thing, whatever be the presence-values of the n properties in the thing.

If properties are represented as squares within a bigger square we can represent any presence-function of them as shadowed part of the big square.

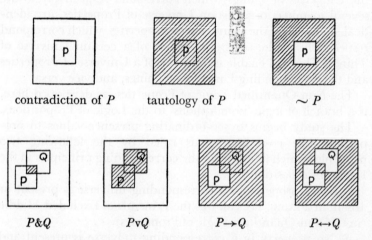

contradiction of P tautology of P $\sim P$

$P \& Q$ $P \vee Q$ $P \rightarrow Q$ $P \leftrightarrow Q$

Since truth-functionship is transitive, presence-functionship is transitive also. (Principle of Transitivity in the Non-Quantified Logic of Properties).

If P and Q are names of properties, we call $\sim P$ the negation-name of P, and $P \& Q$ the conjunction-, $P \vee Q$ the disjunction-, $P \rightarrow Q$ the implication-, and $P \longleftrightarrow Q$ the equivalence-name of P and Q.

A name of a property which is neither the negation-name of another name of a property, nor the conjunction-, disjunction-, implication-, or equivalence-name of two other names of properties is called an atomic name.

By a molecular complex of n names of properties we understand:

i. Any one of the n names themselves.

ii. The negation-name of any molecular complex of the n names, and the conjunction-, disjunction-, implication-, and equivalence-name of any two molecular complexes of the n names.

The n names are called the constituents of their molecular complexes. If the names are atomic, they are called atomic constituents.

A molecular complex of n names of properties is called a negation-, conjunction-, disjunction-, implication-, or equivalence-complex according to whether it is the negation-name of a molecular complex of the n names, or the conjunction-, disjunction-, implication-, or equivalence-name of two molecular complexes of the n names.

As to the use of brackets we adopt the same conventions as in the Logic of Propositions. (Cf. p. 24.)

In virtue of the Principle of Transitivity any molecular complex of n names of properties denotes a presence-function of the properties denoted by the n names themselves.

Which presence-function of the properties denoted by its constituents a molecular complex denotes can be investigated and decided in presence-tables. The technique of constructing presence-tables is strictly analogous to that of constructing truth-tables, which was supposed (p. 25) to be familiar to the reader.

If there are n properties, there are 2^n possible combinations of presence-values of them in a thing and $2^{(2^n)}$ possible presence-functions. A combination of presence-values for which a certain presence-function is present in a thing is called a presence-condition of the presence-function.

If two presence-functions (of the same n properties) have the same presence-conditions, they are called identical (in the realm of the n properties).

If all presence-conditions of one presence-function are also presence-conditions of another presence-function, the first presence-function is said to entail the second.

If two presence-functions of n properties are identical (or if the first entails the second), then any molecular complex of the names of the n properties which denotes the first presence-function is said to be identical with (or to entail) any molecular complex of the names of the n properties which denotes the second presence-function.

If two molecular complexes of the same n names of properties are identical, then their equivalence-name denotes the tautology of the properties denoted by the n names themselves. The converse of this holds also.

If one molecular complex of n names of properties entails another molecular complex of the same n names, then their implication-name denotes the tautology of the properties denoted by the n names themselves. The converse of this holds also.

Entailment is reducible to identity. (Cf. p. 25.)

Be it observed that identity and entailment here mean identity and entailment in the Non-Quantified Logic of Properties.[1]

By a Law of Logic in the Non-Quantified Logic of Properties we understand any proposition to the effect that a certain molecular complex denotes the tautology of the properties denoted by its atomic constituents.

Analogous laws to the Law of Excluded Middle, Contradiction, Double Negation, Contraposition, de Morgan, Commutation, Association, Distribution, the Modus Ponens, and the Modus Tollens of the Logic of Propositions are valid in the Non-Quantified Logic of Properties.

In virtue of the Laws of Association we can henceforth talk of conjunctions and disjunctions of n properties or names of properties (n-termed conjunctions and disjunctions). (Cf. p. 26f.)

In virtue of the Laws of Excluded Middle and Contradiction we call a n-termed disjunction-complex tautologous and a n-termed conjunction-complex contradictory, if at least one of its terms is the negation-name of another of its terms.

Any molecular complex of n names of properties can be transformed into certain so-called normal forms. (Cf. p. 27.)

[1]Cf. fn. on p. 25.

There are the conjunctive and the disjunctive normal forms and the perfect conjunctive and the perfect disjunctive normal forms.

The reader's attention is particularly drawn to the last mentioned normal form. Every molecular complex of n names of properties has a perfect disjunctive normal form in terms of the n names. This is composed of a selection from among 2^n conjunction-complexes. If the complex denotes the contradiction of the properties denoted by its constituents, its perfect disjunctive normal form vanishes, i.e., is a 0-termed disjunction. If the complex denotes the conjunction of the properties denoted by its constituents or by m of them and the negation-names of the $n-m$ remaining ones, its perfect disjunctive normal form is a 1-termed disjunction. If the complex denotes the tautology of the properties denoted by its constituents, its perfect disjunctive normal form is a 2^n-termed disjunction.

3. THE QUANTIFIED LOGIC OF PROPERTIES

If no instance of a property is positive, the property is called empty.

If at least one instance of a property is positive, the property is said to exist.

If all instances of a property are positive, the property is called universal.

The proposition that the property denoted by P exists, will be expressed by the sentence $E P$.

The proposition that the property denoted by P is empty, is the negation-proposition of the above. It can thus be expressed by the sentence $\sim E P$.

The proposition that the property denoted by P is universal, we shall understand as the proposition that the negation of the property denoted by P is empty. It can thus be expressed by the sentence $\sim E \sim P$. As an abbreviation for this sentence we may use $U P$.

(It should be observed that universality, as understood here, does not imply existence. A property may thus be both universal and empty. If this be regarded as 'unnatural', the definition of universality can easily be amended so as to include a condition of existence also.)

If the implication-property of two properties is universal, the first property is said to be included in the second. If P and Q are names of properties, inclusionship can thus be expressed by the sentence $U\ (P \to Q)$. As an abbreviation of this sentence we may also use $P \subset Q$.

If the equivalence-property of two properties is universal, the properties are called co-extensive. If P and Q are names of properties, co-extension can thus be expressed by the sentence $U(P \longleftrightarrow Q)$. As an abbreviation of this sentence we may also use $P \equiv Q$.

It is important not to confuse inclusionship with implication and entailment, nor co-extension with equivalence and identity.

The Quantified Logic of Properties can be regarded as a specialized branch of the Logic of Propositions. It studies propositions, when analysed so as to assert existence, emptiness, or universality of properties, and sentences as symbols of propositions thus analysed.

We shall call such propositions and sentences E- and U-propositions and E- and U-sentences respectively. Since U-sentences are only abbreviations for negation-sentences of certain E-sentences, we use the expression 'E-proposition' and 'E-sentence' to cover U-propositions and -sentences also.

Unlike the Non-Quantified Logic of Properties, the Quantified Logic of Properties is not a branch of logic 'isomorphous' to the Logic of Propositions.

Any molecular complex of E-sentences expresses a truth-function of the E-propositions expressed by its constituents. (Cf. p. 25.)

If the truth-function expressed by a molecular complex of E-sentences is the tautology of the E-propositions expressed by its constituents, then the complex is a Truth of Logic (logically true sentence) in the Quantified Logic of Properties.

The converse of this does not hold. A molecular complex of E-sentences may not express the tautology of the E-propositions expressed by its constituents and yet obviously be 'logically true'. As an example we mention

$$E(P \,\&\, Q) \,\&\, U(Q \to R) \to E(P \,\&\, R)$$

or the *modus dimaris* of traditional logic. If there are red and spherical things and all spherical things are iron things, then

34

there are red and iron things. This sentence does not express the tautology of the propositions expressed by $E(P \& Q)$ and $U(Q \to R)$ and $E(P \& R)$.

Truth of Logic in the Quantified Logic of Properties is, so to speak, two-levelled. It depends partly upon the construction of the molecular complexes of E-sentences by means of the symbols $\sim$, $\&$, v, $\to$ and $\leftrightarrow$, and partly upon the 'inner structure' of the E-sentences. (We shall not here take into account the trivial cases in which the first dependence alone is sufficient to ensure the logical truth of a complex.) The first dependence is in terms of truth-functionship, as known from the Logic of Propositions. We shall endeavour to show that the second dependence is also in terms of truth-functionship.

Existence and emptiness (of properties) are called existence-values.

From the Principles of Excluded Middle and of Contradiction in the Logic of Propositions follow two sub-principles:

i. Every property exists or is empty. We call this the Principle of Excluded Middle (in the Quantified Logic of Properties).

ii. No property exists and is empty. We call this the Principle of Contradiction (in the Quantified Logic of Properties).

We now introduce a special kind of truth-functions (not of presence-functions be it observed) which we call existence-functions.

A property is called an existence-function of n properties, if the existence-value of the former is uniquely determined by the existence-values of the latter.

It is 'intuitively clear' that not any property which is a presence-function of other properties is also an existence-function of them. (Otherwise the Quantified Logic of Properties would be 'isomorphous' to the Logic of Propositions.) For example the conjunction of two properties is not an existence-function of them. From the existence of red things and the existence of spherical things nothing can be concluded as to the existence or not of things which are both red and spherical.

It is also 'intuitively clear' that any property which is the disjunction of two properties is an existence-function of them. It exists, if and only if at least one of the two properties exists. There are things which are red or spherical (or both), if and only

35

if there are things which are red or things which are spherical. This we lay down as a Principle of Existence:

If a property is the disjunction of two properties, then the proposition that the property exists is the disjunction of the propositions that the first of the two properties exists and that the second of the two properties exists.

(Thanks to the associative character of disjunction we can extend this principle to disjunctions of n properties and propositions respectively.)

As will be remembered, any molecular complex of n names of properties has a perfect disjunctive normal form. This is a 0-, 1- or more-than-1-termed disjunction-complex, the terms of which are selected from among 2^n n-termed conjunction-complexes. In virtue of the Principle of Existence any molecular complex of n names of properties denotes an existence-function of the properties denoted by the conjunction-complexes of its perfect disjunctive normal form.

By the existence-constituents of a molecular complex of n names of properties we shall understand the conjunction-complexes of its perfect disjunctive normal form. Similarly, by the E-constituents of the E-sentence expressing the proposition that the property denoted by a molecular complex of n names of properties exists we shall understand the E-sentences expressing the propositions that the properties denoted by the conjunction-complexes of its perfect disjunctive normal form exist.

If the tautology of n properties is represented by a square, the 2^n properties denoted by the existence-constituents of any molecular complex of the names of the n properties can be represented as mutually exclusive and collectively exhaustive sub-areas of the square, and the properties denoted by any molecular complex itself as a sum of 0, 1, or . . . or 2^n such sub-areas. (Cf. diagram p. 37.)

The diagram is a representation of the properties denoted by the eight existence-constituents $P \& Q \& R$, $P \& Q \& \sim R$, $P \& \sim Q \& R$, $P \& \sim Q \& \sim R$, $\sim P \& Q \& R$, $\sim P \& Q \& \sim R$, $\sim P \& \sim Q \& R$, and $\sim P \& \sim Q \& \sim R$ of any molecular complex which can be constructed of the three names P, Q and R.

Which existence-function of (some of) its 2^n existence-constituents a molecular complex of n names of properties denotes can be investigated and decided in existence-tables. Existence-tables are a species of truth-tables.

$P \mathbin{\&} Q \mathbin{\&} \sim R$	$\sim P \mathbin{\&} Q \mathbin{\&} \sim R$
$P \mathbin{\&} Q \mathbin{\&} R$ $\quad$ $\sim P \mathbin{\&} Q \mathbin{\&} R$	
$P \mathbin{\&} \sim Q \mathbin{\&} R$ $\quad$ $\sim P \mathbin{\&} \sim Q \mathbin{\&} R$	
$P \mathbin{\&} \sim Q \mathbin{\&} \sim R$	$\sim P \mathbin{\&} \sim Q \mathbin{\&} \sim R$

Let there be two names of properties P and Q. Any molecular complex of them denotes an existence-function of (some of) the four properties denoted by $P \mathbin{\&} Q$, $P \mathbin{\&} \sim Q$, $\sim P \mathbin{\&} Q$, and $\sim P \mathbin{\&} \sim Q$. We shall here construct an existence-table for the complexes P, $\sim P$, $P \mathbin{\&} Q$, $P \vee Q$, $P \rightarrow Q$, $P \leftrightarrow Q$, $P \vee \sim P$, and $P \mathbin{\&} \sim P$. Their perfect disjunctive normal forms, in terms of P and Q, are $P \mathbin{\&} Q \vee P \mathbin{\&} \sim Q$, $\sim P \mathbin{\&} Q \vee \sim P \mathbin{\&} \sim Q$, $P \mathbin{\&} Q$, $P \mathbin{\&} Q \vee P \mathbin{\&} \sim Q \vee \sim P \mathbin{\&} Q$, $P \mathbin{\&} Q \vee \sim P \mathbin{\&} Q$ $\vee \sim P \mathbin{\&} \sim Q$, $P \mathbin{\&} Q \vee \sim P \mathbin{\&} \sim Q$, and the disjunction of all four, and the disjunction of none of the existence-constituents respectively. Truth is abbreviated by T and falsehood by F.

As seen from the table (p. 38), there is an interesting asymmetry between the tautological and the contradictory property. The latter never exists, for which reason the proposition *that* it exists is always false. The former, however, does not always exist, for which reason the proposition *that* it exists is not always true. If and only if there are no things in the universe, the tautological property is empty.

By the E-constituents of a molecular complex of E-sentences we understand the E-constituents of the E-sentences subject to the additional qualification that the perfect disjunctive normal forms of the molecular complexes of names of properties are in terms of *all* the atomic names of properties (in the same Universe of Properties) which occur in the entire molecular complex of *E*-sentences.

We have seen that any *E*-sentence expresses a truth-function of the propositions expressed by its *E*-constituents. Since any molecular complex of *E*-sentences expresses a truth-function of

Row	1	2	3	4	5	6	7	8	9	10	11	12	13	14	15	16
$E(P\&\sim P)$	F	F	F	F	F	F	F	F	F	F	F	F	F	F	F	F
$E(P\vee\sim P)$	T	T	T	T	T	T	T	T	T	T	T	T	T	T	T	F
$E(P\rightarrow Q)$	T	T	T	T	T	T	T	T	T	F	T	T	T	T	T	F
$E(P\rightarrow Q)$	T	T	T	T	T	T	T	T	T	T	T	F	T	T	T	F
$E(P\vee Q)$	T	T	T	T	T	T	T	T	T	T	T	T	T	T	F	F
$E(P\&Q)$	T	T	T	T	T	T	T	T	F	F	F	F	F	F	F	F
$E\sim P$	T	T	T	F	T	T	T	F	T	T	T	F	T	T	T	F
$E\,P$	T	T	T	T	T	T	T	T	T	T	T	F	F	F	F	F
$E(\sim P\&\sim Q)$	F	F	T	F	T	F	T	F	T	F	T	F	T	T	T	F
$E(\sim P\&Q)$	T	T	F	T	T	F	T	T	T	F	T	T	F	T	F	F
$E(P\&\sim Q)$	T	T	T	F	F	F	F	T	T	T	T	F	F	F	F	F
$E(P\&Q)$	T	T	T	T	T	T	T	F	F	F	F	F	F	F	F	F

the propositions expressed by the E-sentences themselves (p. 34) and since the property of being a truth-function is transitive (p. 23), we can conclude that any molecular complex of E-sentences expresses a truth-function of the propositions expressed by its E-constituents.

Which truth-function of the propositions expressed by its E-constituents a molecular complex of E-sentences expresses can be investigated and decided in truth-tables. This fact constitutes a solution of the so-called problem of decision (*Entscheidungsproblem*) in the Quantified Logic of Properties.

The technique of constructing truth-tables in the Quantified Logic of Properties will be illustrated by an example.

We take the molecular complex of E-sentences $E(P \& Q) \& U(Q \to R) \to E(P \& R)$. As known, $U(Q \to R)$ is an abbreviation for $\sim E \sim(Q \to R)$. The perfect disjunctive normal form, in terms of P, Q, and R, of $P \& Q$ is $P \& Q \& R \vee P \& Q \& \sim R$, of $\sim(Q \to R)$ is $P \& Q \& \sim R \vee \sim P \& Q \& \sim R$, and of $P \& R$ is $P \& Q \& R \vee P \& \sim Q \& R$. The E-constituents of the molecular complex are thus $E(P \& Q \& R)$, $E(P \& Q \& \sim R)$, $E(\sim P \& Q \& \sim R)$, and $E(P \& \sim Q \& R)$.

We first construct an existence-table for the three E-sentences the molecular complex of which we are investigating:

E(P&Q&R)	E(P&Q&~R)	E(~P&Q&~R)	E(P&~Q&R)	E(P&Q)	E~(Q→R)	E(P&R)
T	T	T	T	T	T	T
T	T	T	F	T	T	T
T	T	F	T	T	T	T
T	T	F	F	T	T	T
T	F	T	T	T	T	T
T	F	T	F	T	T	T
T	F	F	T	T	F	T
T	F	F	F	T	F	T
F	T	T	T	T	T	T
F	T	T	F	T	T	F
F	T	F	T	T	T	T
F	T	F	F	T	T	F
F	F	T	T	F	T	T
F	F	T	F	F	T	F
F	F	F	T	F	F	T
F	F	F	F	F	F	F

We thereupon construct a truth-table for the molecular complex itself. (Identical combinations of truth-values in the three constituents need not be repeated.) The table looks as follows:

$E(P\&Q)$	$E\sim(Q{\to}R)$	$E(P\&R)$	$\sim E\sim(Q{\to}R)$	$E(P\&Q)\&\sim E\sim(Q{\to}R)$	modus dimaris
T	T	T	F	F	T
T	F	T	T	T	T
T	T	F	F	F	T
F	T	T	F	F	T
F	T	F	F	F	T
F	F	T	T	F	T
F	F	F	T	F	T

It is seen that the molecular complex of E-sentences which we are investigating expresses the tautology of the propositions expressed by its E-constituents. (The tautological character of the sentence, one might say, emerges from the second truth-table thanks to the fact that the combination of truth-values $T F F$ does not occur (to the right) in the first truth-table.)

It is not necessary, be it observed, that the names of properties occurring in the different E-sentences of the molecular complex should be names of properties of the same Universe of Properties.

For the construction of truth-tables in the Quantified Logic of Properties the following rule could be given:

Given a molecular complex of sentences in the Quantified Logic of Properties. 1. Replace U-sentences by the E-sentences of which they are abbreviations. 2. Transform every molecular complex of names of properties which occurs in any of the E-sentences into its perfect disjunctive normal form, in terms of all atomic names of properties in the same Universe of Properties which occur in the complex. This gives the E-constituents of the complex. 3. Construct, in virtue of the Principle of Existence, truth-(existence-) tables for the E-sentences on the basis of all possible combinations of truth-values in the E-constituents. 4. Finally, construct an ordinary truth-table for the molecular complex itself, on the basis of the combinations of truth-values in the E-sentences which answer to all possible combinations of truth-values in the E-constituents.

A combination of truth-values in (the propositions expressed by) the E-constituents for which the (proposition expressed by) the molecular complex of E-sentences is true, is called a truth-condition of (the proposition expressed by) the complex.

If (the propositions expressed by) two molecular complexes of E-sentences have the same truth-conditions, they are called identical.

If all truth-conditions of one (proposition expressed by a certain) molecular complex of E-sentences are also truth-conditions of another (proposition expressed by a certain) molecular complex of E-sentences, the (proposition expressed by the) first molecular complex is said to entail the (proposition expressed by the) second molecular complex.

If two molecular complexes of E-sentences are identical, then their equivalence-sentence expresses the tautology of the propositions expressed by the E-constituents of the two complexes. The converse of this holds also.

If one molecular complex of E-sentences entails another, then their implication-sentence expresses the tautology of the propositions expressed by the E-constituents of the two complexes. The converse of this holds also.

Entailment is reducible to identity. (Cf. p. 25.)

Be it observed that identity and entailment here mean identity and entailment in the Quantified Logic of Properties.[1]

By a Truth of Logic (a logically true sentence) in the Quantified Logic of Properties we understand any molecular complex of E-sentences which expresses the tautology of the propositions expressed by its E-constituents.

By a Law of Logic in the Quantified Logic of Properties we understand any proposition to the effect that a certain sentence is a Truth of Logic in the Quantified Logic of Properties.

We mention the following well-known Laws of Logic in the Quantified Logic of Properties:

i. Three laws on the relation of existence to universality, and vice versa. If P denotes a property, then

[1]Cf. fn. on p. 25.

(*a*) $U \sim P$ is identical with $\sim E P$, i.e., $U \sim P \leftrightarrow \sim E P$ is a Truth of Logic,

(*b*) $\sim U \sim P$ is identical with $E P$, and

(*c*) $\sim U P$ is identical with $E \sim P$.

(The logical truth of the third law is 'one-levelled' (p. 35), i.e. it is a Truth of Logic already in the Logic of Propositions.)

ii. Four laws for the distribution of the operators E and U. If P and Q denote properties, then

(*a*) $U(P \& Q)$ is identical with $U P \& U Q$,

(*b*) $E(P \vee Q)$ is identical with $E P \vee E Q$,

(*c*) $U P \vee U Q$ entails $U(P \vee Q)$, i.e. $U P \vee U Q \rightarrow U(P \vee Q)$ is a Truth of Logic, and

(*d*) $E(P \& Q)$ entails $E P \& E Q$.

(The second of these laws should not be confused with the Principle of Existence, to which it bears a relation resembling the one between the Law of Excluded Middle and the Principle of Excluded Middle in the Logic of Propositions.)

iii. The nineteen traditional modes of the categorical syllogism with the exception of *darapti, bramantip, felapton,* and *fesapo*.

iv. If P, Q, and R denote properties, then

(*a*) $E P \& U(P \rightarrow Q) \& U(P \rightarrow R)$ entails $E(R \& Q)$ (amended form of *darapti*),

(*b*) $E P \& U(P \rightarrow Q) \& U(Q \rightarrow R)$ entails $E(R \& P)$ (amended form of *bramantip*),

(*c*) $E P \& U(P \rightarrow \sim Q) \& U(P \rightarrow R)$ entails $E(R \& \sim Q)$ (amended form of *felapton*), and

(*d*) $(E P) \& (E Q) \& U(P \rightarrow \sim Q) \& U(Q \rightarrow R)$ entails $E(R \& \sim P)$ (amended form of *fesapo*).

Any molecular complex of E-sentences has what we propose to call an absolutely perfect disjunctive normal form. This we get by replacing any one of the E-sentences by a disjunction of E-constituents of the complex and transforming the molecular complex of E-sentences thus obtained into its perfect disjunctive normal form. The absolutely perfect disjunctive normal form shows with which ones of the possible combinations of truth-values in its E-constituents the molecular complex expresses agreement and with which ones it expresses disagreement. If it agrees with all possibilities it is a Truth of Logic.

ON THE IDEA OF LOGICAL TRUTH

Note. Any formula of the (lower) functional calculus of symbolic logic, which contains only one-place predicates and no sentence variable and no free individual variable, can, within the calculus, be transformed so as to become 'translatable' into the symbolism of our Quantified Logic of Properties. This implies that it has an absolutely perfect disjunctive normal form, from which can be immediately seen with which ones of a finite number of enumerated truth-possibilities the formula expresses agreement (and with which ones it expresses disagreement). Agreement with all possibilities is a necessary and sufficient condition for the formula to be 'identical' in the usual sense, i.e., satisfiable in all realms of individual things.

Be it observed that in the 'traditional' calculus the possibility of an empty Universe of Things is excluded. Thus, e.g., the formula which is translated into our symbolism as $U P \to E P$ can be proved in it. This, however, is no Truth of Logic. It disagrees with the possibility that the universe may be empty. It can be regarded as a degenerated form of $E(P \vee \sim P) \to (U P \to E P)$ which is a Truth of Logic.

Be it finally observed that our idea of a solution of the *Entscheidungsproblem* of the Quantified Logic of Properties and of the functional calculus with only one-place predicates respectively is implicit in the idea of Lewis Carroll-diagrams.

43

ON DOUBLE QUANTIFICATION

(1952)

ONE variable x and n predicates $P_1, \ldots, P_n$ are introduced for the purpose of forming n 'basic' sentences $P_1x, \ldots, P_nx$.

By a Cx-sentence we understand a molecular complex of (some or all of) the basic sentences. For instance: P_1x v $\sim P_2x$ is a Cx-sentence.

By a $ExCx$-sentence we understand a Cx-sentence which has been existentially quantified in the variable x. For instance: $(Ex)(P_1x$ v $\sim P_2x)$ is a $ExCx$-sentence.

By a $CExCx$-sentence, finally, we understand a molecular complex of $ExCx$-sentences. For instance: $(Ex)(P_1x$ v $\sim P_2x) \rightarrow \sim (Ex) \sim P_1x$ is a $CExCx$-sentence.

(Trivially, $ExCx$-sentences are themselves $CExCx$-sentences. For $\sim (Ex) \sim$ we can introduce the abbreviation (x).)

$CExCx$-sentences will be called formulae (sentences) of the first degree.

The study of the fragment of the lower functional calculus, which contains only formulae of the first degree, might be called the theory of simple quantification.

Any formula of the lower functional calculus, which contains only one-place predicates and no free individual variable, is equivalent to a formula of the first degree.

The decision problem can be effectively solved for formulae of the first degree The solution of the problem is implicit in some of the classical treatments (by Venn, Lewis Carroll, and others) of the syllogism, using diagrams. The first systematic solution is due to Löwenheim.[1] A different solution is described in my paper 'On the Idea of Logical Truth (I)'. Substantially the same solution had been given before by several authors.[2]

*

[1]'Über Möglichkeiten im Relativkalkül' in *Mathematische Annalen*, **76**, 1915.
[2]Cf. the review by Alonzo Church in *The Journal of Symbolic Logic*, **15**, 1950, pp. 58f., 199 and 280.

ON DOUBLE QUANTIFICATION

Two variables, x and y, and n names of relations R_1, . . . , R_n are introduced for the purpose of forming $3n$ 'basic' sentences R_1xy, R_1yx, R_1xx, . . ., R_nxy, R_nyx, R_nxx.

By a Cxy-sentence we understand a molecular complex of (some or all of) the basic sentences. For instance: R_1xy v $\sim R_2yx$ is a Cxy-sentence.

By a $EyCxy$-sentence we understand a Cxy-sentence which has been existentially quantified in the variable y. For instance: (Ey) $(R_1xy$ v $\sim R_2yx)$ is a $EyCxy$-sentence.

By a $CEyCxy$-sentence we understand a molecular complex of $EyCxy$-sentences. For instance: (Ey) $(R_1xy$ v $\sim R_2yx)$ → (Ey) $(R_2xx$ & $R_3xy)$ is a $CEyCxy$-sentence.

By a $ExCEyCxy$-sentence we understand a $CEyCxy$-sentence which has been existentially quantified in the variable x. For instance: (Ex) $[(Ey)$ $(R_1xy$ v $\sim R_2yx)$ → (Ey) $(R_2xx$ & $R_3xy)]$ is a $ExCEyCxy$-sentence.

By a $CExCEyCxy$-sentence, finally, we understand a molecular complex of $ExCEyCxy$-sentences. For instance:(Ex) $[(Ey)$ $(R_1xy$ v $\sim R_2yx)$ → (Ey) $(R_2xx$ & $R_3xy)]$ ⟷ (Ex) (Ey) R_1xy is a $CExCEyCxy$-sentence.

$CExCEyCxy$-sentences (and formulae which are equivalent to $CExCEyCxy$-sentences) will be called formulae (sentences) of the second degree.

The study of the fragment of the lower functional calculus, which contains only formulae of the second degree, might be called the theory of double quantification.

The decision problem can be effectively solved also for formulae of the second degree. I have treated this class of formulae in my paper 'On the Idea of Logical Truth (II)'.[1] The working of the decision method was there illustrated on formulae of the second degree containing only one atomic relation-name. Its working for all cases may not have been quite obvious from the illustration. I shall, therefore, in this paper produce a general solution of the decision problem in question.[2] Further,

[1]In Soc. Scient. Fenn., Comm. Phys.-Math. xv, 10, 1950.
[2]As shown by Dr. W. Ackermann in The Journal of Symbolic Logic, 17, 1952, pp. 201ff. this problem is a special case of a more comprehensive decision problem, previously solved by Gödel, Kalmar, and Schütte. Cf. also Ackermann, Solvable Cases of the Decision Problem, Amsterdam 1954, pp. 88f. (1955)

I shall prove that all (consistent) formulae of the second degree have an *Erfüllung* in a finite realm of individuals.

*

Every Cxy-sentence has a perfect (*ausgezeichnete*) disjunctive normal form in terms of the basic sentences. This normal form is a 0-, 1-, . . . or 2^{3n}-termed disjunction of $3n$-termed conjunctions of basic sentences and/or their negations. (n, it will be remembered, is the number of relations).

By a $Ccxy$-conjunction we understand a conjunction in the normal form of some Cxy-sentence.

By a $EyCcxy$-sentence we understand a $Ccxy$-conjunction which has been existentially quantified in the variable y.

The existential quantifier before a disjunction can be distributed.

Hence, every $EyCxy$-sentence is equivalent to a disjunction of $EyCcxy$-sentences.

Every $CEyCxy$-sentence has a perfect disjunctive normal form in terms of the $EyCcxy$-sentences. This normal form is a 0-, 1-, . . . or $2^{(2^{3n})}$-termed disjunction of 2^{3n}-termed conjunctions of $EyCcxy$-sentences and/or their negations.

By a $CcEyCcxy$-conjunction we understand a conjunction in the normal form of some $CEyCxy$-sentence.

If an individual has a certain relation to itself, then the individual in question has this relation to some individual and some individual has this relation to the individual in question.

It follows that a $CcEyCcxy$-conjunction which contains a sentence $\sim (Ey)$ ($. . . R_i xy$ & $R_i yx$ & $R_i xx . . .$) or $\sim (Ey)$ ($. . . \sim R_i xy$ & $\sim R_i yx$ & $\sim R_i xx . . .$) is self-contradictory. ($1 \leq i \leq n$.)

Trivially a $CcEyCcxy$-conjunction which contains both $R_i xx$ and $\sim R_i xx$ is self-contradictory.

It is easy to calculate that the number of consistent $CcEyCcxy$-conjunctions is 2 with the exponent $2^{2n} + n - 1$.

Self-contradictory members of a disjunction can be omitted.

Hence, every $CEyCxy$-sentence is equivalent to a 0-, 1-, . . . or $2^{(2^{2n}+n-1)}$-termed disjunction of consistent 2^{3n}-termed conjunctions of $EyCcxy$-sentences and/or their negations.

By a $ExCcEyCcxy$-sentence we understand a $CcEyCcxy$-

conjunction which has been existentially quantified in the variable x. If the conjunction is consistent, we call the quantified sentence an existence-constituent or E-constituent.

Thus the number of E-constituents is the same as the number of consistent $CcEyCcxy$-conjunctions i.e., 2 with the exponent $2^{2n} + n - 1$.

Every $ExCEyCxy$-sentence is equivalent to a disjunction of $ExCcEyCcxy$-sentences of the sort which we have called E-constituents.

Every $CExCEyCxy$-sentence, i.e. every formula of the second degree, has a perfect disjunctive normal form in terms of E-constituents. This normal form is a 0-, 1-, . . . or (2 with the exponent $2^{(2^{2n}+n-1)}$-termed disjunction of $2^{(2^{2n}+n-1)}$-termed conjunctions of E-constituents and/or their negations.

By a $CcExCcEyCcxy$-conjunction we understand a conjunction of E-constituents and/or their negations.

Of the $CcExCcEyCcxy$-conjunctions a certain number are self-contradictory. Let the number of consistent conjunctions be μ.

Hence, every $CExCEyCxy$-sentence is equivalent to a 0-, 1-, . . . or μ-termed disjunction of consistent $2^{(2^{2n}+n-1)}$-termed conjunctions of E-constituents and/or their negations. If and only if it is equivalent to the disjunction of all the consistent conjunctions in question, it expresses a logically true proposition.

The decision problem for formulae of the second degree has now become 'reduced' to the following question:

How is it to be decided, whether a given $CcExCcEyCcxy$ conjunction is consistent, or not?

*

A basic sentence $R_i xy$ can be pictured in the following way:

(1)

The patch to the left pictures x. The patch to the right pictures y. The arrow indicates that the relation subsists between x and y *in that order*.

47

(A relation which subsists reflexively is indicated by an arrow which returns to its point of departure.)

If there are several (basic) relations, they ought to be somehow distinguished from each other in the pictures. We may, e.g., use arrows of different colours for the different relations.

A *Ccxy*-conjunction can be pictured in the following way:

There is one patch which pictures *x* and another patch which pictures *y*. The patches are joined by arrows as indicated by the basic sentences which occur in the conjunction.

Example. Let there be only two basic relations. We call them *R* and *S*. To indicate *R* we use an 'ordinary' arrow and to indicate *S* we use a dotted arrow. There are 2^6 or 64 *Ccxy*-conjunctions. One of them is *Rxy* & *Ryx* & *Rxx* & *Sxy* & $\sim$ *Syx* & $\sim$ *Sxx*. Its picture looks as follows:

(2)

(To indicate that a relation subsists 'both ways' between two individuals we use a double-arrow (instead of two arrows).)

We shall say that the patch which pictures *x* has a certain *Cc*-relation to the patch which pictures *y*, and that the patch which pictures *y* has the converse (relation) of this *Cc*-relation to the patch which pictures *x*.

There are as many *Cc*-relations between patches as there are ways, in which *n* relations and their converse relations can subsist or not subsist between two individuals. The number of different *Cc*-relations is thus 2^{2n}.

Some *Cc*-relations are symmetrical, others are not. The converse of every *Cc*-relation is itself a *Cc*-relation.

A patch also has a certain *Cc*-relation to itself.

If there are no arrows joining two patches (one patch to itself), we say that the patches (patch) are (is) in the o-relation to each other (itself). — The o-relation is a *Cc*-relation.

The picture of a *Ccxy*-conjunction is also a picture of a *EyCcxy*-sentence.

A (consistent) *CcEyCcxy*-conjunction can be pictured in the following way:

There is one patch which pictures *x*. It is surrounded by (at least) as many patches as there are (unnegated) *EyCcxy*-sentences in the conjunction. The patch which pictures *x* has to the surrounding patches and to itself *Cc*-relations as indicated by the *EyCcxy*-sentences. The surrounding patches have the o-relation to themselves and to each other.

Example. In the case of the two relations called *R* and *S* this is a *CcEyCcxy*-conjunction:

$$(Ey) \ (Rxy \ \& \ Ryx \ \& \ Rxx \ \& \ Sxy \ \& \ Syx \ \& \ Sxx) \ \&$$
$$\sim (Ey) \ (Rxy \ \& \ Ryx \ \& \ Rxx \ \& \ Sxy \ \& \ \sim Syx \ \& \ Sxx) \ \&$$
$$\sim (Ey) \ (Rxy \ \& \ Ryx \ \& \ Rxx \ \& \ \sim Sxy \ \& \ Syx \ \& \ Sxx) \ \&$$
$$\sim (Ey) \ (Rxy \ \& \ Ryx \ \& \ Rxx \ \& \ \sim Sxy \ \& \ \sim Syx \ \& \ Sxx) \ \&$$
$$\sim (Ey) \ (Rxy \ \& \ \sim Ryx \ \& \ Rxx \ \& \ Sxy \ \& \ Syx \ \& \ Sxx) \ \&$$
$$\sim (Ey) \ (Rxy \ \& \ \sim Ryx \ \& \ Rxx \ \& \ Sxy \ \& \ \sim Syx \ \& \ Sxx) \ \&$$
$$\sim (Ey) \ (Rxy \ \& \ \sim Ryx \ \& \ Rxx \ \& \ \sim Sxy \ \& \ Syx \ \& \ Sxx) \ \&$$
$$(Ey) \ (Rxy \ \& \ \sim Ryx \ \& \ Rxx \ \& \ \sim Sxy \ \& \ \sim Syx \ \& \ Sxx) \ \&$$
$$\sim (Ey) \ (\sim Rxy \ \& \ Ryx \ \& \ Rxx \ \& \ Sxy \ \& \ Syx \ \& \ Sxx) \ \&$$
$$\sim (Ey) \ (\sim Rxy \ \& \ Ryx \ \& \ Rxx \ \& \ Sxy \ \& \ \sim Syx \ \& \ Sxx) \ \&$$
$$\sim (Ey) \ (\sim Rxy \ \& \ Ryx \ \& \ Rxx \ \& \ \sim Sxy \ \& \ Syx \ \& \ Sxx) \ \&$$
$$\sim (Ey) \ (\sim Rxy \ \& \ Ryx \ \& \ Rxx \ \& \ \sim Sxy \ \& \ \sim Syx \ \& \ Sxx) \ \&$$
$$\sim (Ey) \ (\sim Rxy \ \& \ \sim Ryx \ \& \ Rxx \ \& \ Sxy \ \& \ Syx \ \& \ Sxx) \ \&$$
$$\sim (Ey) \ (\sim Rxy \ \& \ \sim Ryx \ \& \ Rxx \ \& \ Sxy \ \& \ \sim Syx \ \& \ Sxx) \ \&$$
$$\sim (Ey) \ (\sim Rxy \ \& \ \sim Ryx \ \& \ Rxx \ \& \ \sim Sxy \ \& \ Syx \ \& \ Sxx) \ \&$$
$$\sim (Ey) \ (\sim Rxy \ \& \ \sim Ryx \ \& \ Rxx \ \& \ \sim Sxy \ \& \ \sim Syx \ \& \ Sxx).$$

Its picture looks as follows:

(3)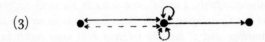

(If the patch which pictures *x* stands to *one* other patch (or to itself) in a certain *Cc*-relation, we can introduce into the diagram *any number* of new patches to which the patch which pictures *x* has the same *Cc*-relation.)

The picture of a (consistent) *CcEyCcxy*-conjunction is also a picture of a (consistent) *ExCcEyCcxy*-sentence or *E*-constituent.

We shall say that the patch which pictures *x* *together with the patches surrounding it* constitutes a picture of the *E*-constituent. We call the patch which pictures *x* *constituent-individual*. Two constituent-individuals are said to be *of the same kind* if they, together with the patches surrounding each of them, constitute pictures of the same *E*-constituent. Otherwise they are said to be of different kinds.

A *CcExCcEyCcxy*-conjunction says that there are constituent-individuals of certain kinds and not constituent-individuals of certain other kinds ('in the world').

The problem of constructing a picture of a given *CcExCcEyCcxy*-conjunction, therefore, is the problem of constructing a diagram of patches and arrows in such a way that

(*a*) each existing kind of constituent-individual is represented by at least one patch, and

(*b*) each patch represents an existing kind of constituent-individual.

We shall call part (*a*) of the problem the Fitting-in-Problem and part (*b*) the Completing-Problem.

A *CcExCcEyCcxy*-conjunction is consistent, if and only if it has a picture.

The decision problem for formulae of the second degree has now become 'reduced' to the problem of giving effective criteria for the solvability of the two problems which we have called the Fitting-in-Problem and the Completing-Problem.

*

The solution of the Fitting-in-Problem is governed by the following Criterion of Compatibility:

Two constituent-individuals, i and i', can occur in the same diagram, if and only if there is a Cc-relation r such that i has the relation r to some patch in its surrounding and i' has the relation ř to some patch in its surrounding.[1]

Example. Consider the *E*-constituents, of which (3) above and (4) below are pictures. (We leave it as an exercise to the reader to 'reconstruct' the *ExCcEyCcxy*-sentence containing the names *R* and *S*, of which (4) is a picture.)

(4)

The constituent-individuals of the two pictures can be fitted into one and the same diagram as follows:

[1] ˘ is the symbol for converse.

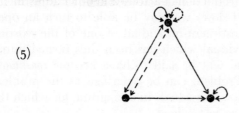

(5)

Consider the E-constituent, of which (6) is a picture.

(6)

It is not possible for the constituent-individual of this picture to occur in the same diagram as the constituent-individuals of either (3) or (4).

Since the number of Cc-relations is necessarily finite, it is always possible to tell from the pictures of the E-constituents, whether any given number of kinds of constituent-individual can be represented in the same diagram, or not.

(I have not been able to find the number of consistent conjunctions of (unnegated) E-constituents in the general case, when there are n basic relations. In the simplest possible case, when there is only one basic relation, the number if 13312. The calculation of the number is a fairly laborious operation.[1])

The Criterion of Compatibility can be said to 'reflect' in the language of diagram-constructing the following important truth about relations.

If something has to everything a certain relation, then everything has to something the converse of this relation.

Consider a diagram, for which the Fitting-in-Problem has been solved. (It is thus being assumed that the existing kinds of constituent-individual are mutually compatible and represented by at least one patch in the diagram).

In such a diagram there will usually occur other patches beside fitted in constituent-individuals. We shall call these patches open individuals. The open individuals have the o-relation to themselves and to each other.

[1]Cf. 'On the Idea of Logical Truth (II)', pp. 42-44.

By means of the introduction of arrows and other adjustments in the diagram (cf. below) we may be able to turn an open individual into a constituent-individual of one of the existing kinds. An open individual which has been thus turned into a constituent-individual will be said to have become *constituted*.

The Completing-Problem can be described as the problem of constituting all open individuals in a diagram, for which the Fitting-in-Problem has been solved.

The solution of the Completing-Problem is governed by the following Criterion of Constitutability:

An open individual o can be constituted, if and only if there is no Cc-relation r such that o has the relation r to some constituent-individual but no constituent-individual has the relation r to any patch in the diagram.

Since the number of Cc-relations and existing kinds of constituent-individual is necessarily finite, it is always possible to tell from a diagram, for which the Fitting-in-Problem has been solved, whether or not the above criterion is satisfied for the open individuals. It remains, however, to be proved that the criterion actually is necessary as well as sufficient for constitutability.

Consider an open individual o. We make a list of the Cc-relations which o has to the other patches in the diagram. The following three cases can now be distinguished:

i. The Cc-relations which o has to the surrounding patches are those and only those Cc-relations which some constituent-individual, say i, in the diagram has to the surrounding patches.

ii. There is (at least) one Cc-relation which o has to some constituent-individual in the diagram, but which no constituent-individual in the diagram has to any patch.

iii. The Cc-relations in the list satisfy neither i nor ii.

In the first case, o can be constituted as a constituent-individual of the same kind as i. The constitution of o is accomplished by joining o to itself with arrows in the same way as i is joined to itself with arrows.

Example. In the diagram (5) above there are two constituent-individuals and one open individual, viz. the one to the left. The open individual has exactly the same Cc-relations to the two other patches as has the constituent-individual on the top. Thus we accomplish the constitution of the open individual by joining it to itself with an 'ordinary' arrow and a dotted arrow. When completed, the diagram looks as follows:

(7)

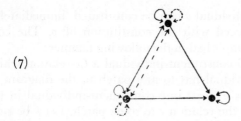

In the second case, o cannot be constituted.

Example. In the diagram (6) above there is one constituent-individual and one open individual, viz. the one to the right. The Cc-relation which subsists between the patches is not symmetrical. Hence, the open individual has to the constituent-individual a Cc-relation, which the constituent-individual has to no patch in the diagram. It is not possible to constitute the open individual and thus complete the diagram. (We assumed that the Fitting-in-Problem had been solved.)

In the third case, o can be constituted as a constituent-individual of any one of the existing kinds. This has to be proved.

Consider an arbitrary constituent-individual i in the diagram. We divide the Cc-relations which o has to the surrounding patches into the following three classes:

1. Cc-relations which o has to some patch and i has to some patch.

2. Cc-relations which o has to some patch but i has to no patch.

3. Cc-relations which i has to some patch but o has to no patch.

Cc-relations of the first class are left unaltered in the diagram.

Let r be a Cc-relation of the second class. Consider a constituent-individual p to which o has the relation r. By removing and/or introducing suitable arrows we 'cut off' the existing connexion between o and p and establish between them the Cc-relation which i has to p.

If o happened to be the only patch which has the relation r to p, we ought to introduce into the diagram a new open individual a which has the relation r to p. We call a *auxiliary individual*.

The auxiliary individual a can be constituted 'immediately', i.e. before we proceed with the constitution of o. The constitution of a is accomplished in the following manner:

Since o has to no constituent-individual a Cc-relation which no constituent-individual has to any patch in the diagram, it follows that there is at least one constituent-individual in the diagram which has the relation r to some patch. Let k be such a constituent-individual and let r' be the relation which k has to p. We maintain that a can be constituted as a constituent-individual of the same kind as k. Two cases ought to be distinguished:

α. The relation r' is symmetrical or p is not the only patch to which k has the relation r' or $r' = r$. If r' is symmetrical, we establish between a and k the relation r'. If r' is not symmetrical, we establish between a and k the Cc-relation which k has to itself. Between a and itself we establish the Cc-relation which k has to itself. Between a and the remaining patches in the diagram we establish the Cc-relations which k has to them. This completes the constitution of a. (If a has the relation r' to some other patch but k, we may establish between a and k any Cc-relation, which k has to some patch and some patch has to k.)

Example. In the diagram (8) below o was originally connected with p by a double-arrow. Since p was not connected with any other patch by a double-arrow, the constitution of o as a constituent-individual of the same kind as i necessitated the introduction of $a.p$ fulfils the requirement which k above had to satisfy. We therefore, identify k with p. The constitution of a is completed by emitting an arrow from a to o and i.

(8)

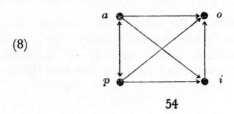

It should be observed that i, p and a are constituted in (8), but not yet o. (Cf. below.)

β. The relation r' is not symmetrical and p is the only patch to which k has the relation r' and $r' \neq r$. In this case we have to introduce an additional auxiliary individual a'. Between a and a' we establish the relation r'. Thereupon we complete the constitution of a in exactly the same way as under the alternative α above.

Between a' and k we establish the relation $\check{r}$. Between a' and p we establish the Cc-relation which p has to itself. Between a' and itself we establish the Cc-relation which p has to itself. Between a' and the remaining patches in the diagram (i.e. all patches but a, k, and p) we establish the Cc-relation which p has to them. This completes the constitution of a' as a constituent-individual of the same kind as p.

Example. The relations which p has to a, a to a', a' to k, and k to p might, e.g., be as indicated in the diagram.

(9)

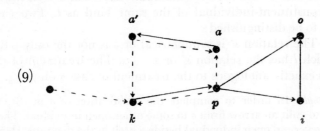

We leave it as an exercise to the reader to constitute a as a constituent-individual of the same kind as k and a' as a constituent-individual of the same kind as p.

If the operation which we have described is repeated, first for every patch (if any) beside p, to which o has the relation r, and then for every relation (if any) beside r, which o but not i has to some constituent-individual, we shall ultimately achieve that there is no longer any Cc-relation which o has to some constituent-individual but i to no patch in the diagram.

Let s be a Cc-relation of the third class. By introducing suitable arrows we establish between o and some other open individual in the diagram the relation s. If this operation is repeated for every relation (if any) beside s, which i but not o has to some patch, we shall ultimately achieve that there is no longer any Cc-relation of the third class.

Lastly, if i has the o-relation to no patch, we establish between o and such open individuals (if any) in the diagram, to which o still has the o-relation, the Cc-relation which i has to them. This completes the constitution of o as a constituent-individual of the same kind as i.

If there is not a sufficient number of open individuals left in the diagram for dealing with Cc-relations of the third class, we ought to introduce auxiliary individuals for the purpose.

Let b be such an auxiliary individual. o has to b the relation s.

Since we have already accomplished the constitution of all open individuals beside o, which originally appeared in the diagram, it follows that there is at least one constituent-individual in the diagram, to which some patch has the relation s. Let l be such a constituent-individual and let s' be the relation which l has to o. We maintain that b can be constituted as a constituent-individual of the same kind as l. Two cases ought to be distinguished:

α'. The relation s' is symmetrical or o is not the only patch to which l has the relation s' or $s' = s$. The treatment of this case is exactly analogous to the treatment of case α on p. 54.

Example. In order to complete the constitution of o in (8), we ought to emit an arrow from o to some other open individual. There is, however, no open individual beside o itself in the diagram. Hence we introduce b and emit an arrow from o to b. i fulfils the requirement which l above had to satisfy. We, therefore, identify l with i. The constitution of b is completed by emitting an arrow from a and p to b and from b to i.

(10)

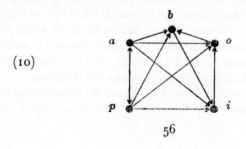

β'. The relation s' is not symmetrical and o is the only patch to which l has the relation s' and $s' \neq s$. The treatment of this case is exactly analogous to the treatment of case β on p. 55. (An additional auxiliary individual b' will have to be introduced. b' is constituted as a constituent-individual of the same kind as o).

We have now proved the necessary and sufficient character of the Criterion of Constitutability.

As seen, the constitution of an open individual may require the introduction of auxiliary open individuals. The constitution of an auxiliary open individual may require the introduction of one but never of more than one additional auxiliary open individual. The fact that the process of introducing auxiliary individuals thus necessarily 'comes to an end' means that the picture of a (consistent) $CcExCcEyCcxy$-conjunction will necessarily contain only a finite number of patches.[1]

(I have not been able to find the number of consistent conjunctions of E-constituents and/or their negations in the general case, when there are n basic relations. In the simplest possible case, when there is only one basic relation, the number is 13112.[2])

The Criterion of Constitutability can be said to 'reflect' in the language of diagram-constructing the following important truth about relations:

Something has to something a certain relation, if, and only if, something has to something the converse of this relation.

---

[1] In dealing with formulae of the third degree or $CExCEyCEzCxyz$-sentences (not defined in this paper) the following situation sometimes occurs: The picture of a certain $CcExCcEyCcEzCcxyz$-conjunction can be completed, i.e. every open individual can be constituted, but the constitution of some open individuals necessitates the introduction of an auxiliary open individual, the constitution of which necessitates the introduction of an additional auxiliary open individual, and so on *ad infinitum*. Such a conjunction is said to have an *Erfüllung* only in an infinite realm of individuals.

[2] Cf. 'On the Idea of Logical Truth (II)', p. 45.

DEONTIC LOGIC

(1951)

So called modal concepts might conveniently be divided into three or four main groups. There are the alethic modes or modes of truth. These are concepts such as the necessary (the necessarily true), the possible (the possibly true), and the contingent (the contingently true). There are the epistemic modes or modes of knowing. These are concepts such as the verified (that which is known to be true), the undecided, and the falsified (that which is known to be false). There are the deontic[1] modes or modes of obligation. These are concepts such as the obligatory (that which we ought to do), the permitted (that which we are allowed to do), and the forbidden (that which we must not do). As a fourth main group of modal categories one might add the existential modes or modes of existence. These are concepts such as universality, existence, and emptiness (of properties or classes).

There are essential similarities but also characteristic differences between the various groups of modalities. They all deserve, therefore, a special treatment. The treatment of the existential modes is usually known as quantification theory. The treatment of the alethic modes covers most of what is traditionally known as modal logic. The epistemic modes have not to any great extent and the deontic modes hardly at all been treated by logicians.

In the present paper an elementary formal logic of the deontic modalities will be outlined.

2. First a preliminary question must be settled. What are the 'things' which are pronounced obligatory, permitted, forbidden, etc.?

[1]For the term 'deontic' I am indebted to Professor C. D. Broad.

We shall call these 'things' acts.

The word 'act', however, is used ambiguously in ordinary language. It is sometimes used for what might be called act-qualifying properties, e.g. theft. But it is also used for the individual cases which fall under these properties, e.g. the individual thefts.

The use of the word for individual cases is perhaps more appropriate than its use for properties. For the sake of verbal convenience, however, we shall in this paper use 'act' for properties and not for individuals. We shall say that theft, murder, smoking, etc., are acts. The individual cases that fall under theft, murder, smoking, etc., we shall call act-individuals. It is of acts and not of act-individuals that deontic words are predicated.

The performance or non-performance of a certain act (by an agent)we shall call performance-values (for that agent). An act will be called a performance-function of certain other acts, if its performance-value for any given agent uniquely depends upon the performance-values of those other acts for the same agent.

The concept of a performance-function is strictly analogous to the concept of a truth-function in propositional logic.

Particular performance-functions can be defined in strict correspondence to the particular truth-functions.

Thus by the negation (-act) of a given act we understand that act which is performed by an agent, if and only if he does not perform the given act. For example: the negation of the act of repaying a loan is the act of not repaying it. If A denotes (is the name of) an act, $\sim A$ will be used as a name of its negation (-act).

Similarly, we can define the conjunction-, disjunction-, implication-, and equivalence-act of two given acts. (The implication-act, e.g., of two given acts is the act which is performed by an agent, if and only if it is not the case that the first act is performed and the second act is not performed by the agent in question.) If A and B denote acts, $A \& B$ will be used as a name of their conjunction, $A \vee B$ as a name of their disjunction, $A \to B$ as a name of their implication, and $A \longleftrightarrow B$ as a name of their equivalence.

59

Finally, we can define the tautology- and contradiction (-act) of *n* given acts. The first is the act which is performed and the second the act which is not performed by an agent, whatever be the performance-values of the *n* given acts for the agent in question.

We shall call $\sim A$ the negation-name of A, and A & B the conjunction-, A v B the disjunction-, $A \to B$ the implication-, and $A \longleftrightarrow B$ the equivalence-name of A and B.

A name of an act which is neither the negation-name of another name of an act, nor the conjunction-, disjunction-, implication-, or equivalence-name of two other names of acts we shall call an atomic name.

By a molecular complex of *n* names of acts we understand:

(i) Any one of the *n* names themselves.

(ii) The negation-name of any molecular complex of the *n* names, and the conjunction-, disjunction-, implication-, and equivalence-name of any two molecular complexes of the *n* names.

The *n* names are called constituents of their molecular complexes. If they are atomic names, they are called atomic constituents.

As to the use of brackets we adopt the convention that the symbol & has a stronger combining force than v, $\to$, and $\longleftrightarrow$; the symbol v than $\to$ and $\longleftrightarrow$; and the symbol $\to$ than $\longleftrightarrow$. Thus, e.g., we write for $([(A \ \& \ B) \ v \ C] \to D) \longleftrightarrow E$ simply $A \ \& \ B \ v \ C \to D \longleftrightarrow E$.

The symbols $\sim$, &, v, $\to$, and $\longleftrightarrow$ will be used for truth-functions as well as for performance-functions. This ambiguity does not easily lead to confusion and is, therefore, to be preferred to the introduction of two special sets of symbols.

3. As an undefined deontic category we introduce the concept of permission. It is the only undefined deontic category which we need.

If an act is not permitted, it is called forbidden. For instance: Theft is not permitted, hence it is forbidden. We are *not allowed to* steal, hence we *must not* steal.[1]

[1]It need hardly be stressed that the question of validity of various deontic propositions (other than those which are true on formal grounds) does not concern us in this paper.

If the negation of an act is forbidden, the act itself is called obligatory. For instance: it is forbidden to disobey the law, hence it is obligatory to obey the law. We *ought to* do that which we are *not allowed not to* do.

If an act and its negation are both permitted, the act is called (morally) indifferent. For instance: in a smoking compartment we may smoke, but we may also not smoke. Hence smoking is here a morally indifferent form of behaviour.

It should be observed that indifference is thus a narrower category than permission. Everything indifferent is permitted, but everything permitted is not indifferent. For, what is obligatory is also permitted, but not indifferent.

(The difference between the permitted and the indifferent among the deontic modes is analogous to the difference between the possible and the contingent among the alethic modes.)

The above deontic concepts apply to a single act (or performance-function of acts). There are also deontic concepts which apply to pairs of acts.

Two acts are morally incompatible, if their conjunction is forbidden (and compatible if it is permitted). For instance: giving a promise and not keeping it are (*morally*) incompatible acts.

Doing one act commits us to do another act, if the implication of the two acts is obligatory. For instance: giving a promise commits us to keep it.

The proposition[1] that the act named by A is permitted will be expressed in symbols by PA.

The proposition that the act named by A is forbidden, is the negation of the proposition that it is permitted. It can thus be symbolized by $\sim P A$.

The proposition that the act named by A is obligatory, is the negation of the proposition that the negation of the act is permitted. It can thus be symbolized by $\sim P \sim A$. We shall also use the shorter expression $O A$.

The proposition that the act named by A is (morally) indifferent can be symbolized by $P A \mathbin{\&} P \sim A$.

The proposition that the acts named by A and by B are

[1] See above Preface, p. vii.

(morally) incompatible can be symbolized by $\sim P(A \ \& \ B)$.

The proposition that the performance of the act named by A commits us to perform the act named by B can be symbolized by $O(A \to B)$. But $O(A \to B)$ means the same as $\sim P \sim (A \to B)$, and this means the same as $\sim P(A \ \& \ \sim B)$. Commitment can thus be explained in terms of compatibility.[1]

P and O are called the deontic operators. Sentences of the type 'P ', where a name of an act (or a molecular complex of names of acts) has to be inserted in the blank, we shall call P-sentences. Similarly, we shall call sentences of the type 'O ' O-sentences.

The system of Deontic Logic, which we are outlining in this paper, studies propositions (and truth-functions of propositions) about the obligatory, permitted, forbidden, and other (derivative) deontic characters of acts (and performance-functions of acts).

We shall call the propositions which are the object of study deontic propositions. The sentences, in which they are expressed in our system, are P- and O-sentences or molecular complexes of such sentences.

4. A task of particular importance which Deontic Logic sets itself is to develop a technique for deciding, whether the propositions it studies are logically true or not. (The decision problem.)

Sometimes molecular complexes of P- and O-sentences express truths of logic for reasons which have nothing to do with the specific character of deontic concepts. For instance: if A is permitted, if B is permitted, then B is forbidden, if A is forbidden. In symbols: $(P B \to P A) \to (\sim P A \to \sim P B)$. This is a truth of logic. It is an application of a variant of the so-called *modus tollens* which is valid for any sentences, whether deontic or not. It is, therefore, a trivial truth from the point of view of our Deontic Logic.

Sometimes, however, molecular complexes of P- and O-sentences express truths of logic for reasons which depend upon

---

[1]This view of commitment is open to criticism. See A. N. Prior, 'The Paradoxes of Derived Obligation', *Mind* **63**, p. 67f., and my reply 'A Note on Deontic Logic and Derived Obligation', *Mind* **65**, p. 507f.

the specific (logical) character of deontic concepts. For instance: If A is obligatory and if doing A commits us to do B, then B is obligatory too. In symbols: $O\,A\ \&\ O(A \to B) \to O\,B$. It is intuitively obvious that this is a truth of logic, i.e. something which is valid on purely formal grounds. It is, however, not an application of any scheme which is valid for *any* sentences, whether deontic or not. The existence of logical truths which are peculiar to deontic concepts is what makes the study of Deontic Logic interesting.

If a molecular complex of P- and O-sentences expresses logical truth for reasons which are independent of the specific nature of deontic concepts, then its truth can be established or proved in a truth-table of propositional logic.

If, however, a molecular complex of P- and O-sentences expresses logical truth for reasons which depend on the specific nature of deontic concepts, then its truth cannot be established by the means of propositional logic alone. The question therefore arises: What is the necessary and sufficient criterion which a molecular complex of P- and/or O-sentences must satisfy in order to express a logically true proposition?

5. Let us call 'permitted' and 'forbidden' the two deontic values.

An act will be called a deontic function of certain other acts, if the deontic value of the former uniquely depends upon the deontic values of the latter.

It is easy to see that not any act which is a performance-function of certain other acts is also a deontic function of them. (Otherwise the logic of deontic concepts would be trivial.)

Consider first the negation of a given act. From the fact that A is performed, we can conclude to the fact that $\sim A$ is not performed. But from the fact that A is permitted, we can conclude nothing as to the permitted or forbidden character of $\sim A$. Sometimes $\sim A$ is permitted, sometimes not. If A is what we have called indifferent, then $\sim A$ is also permitted, but if A happened to be obligatory as well as permitted, then $\sim A$ would be forbidden. In the smoking compartment, e.g., not-smoking is permitted and also smoking. But in the non-smoking compartment, not-smoking is permitted and smoking forbidden.

Consider next the conjunction of two acts. From the fact that A and B are both performed, it follows that A & B is performed. But from the fact that A and B are both permitted, it does not follow that A & B is permitted. Sometimes A & B is permitted, sometimes not. For, A and B may both be permitted, but doing either of them may commit us not to do the other. I may be free to promise and also not to promise to give a certain thing to a person, and free to give and also not to give this thing to him, but forbidden to promise to give and yet not give it.

Consider, finally, the disjunction of two acts. From the fact that at least one of the two acts A and B is performed, it follows that A v B is performed, and from the fact that none of the two acts A and B is performed, it follows that A v B is not performed. Similarly, from the fact that at least one of the acts is permitted, it follows that their disjunction is permitted, and from the fact that both acts are forbidden, it follows that their disjunction is forbidden. In other words: the disjunction of two acts is permitted, if and only if at least one of the acts is permitted. Speaking loud or smoking is permitted in the reading-room, if and only if speaking loud is permitted or smoking is permitted.[1]

Thus deontic functions are similar to performance-functions (and truth-functions) in regard to disjunction, but not similar in regard to negation and conjunction. The similarity can be laid down as a Principle of Deontic Distribution:

If an act is the disjunction of two other acts, then the proposition that the disjunction is permitted is the disjunction of the proposition that the first act is permitted and the proposition that the second act is permitted.

(This principle can, naturally, be extended to disjunctions with any number n of members.)

---

[1] The meaning of 'or' in ordinary language is not quite settled. When we say that we are permitted to do A or B, we sometimes mean, by implication, that we are allowed to do both. Sometimes, however, we mean that we are allowed to do one only of the two acts. Which meaning the 'or' conveys by implication depends upon the material nature of the individual case, in which it is used. It ought to be stressed that our use of 'or' in this paper is neutral with regard to such material differences in the individual situations. That we are permitted to do A or B means here that we are permitted to do at least one of the two acts, and neither excludes nor includes, by implication, the permission to do both.

In virtue of familiar principles of formal logic, any molecular complex of n names of acts has what we propose to call a perfect disjunctive normal form. This is a 0-, 1-, or more-than-1-termed disjunction-name of n-termed conjunction-names. Each of the n original names or its negation-name occurs in every one of the conjunction-names.

In virtue of the above Principle of Deontic Distribution, any molecular complex of n names of acts denotes a deontic function of the acts denoted by the conjunction-names in its perfect disjunctive normal form.

Consider now a P-sentence $P\,c$, where c stands for (an atomic name of an act or) a molecular complex of names of acts. Let $c_1, \ldots c_k$ stand for the conjunction-names in the perfect disjunctive normal form of c. The sentences $Pc_1, \ldots, Pc_k$ we shall call the P-constituents of $P\,c$.

Since, in virtue of the Principle of Deontic Distribution, c denotes a deontic function of the acts named by $c_1, \ldots, c_k$, it follows that $P\,c$ expresses a truth-function of the propositions expressed by $Pc_1, \ldots, Pc_k$. Generally speaking: a P-sentence expresses a truth-function of the propositions expressed by its P-constituents.

Consider n names of acts $A_1, \ldots, A_n$. There are in all 2^n conjunction-names which can be formed by selecting m ($0 \le m \le n$) out of the n names and taking the negation-names of the remaining n-m names. (The order of the names in a conjunction-name is irrelevant.) By the deontic units in the deontic realm of the acts named by $A_1, \ldots, A_n$ we shall understand the propositions that the respective acts named by those 2^n conjunction-names are permitted. By the deontic realm itself we shall understand the disjunction of all the deontic units.

Thus, e.g., the deontic units of the deontic realm of the sole act named by A are the propositions expressed by $P\,A$ and $P \sim A$. The deontic realm itself is the proposition expressed by $P\,A \lor P \sim A$. The deontic units of the deontic realm of the acts named by A and B are the propositions expressed by $P(A \,\&\, B)$ and $P(A \,\&\sim B)$ and $P(\sim A \,\&\, B)$ and $P(\sim A \,\&\sim B)$. Etc.

The deontic units of the deontic realm of given acts are logically independent of one another, meaning that they can be true or false in any combination of truth-values. There is, however, one point at which this independence might be questioned. Could *all* the deontic units be false?

Let *A* be the name of an act. That all (both) the deontic units in the deontic realm of this act are false means that the act itself and its negation are both forbidden. In symbols: $\sim P\,A\,\&\,\sim P \sim A$. Since the act *or* its negation is performed by any agent whenever he acts, the falsehood of all the deontic units means that we are forbidden to act in any way whatsoever.

Is such a prohibition illogical? Its counterpart in the logic of the alethic modalities would be the case, when a proposition and its negation are both impossible, and its counterpart in the logic of the epistemic modalities would be the case, when a proposition and its negation are both known to be false. *These* cases are obviously logical impossibilities. On the other hand, in the logic of the existential modalities the corresponding case is, when a property and its negation are both empty. *This* is not an impossibility, since the Universe of Discourse may have no members. The question, therefore is, whether the deontic modes at this point resemble the alethic and the epistemic modes or whether they resemble the existential modes.

Ordinary language and our common sense logical intuitions seem at first not to provide us with a clear answer. A simple logical transformation, however, will help us to make up our minds.

That the negation of an act is forbidden means that the act itself is obligatory. Thus we can for $\sim P \sim A$ write $O\,A$. That an act and its negation are both forbidden means the same as that the act itself is both obligatory and forbidden.

At this point an appeal to ordinary language will, I think, be decisive. We seem prepared to reject a use of the words, according to which one and the same act could be truly called both obligatory and forbidden.[1] If, however, we reject this use, we must also reject the idea that all the units in a deontic realm could be false.

Thus, on the point at issue, the deontic modalities appear to resemble the alethic and the epistemic modalities rather than the existential ones.

[1] For the 'relativity' of deontic propositions cf. below, p. 74.

66

The restriction on the logical independence of the deontic units, which we are forced to accept, can be laid down as a Principle of Permission:

Any given act is either itself permitted or its negation is permitted.

There are alternative formulations of the principle. We might also have said: If the negation of an act is forbidden, then the act itself is permitted. And this again is equivalent to saying: If an act is obligatory, then it is permitted.

6. Which truth-function of its P-constituents a P-sentence expresses can be investigated and decided in truth-tables.

We shall here construct a truth-table for the following P-sentences: $P A$ and $P \sim A$ and $P(A \& B)$ and $P(A \vee B)$ and $P(A \to B)$ and $P(A \longleftrightarrow B)$ and $P(A \vee \sim A)$. The perfect disjunctive normal form of A (in terms of A and B) is $A \& B \vee A \& \sim B$. The normal form of $\sim A$ is $\sim A \& B \vee \sim A \& \sim B$. The normal form of $A \& B$ is $A \& B$. The normal form of $A \vee B$ is $A \& B \vee A \& \sim B \vee \sim A \& B$. The normal form of $A \to B$ is $A \& B \vee \sim A \& B \vee \sim A \& \sim B$. The normal form of $A \longleftrightarrow B$ is $A \& B \vee \sim A \& \sim B$. The normal form of $A \vee \sim A$ is $A \& B \vee A \& \sim B \vee \sim A \& B \vee \sim A \& \sim B$. Thus the seven P-sentences have in all four P-constituents, viz. $P(A \& B)$ and $P(A \& \sim B)$ and $P(\sim A \& B)$ and $P(\sim A \& \sim B)$. They express the deontic units of the deontic realm of the two acts named by A and by B.

In distributing truth-values over the deontic units (or the P-constituents) we have to observe the restriction imposed by the Principle of Permission. The subsequent calculation of truth-values for the seven deontic propositions (or the seven P-sentences) depends only on the Principle of Deontic Distribution. The table looks as on page 68.

What is the truth-table for $P(A \& \sim A)$? The perfect disjunctive normal form of $A \& \sim A$ is 'empty', i.e. a 0-termed disjunction. Thus $P(A \& \sim A)$ too is a 0-termed disjunction of P-constituents. It might be argued that a disjunction is true, if and only if at least one of its members is true, and that a 0-termed disjunction, since it has no members, is never true (always false). If, however, $P(A \& \sim A)$ is always false, its negation $\sim P(A \& \sim A)$ is always true. But $\sim P(A \& \sim A)$

means the same as $O(A \vee \sim A)$. Thus, on the above criterion for the truth of a o-termed disjunction, it follows that $O(A \vee \sim A)$ is a deontic tautology.

It might, however, be questioned whether it can be regarded as a truth of logic that a tautologous act is obligatory (and a contradictory act forbidden). The corresponding proposition in the logic of the alethic modalities is that a tautologous pro-

P(A&B)	P(A&~B)	P(~A&B)	P(~A&~B)	P A	P~A	P(A&B)	P(AvB)	P(A→B)	P(A⟶B)	P(Av~A)
T	T	T	T	T	T	T	T	T	T	T
T	T	T	F	T	T	T	T	T	T	T
T	T	F	T	T	T	T	T	T	T	T
T	T	F	F	T	F	T	T	T	T	T
T	F	T	T	T	T	T	T	T	T	T
T	F	T	F	T	T	T	T	T	T	T
T	F	F	T	T	T	T	T	T	T	T
F	F	F	F	T	F	F	T	T	T	T
F	T	T	T	T	T	F	T	T	T	T
F	T	T	F	T	T	F	T	T	F	T
F	T	F	T	T	T	F	T	T	T	T
F	T	F	F	T	F	F	T	F	F	T
F	F	T	T	F	T	F	T	T	T	T
F	F	T	F	F	T	F	F	T	F	T

position is necessary (and a contradictory proposition impossible), and the corresponding proposition in the logic of the existential modalities is that a tautologous property is universal (and a contradictory property empty). *These* corresponding cases are obviously logical truths. On the other hand, the corresponding propositions in the logic of the epistemic modalities is that a tautologous proposition is verified (and a contradictory proposition falsified). *This* is not a logical truth. For, a proposition may be tautologous (contradictory) without our knowing it. The question therefore is, whether the deontic modes at this point resemble the alethic and the existential modes, or whether they resemble the epistemic modes.

Ordinary language and our common sense logical intuitions seem not to provide us with any clear answer. It appears, moreover, that no further logical considerations can help us to decide on the issue. It may be thought 'awkward' to permit contradictory actions[1] but it is difficult to conceive of any logical argument against this permission. From the point of view of logic, therefore, the most plausible course seems to be to regard $P(A \& \sim A)$ and $O(A \text{ v} \sim A)$ as expressing contingent propositions which can be either true or false.

Thus, on the point at issue, the deontic modalities appear to resemble the epistemic rather than the alethic and the existential modalities.

We suggest the following Principle of Deontic Contingency:

A tautologous act is not necessarily obligatory, and a contradictory act is not necessarily forbidden.[2]

7. Let us consider a molecular complex of *P*- and/or *O*-sentences. *O*-sentences can be regarded as abbreviations for negation-sentences of certain *P*-sentences. (Cf. above, p. 61.) If the molecular complex happened to contain *O*-sentences, we replace them by negation-sentences of *P*-sentences. Thus we

---

[1]Contradictory acts should not be confused with (morally) indifferent acts. The former are acts which, by definition, are never performed by an agent. The latter are acts which we are permitted to perform, but also not to perform.

[2]I now consider this solution to the problem unsatisfactory. I am inclined to think that what are here called 'tautologous' and 'contradictory' acts do not qualify as 'acts' at all. It seems to be of the essence of an *act* (i.e., of anything that can be subject to norm) that it should be in the agent's power *both* to perform *and* to neglect it. (1955)

get a new molecular complex, all the constituents of which are
P-sentences.

We now turn our attention to the (molecular complexes of)
names of acts which follow after the modal operators in this new
molecular complex of P-sentences. We make an inclusive list
of all atomic names which are constituents of at least one of the
(molecular complexes of) names of acts in question. Thereupon
we transform these (molecular complexes of) names of acts into
their perfect disjunctive normal forms in terms of all atomic
names which occur in our list. The respective conjunction-
names in these normal forms preceded by the deontic operator P
we shall call the P-constituents of the initially given molecular
complex of P- and/or O-sentences. (Cf. the example given
below.)

We know already that any P-sentence expresses a truth-
function of the propositions expressed by its P-constituents.
Since any molecular complex of P- and/or O-sentences expresses
a truth-function of the propositions expressed by the P- and/or
O-sentences themselves, it follows that any molecular complex
of P- and/or O-sentences expresses a truth-function of the propositions expressed by its P-constituents.

Which truth-function of the propositions expressed by its P-
constituents a molecular complex of P- and/or O-sentences
expresses can be investigated and decided in a truth-table.
This fact constitutes a solution of the decision problem for the
system of Deontic Logic which we are outlining in this paper.

The technique of constructing truth-tables in Deontic Logic
will be illustrated by an example.

Let the molecular complex be O A & $O(A \to B) \to O$ B.
(Cf. above, p. 63.)

O A is an abbreviation for $\sim P \sim A$, $O(A \to B)$ for $\sim P$
$(A$ & $\sim B)$, and O B for $\sim P \sim B$. By replacing O-sentences
by P-sentences in our initial complex, we get the new complex
$\sim P \sim A$ & $\sim P(A$ & $\sim B) \to \sim P \sim B$.

The atomic names of acts which are constituents of (at least
one of) the molecular complexes 'inside' the operator P are A
and B. The perfect disjunctive normal form of $\sim A$ in terms of
A and B is $\sim A$ & B v $\sim A$ & $\sim B$. The normal form of A &
$\sim B$ is A & $\sim B$. The normal form of $\sim B$ is A & $\sim B$ v $\sim A$

& $\sim B$. The P-constituents of the initially given molecular complex, therefore, are $P(A \ \& \ \sim B)$ and $P(\sim A \ \& \ B)$ and $P(\sim A \ \& \ \sim B)$.

Since the P-constituents do not represent all the deontic units of the deontic realm of the acts named by A and by B (cf. above p. 65) the Principle of Permission does not here impose any restrictions upon the combinations of truth-values. The calculation of truth-values depends only upon the Principle of Deontic Distribution (and principles of propositional logic). The table looks as follows:

$P(A\&\sim B)$	$P(\sim A\&B)$	$P(\sim A\&\sim B)$	$O\ A$	$O(A \rightarrow B)$	$OA\&O(A \rightarrow B)$	$O\ B$	$\rightarrow$
T	T	T	F	F	F	F	T
T	T	F	F	F	F	F	T
T	F	T	F	F	F	F	T
T	F	F	T	F	F	F	T
F	T	T	F	T	F	F	T
F	T	F	F	T	F	T	T
F	F	T	F	T	F	F	T
F	F	F	T	T	T	T	T

It is seen that the molecular complex which we are investigating (indicated by '$\rightarrow$' in the column to the extreme right) expresses the tautology of the propositions expressed by its P-constituents.

8. A molecular complex of P- and/or O-sentences which expresses the tautology of the propositions expressed by its P-constituents, is said to express a truth of Deontic Logic or a deontic tautology.

A (true) proposition to the effect that a certain molecular complex of P- and/or O-sentences expresses a deontic tautology will be called a law of Deontic Logic.

We mention below some examples of such laws. When we call two molecular complexes of P- and/or O-sentences identical, we mean that their equivalence-sentence expresses a deontic tautology. When we say that (the proposition expressed by) one molecular complex of P- and/or O-sentences entails (the proposition expressed by) another, we mean that their implication-sentence expresses a deontic tautology. The propositions expressed by the molecular complexes of sentences given below (or by the equivalence- or implication-sentences in question) are easily shown by truth-tables to be tautologies.

i. Two laws on the relation of permission to obligation, and vice versa:

(a) $P A$ is identical with $\sim O \sim A$, i.e. $P A \longleftrightarrow \sim O \sim A$ expresses a deontic tautology.

(b) $O A$ entails $P A$, i.e. $O A \to P A$ expresses a deontic tautology.

The second of these laws should not be confused with the above (alternative formulation of the) Principle of Permission (p. 67). In the proof of i.(b) this principle is already assumed.

ii. Four laws for the distribution of deontic operators:

(a) $O(A \ \& \ B)$ is identical with $O A \ \& \ O B$.

(b) $P(A \lor B)$ is identical with $P A \lor P B$.

(c) $O A \lor O B$ entails $O(A \lor B)$.

(d) $P(A \ \& \ B)$ entails $P A \ \& \ P B$.

The second of these laws should not be confused with the Principle of Deontic Distribution (p. 64). In the proof of ii.(b) this principle is already assumed.

iii. Six laws on 'commitment':

(a) $O A \ \& \ O(A \to B)$ entails $O B$. If doing what we ought to do commits us to do something else, then this new act is also something which we ought to do. (This was the example of a deontic tautology which we discussed above.)

(b) $P A \ \& \ O(A \to B)$ entails $P B$. If doing what we are free to do commits us to do something else, then this new act is also something which we are free to do. In other words: doing the permitted can never commit us to do the forbidden.

(c) $\sim P B \ \& \ O(A \to B)$ entails $\sim P A$. This is but a new version of the previous law. If doing something commits us to do the forbidden, then we are forbidden to do the first thing. For instance: if it is obligatory to keep one's promises and if we promise to do something which is forbidden, then the act of promising this thing is itself forbidden.

(d) $O(A \to B \lor C) \ \& \ \sim P B \ \& \ \sim P C$ entails $\sim P A$. This is a further version of the two previous laws. An act which commits us to a choice between forbidden alternatives is forbidden.

(e) $\sim [O\ (\ A\ \mathrm{v}\ B)\ \&\ \sim P\ A\ \&\ \sim P\ B]$. It is logically impossible to be obliged to choose between forbidden alternatives.[1]

(f) $O\ A\ \&\ O(A\ \&\ B\ \rightarrow\ C)$ entails $O(B\ \rightarrow\ C)$. If doing two things, the first of which we ought to do, commits us to do a third thing, then doing the second thing alone commits us to do the third thing. 'Our commitments are not affected by our (other) obligations.'

(g) $O\ (\sim A\ \rightarrow\ A)$ entails $O\ A$. If failure to perform an act commits us to perform it, then this act is obligatory.

The truth of all these laws follows from our intuitive notions of obligation and permission. Not all of the laws themselves, however, are intuitively obvious. In the case of some of the laws, moreover, it is not intuitively clear whether their truth is a matter of logic or a matter of moral code. This proves that the decision procedure of Deontic Logic which we have outlined is not void of philosophical interest.

Any molecular complex of P- and/or O-sentences has what we propose to call an absolutely perfect disjunctive normal form. This we get by replacing every one of the P- and/or O-sentences by a disjunction-sentence of P-constituents of the complex and transforming the molecular complex of P-sentences thus obtained into its perfect disjunctive normal form. If the normal form contains the conjunction of the negation of all P-constituents, we omit it from the normal form.

The absolutely perfect disjunctive normal form shows with which ones of the possible combinations of truth-values in its P-constituents the molecular complex in question expresses agreement and with which ones it expresses disagreement. If it agrees with all possibilities, it expresses a deontic tautology, i.e., is a truth of Deontic Logic.

---

[1]Aquinas several times refers to the laws *d* and *e*. He distinguishes between a man's being *perplexus simpliciter* and his being *perplexus secundum quid*. The former is the case, if he is, as such, obliged to choose between forbidden alternatives. The latter is the case, if he by a previous wrong act commits himself to a choice between forbidden alternatives. Aquinas rightly denies that a man could be *perplexus simpliciter* (*e*) and affirms that a man might be *perplexus secundum quid* (*d*). Cf. *De Veritate*, Q. 17, art. 4; *Summa Theologica*, iaiiae Q. 19, art. 6; *Summa Theologica*, iiia, Q. 64, art. 6. For these observations I am indebted to Mr. P. Geach.

9. There is one relevant respect, in which the deontic modalities differ from the alethic, epistemic, and existential modalities. It can be illustrated as follows: If a proposition is true, then it is possible, and if a proposition is true, then it is not falsified, and if a property is true of a thing, then the property exists. But if an act is performed (or not performed), then nothing follows as regards its obligatory, permitted or forbidden character. There is thus an important sense in which the deontic modalities unlike the alethic, epistemic, and existential ones have no logical connexions with matters of fact (truth and falsehood). This is a point about deontic categories which has often been stressed by moral philosophers.

10. In this paper deontic propositions have been treated as 'absolute'. They can, however, be made 'relative' in several ways.

First of all, it might be argued that deontic propositions are sometimes, or perhaps always, relative to some so-called moral code. What is obligatory within one moral code, may be forbidden within another.

Secondly, instead of simply considering whether an act is obligatory, permitted or forbidden, we may consider propositions of the following type: x is permitted to do A, or x permits y to do A. Introducing quantifiers we then get propositions of the type: somebody is permitted to do A, or somebody permits everybody to do A, etc. The logical systems which we get by such extensions are of considerable complexity. Their decision-problem can be solved for many interesting cases, but not for all cases.[1]

[1]Some such extensions of Deontic Logic are studied in my paper 'On the Logic of some Axiological and Epistemological Concepts', *Ajatus* 17, 1952.

INTERPRETATIONS OF MODAL LOGIC

(1952)

I

SOME of the notorious difficulties in connexion with modal concepts concern the relation of what we shall call higher order modalities to lower order modalities.

It is a 'received truth' of modal logic that if a proposition is true, then it is also possibly true. (*Ab esse ad posse valet consequentia.*) By an application of this principle to the case when the proposition concerned is to the effect that a further proposition is possibly true or not possibly true, we conclude:

If (it is true that) a proposition is possibly true, then the proposition in question is also possibly possibly true, and if (it is true that) a proposition is not possibly true, then the proposition in question is also possibly not possibly true.

It cannot be a universally valid truth of modal logic that if a proposition is possibly true, then it is (certainly) true. In the special case, however, when the possibly true proposition is to the effect that a further proposition is possibly true, it might be thought that possibility entails truth. In other words: it might be suggested that, if a proposition is possibly possibly true, then (it is true that) the proposition in question is possibly true.

In view of what was concluded above from the *ab esse ad posse* principle, this suggestion would entail an identity between what is possible and what is possibly possible. We shall refer to this as the First Identity.

It cannot be a universally valid truth of modal logic that if a proposition is possibly false, then it is (certainly) false. In the special case, however, when the possibly false proposition is to the effect that a further proposition is possibly true, it might be thought that possible falsehood entails falsehood. In other words, it might be suggested that, if a proposition is possibly not possibly true, then (it is true that) the proposition in question is not possibly true.

In view of what was concluded above from the *ab esse ad posse* principle, this suggestion would entail an identity between what is impossible (not possible) and what is possibly impossible. We shall refer to this as the Second Identity.

Possibility and necessity are interdefinable. What is necessarily true is what is not possibly false, and vice versa. The reader can easily satisfy himself that, if we prefer to speak in terms of necessity rather than in terms of possibility, then our First Identity becomes an identity between what is necessary and what is necessarily necessary, and our Second Identity becomes an identity between what is not necessary and what is necessarily not necessary.

It can be shown that the First Identity is weaker than the Second. This means: We can accept the First Identity without accepting the Second, but we cannot accept the Second Identity without also accepting the First. (Cf. below, Sections V and VII.)

The two identities are consistent with what we shall call the 'received system' of modal logic. The notion of a 'received system', however, is not clear in itself. We might identify it with Lewis's $S2$. I shall, however, here identify it with a more comprehensive system, which includes $S2$ and which differs substantially from $S2$ only in that it allows us to conclude from any given theorem of the system to the necessary truth of that theorem. I call this system 'received', because I do not think that anyone would seriously question the necessary and universal validity of its theorems for the notions of possibility and necessity.[1]

The identity of what is possible with what is possibly possible is the constitutive feature of the system of modal logic known as $S4$, and the identity of what is impossible with what is possibly impossible is the constitutive feature of $S5$.

The test of truth for the two identities is thus not a test of consistency with other, accepted truths. The question then arises:

---

[1]A more detailed study of this system will be found in my publication *An Essay in Modal Logic*, Amsterdam, 1951.

On what grounds, if on any, can it be decided whether the two identities are valid, or not?

Our 'logical intuitions', apparently, give no strong indication in favour of any definite answer to the question of truth here. One of the main reasons for this, it seems to me, is the fact that higher order modal expressions like 'possibly possible' or 'possibly impossible' have hardly any *use* at all in ordinary or scientific discourse (outside modal logic).

A problem of primary importance, therefore, is to *invent a use* or some kind of 'equivalent' of a use for the expressions in question (outside modal logic). This done, the problem of truth mentioned above can be tackled on a firmer basis. We shall return to this problem in the concluding section of the present paper.

II

We shall first consider a geometrical interpretation of ('classical') propositional logic.

The variables of the calculus are p, q, r, . . . (an unlimited multitude). The constants which we are going to use are $\sim$ for negation, & for conjunction, v for disjunction, $\rightarrow$ for material implication, and $\longleftrightarrow$ for material equivalence. The class of well-formed formulae (wff: s) is defined recursively in the usual way. Rules for brackets are given.

We consider an arbitrary line of unit length 1. All wff: s can be represented by segments of the unit line in accordance with the following rules of interpretation:

i. The variables are represented by arbitrary segments. (A segment may consist of parts which are disconnected.) For example:

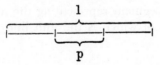

ii. The negation of a wff. is represented by that part of the unit line which is not covered by the segment representing the wff. itself. We shall call the segment representing the negation of a wff. the *complement* of the segment representing the wff. itself.

iii. The conjunction of two wff: s is represented by the common part, if any, of the segments representing the wff: s themselves.

It follows from these rules that the disjunction of two wff: s is represented by the part of the unit line covered jointly by the segments representing the wff: s themselves; that the implication of an antecedent and a consequent wff. is represented by the part of the unit line covered jointly by the segments representing the consequent wff. and the negation of the antecedent wff.; and that the equivalence of two wff: s is represented by the part of the unit line covered jointly by the segments representing the conjunction of the two wff: s and the conjunction of the negations of the two wff: s.

A wff. is a tautology of propositional logic, if and only if its representation in accordance with Rules i.–iii. is the unit line, independently of the choice of segments to represent the variables. For example: the segment representing $p \vee \sim p$ is the part covered jointly by an arbitrary segment of the unit line (representing p) and its complement. Hence the representation of $p \vee \sim p$ must be the unit line itself.

If and only if the representation of the implication of two wff: s is the unit line, the representation of the antecedent is a segment of the representation of the consequent. For suppose, e.g., that the representation of $p \rightarrow q$ is the unit line. This means that the representation of $\sim p$ covers at least those portions of the unit line which are not covered by the representation of q. Hence the representation of p 'falls inside', i.e., is a segment of, the representation of q.

If and only if the representation of the equivalence of two wff: s is the unit line, the wff: s are represented by the same segment.

As a name of the unit line itself we shall use the symbol 1. As a name of the segment representing the negation of a wff., the representation of which is the unit line, we shall use the symbol 0.

III

To the calculus of propositional logic we add one new constant M. It is prefixed to wff: s in the same way as $\sim$ is prefixed. We modify the definition of the class of wff: s so as to include mention of M. No new rules for brackets are needed.

Just as we by the negation of a given wff. understand the wff. which we get, when ∼ is prefixed to the given wff., we shall by the *modal* of a given wff. understand the wff. which we get, when *M* is prefixed to the given wff.

All wff: s can be represented as segments of a unit line, if—in addition to the three rules of the previous section—we adopt the following new rules of interpretation:

iv. The modal of a wff. is represented by an arbitrary segment of the unit line which covers the segment representing the wff. itself. For example:

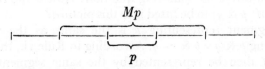

v. The modal of the disjunction of two wff: s is represented by that part of the unit line which is covered jointly by the segments representing the modals of the two wff: s themselves.

vi. If two wff: s are represented by the same segment, then the modals of the two wff: s will have to be represented by the same segment as well.

vii. The representation of the modal of a wff., the representation of which is 0, is 0.

A wff. will be called a *M*-tautology or modal tautology, if and only if its representation in accordance with Rules i.-vii. is the unit line, independently of the choice of segments to represent the variables and the modals.

(Since the wff: s now under consideration include among themselves the wff: s of propositional logic, it follows that the modal tautologies include among themselves the tautologies of propositional logic.)

Let us convince ourselves, relying upon the geometrical interpretation of wff: s, that $M(p \mathbin{\&} q) \to Mp \mathbin{\&} Mq$ is a *M*-tautology. ('If propositions are mutually consistent, they are self-consistent.')

Remembering what was said above about the representation of implications, the task can be reduced to one of showing that the representation of $M(p \mathbin{\&} q)$ must be a segment of the representation of $Mp \mathbin{\&} Mq$.

We start from the picture

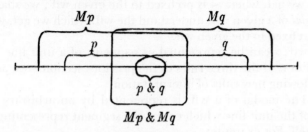

and ask ourselves the following question: How is the representation of $M(p \& q)$ to be fitted into this picture?

The segment representing p is the same as the segment representing $p \& q \vee p \& \sim q$. According to Rule vi., the modal of p must then be represented by the same segment as the modal of $p \& q \vee p \& \sim q$. But in virtue of Rule v., the modal of $p \& q \vee p \& \sim q$ is represented by the same segment as the representation of the disjunction of the modal of $p \& q$ and the modal of $p \& \sim q$. It follows that the representation of $M(p \& q)$ must be a segment of the representation of Mp, which is in the picture.

By an exactly similar argument, it is shown that the representation of $M(p \& q)$ must also be a segment of the representation of Mq, which is in the picture.

The two conditions, thus deduced, which the representation of $M(p \& q)$ has to satisfy, can be simultaneously fulfilled if and only if the representation of $M(p \& q)$ is a segment of the representation of $Mp \& Mq$, which is in the picture.

A second example will be given. Let us convince ourselves that $M(p \to \sim M \sim p)$ is a M-tautology.

The segment representing $p \to \sim M \sim p$ is the same as the segment representing $\sim p \vee \sim M \sim p$. According to Rule vi., the modal of $p \to \sim M \sim p$ must then be represented by the same segment as the modal of $\sim p \vee \sim M \sim p$. But in virtue of Rule v., the modal of $\sim p \vee \sim M \sim p$ is represented by the same segment as the representation of the disjunction of the modal of $\sim p$ and the modal of $\sim M \sim p$.

The representation of $M \sim p \vee \sim M \sim p$ is the unit line. Since, according to Rule iv., the representation of $\sim M \sim p$ is a segment of the representation of $M \sim M \sim p$, it follows that the representation of $M \sim p \vee M \sim M \sim p$ must be the unit line too. Q.E.D.

For any given wff. of the class under consideration can be effectively decided, whether or not it is a M-tautology. The proof will not be given here.

The class of M-tautologies includes within itself the class of theorems of $S2$. The proof will not be given here.

The class of M-tautologies is identical with the class of what is called in this paper the 'received truths' of modal logic.

IV

We consider the same class of wff: s as in the previous section, but add a new rule for the interpretation of modals:

viii. The representation of the modal of the modal of a wff. is the same as the representation of the modal of the wff.

The rule answers to what we called above the First Identity (what is possible $=$ what is possibly possible).

A wff. will be called a M'-tautology, if and only if its representation in accordance with Rules i.–viii. is the unit line, independently of the choice of segments to represent the variables and the modals.

(It follows trivially that M-tautologies are also M'-tautologies.)

Let us convince ourselves, relying upon the geometrical interpretation of wff: s, that $M(Mp \, \& \, M \sim p) \longleftrightarrow Mp \, \& \, M \sim p$ is a M'-tautology. ('The contingent is the same as the possibly contingent.')

Remembering what was said above about the representation of equivalences, the task can be reduced to one of showing that the representation of $M(Mp \, \& \, M \sim p)$ must be the same segment as the representation of $Mp \, \& \, M \sim p$.

We start from the picture

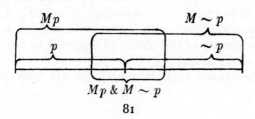

$$Mp \, \& \, M \sim p$$

and ask ourselves the following question: How is the representation of $M(Mp \ \& \ M \sim p)$ to be fitted into this picture?

We know from what was shown in the preceding section that the representation of $M(Mp \ \& \ M \sim p)$ must be a segment of the representation of $MMp \ \& \ MM \sim p$. In virtue of Rule viii., however, the representation of MMp is the same segment as the representation of Mp, and the representation of $MM \sim p$, the same segment as the representation of $M \sim p$. Consequently, the representation of $MMp \ \& \ MM \sim p$ is the same segment as the representation of $Mp \ \& \ M \sim p$, which is already in the picture.

We have now shown that the representation of $M(Mp \ \& \ M \sim p)$ must be a segment of the representation of $Mp \ \& \ M \sim p$. In virtue of Rule iv., on the other hand, the representation of $Mp \ \& \ M \sim p$ must be a segment of the representation of $M(Mp \ \& \ M \sim p.)$ These two features of the representation of $M(Mp \ \& \ M \sim p)$ can be reconciled only if the representation of $M(Mp \ \& \ M \sim p)$ in the picture is the same segment as the representation of $Mp \ \& \ M \sim p$.

For any given wff. of the class under consideration can be effectively decided, whether or not it is a M'-tautology. The proof will not be given here.

The class of M'-tautologies is identical with the class of theorems in $S4$.

V

We consider the same class of wff: s as in Sections III and IV, but add a further rule:

ix. The representation of the modal of the negation of the modal of a wff. is the same as the representation of the negation of a modal of the wff.

This rule answers to what we called above the Second Identity (what is impossible = what is possibly impossible).

A wff. will be called a M''-tautology, if and only if its representation in accordance with Rules i.–vii. and ix. is the unit line, independently of the choice of segments to represent the variables and the modals.

It can be shown that M'-tautologies are also M''-tautologies.

Consider the picture

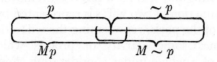

We ask the question: How is the representation of the modal of the modal of p, i.e. MMp, to be fitted into the picture?

In virtue of Rule ix., the representation of the modal of the negation of the modal of p, i.e. $M \sim Mp$, is the same as the representation of the negation of the modal of p, i.e. $\sim Mp$, which is in the picture. In virtue of Rule vi., if two wff: s have the same representation, then their modals have the same representation too. Thus the representation of $M \sim M \sim Mp$ is the same as the representation of the modal of the modal of p i.e. MMp. But in virtue of Rule ix., the representation of $M \sim M \sim Mp$ is the same as the representation of $\sim M \sim Mp$ which was already shown to be the same as the representation of Mp. Thus we conclude that the representation of the modal of the modal of p, i.e. MMp, is the same segment as the representation of the modal of p, i.e. Mp, which is already in the picture.

For any given wff. of the class under consideration can be effectively decided, whether or not it is a M''-tautology. The proof will not be given here.

The class of M''-tautologies is identical with the class of theorems in $S5$.

VI

We shall now consider physical models which are 'isomorphic' with the above geometrical models of propositional logic and various systems of modal logic.

We conceive of the variables p, q, r, . . . as the 'physical' parts of some 'physical' whole. (The parts need not necessarily be spatio-temporally continuous.) For example: p, q, r, . . . can be represented by segments of a metal rod, geographical areas on the earth's surface, populations of human beings, etc. All the wff: s of propositional logic can be interpreted as parts of such wholes, if we adopt the rule that the negation of a wff.

is represented by that part of the whole which remains, when the part representing the wff. itself has been removed, *and* the rule that the conjunction of two wff: s is represented by the common part, if any, of the parts, representing the wff: s themselves.

Consider next some 'activity' or 'process' which may occur in the parts of a whole under consideration. For example: an electric current of a certain strength running through a segment of a metal rod, rainfall in a district, a certain disease occurring among (not necessarily all) members of a population, etc.

Relative to such an assumed activity, we decide to call the parts *fields of activity*.

The activity under consideration may have some 'influence' or 'effect', extending from a part in which the activity is supposed to occur to other parts of the same whole. For example: an electric current running through a segment of a metal rod may have a thermic effect on the surrounding portions of the rod; a change of climate in one country may produce a change of climate in neighbouring countries; a disease among members of one population may spread by contagion to the members of another population, etc.

Relative to an assumed activity and an assumed influence, we decide to call the part, to which the influence may extend, when the activity occurs in a given part, the *field of influence* of (or associated with) the given field of activity.

It will be convenient to understand the concept of a field of influence in such a way that any given field of influence *includes* the associated field of activity.

Relative to an assumed activity and an assumed influence, we further decide to call the part, to which the influence will *not* extend, when the activity occurs in a given part, the *field of resistance* of the surrounding (of the given field of activity).

The activities and influences to be considered are assumed to obey the following three laws:

$L1$. If a field of activity is divided into parts (not necessarily mutually exclusive), then the fields of influence of the parts conceived of as fields of the same activity, are jointly identical with the field of influence of the original field of activity.

$L2$. With the same field of activity is always associated the same field of influence.

$L3$. If the field of activity is non-existent ('the o-field'), then the associated field of influence is also non-existent.

Activities which obey $L1$ can conveniently be called *additive* with regard to their influences. Far from all processes in nature possess this feature of additiveness. But some obviously possess it. For example: if an epidemic occurs among the members of two populations, then the members of the surrounding population which may become infected are exactly those which may get the disease from members of the one *or* the other of the two populations, whenever the disease occurs in them.

We can now give a new interpretation to the class of wff: s considered in Sections III–V (the wff: s formed of the symbols of propositional logic and the symbol M).

We call the parts of a given whole, fields of activity. The variables, negation, and conjunction are interpreted as before. The modal of a wff. is interpreted as the field of influence of the field of activity representing the wff. itself.

(Since, under the terminology adopted, any part of the given whole is called a field of activity, it follows that the fields of influence (and of resistance) are a sub-class of the fields of activity.)

A wff. is a M-tautology, if and only if its representation is the whole, of which the fields of activity are parts, independently of the choice of fields of activity to represent the variables and fields of influence to represent the modals.

VII

Processes in nature which are additive with regard to their effects in the sense of $L1$ above, can be divided into the following three categories:

A. Processes which are such that, if a field of their influence becomes itself a field of activity for the same process, then the field of influence of this new field of activity extends beyond the boundaries of the original field of influence.

B. Processes which are such that, if a field of their influence becomes itself a field of activity for the same process, then the field of influence of this new field of activity does *not* extend beyond the boundaries of the original field of influence.

C. Processes which are such that, if a field of resistance of the neighbourhood of a field of their activity becomes itself a field of activity for the same process, then the field of influence of this new field of activity does not extend beyond the boundaries of the original field of resistance.

Processes of the third kind are also processes of the second kind, but not necessarily vice versa.

The fields of activity, influence, and resistance of processes of the kind B offer a model of a system of modal logic in which the First Identity holds.

The fields of activity, influence, and resistance of processes of the kind C offer a model of a system of modal logic in which the Second Identity holds.

Examples of processes of each of the three kinds can be given. Here we shall consider only one example.

Let us conceive of p as a certain population of human beings. Let the activity, of which p is a field, be an epidemic disease. (We need not suppose, however, that all members of the population actually have or even can get the disease.) $\sim p$ is represented by the population, of which a man is a member if and only if he is not a member of the population representing p. For the sake of convenience, we shall speak of the 'population' and its 'neighbourhood' (population).

Of Mp we conceive as the population itself *and* those members of the neighbourhood, who for some reason or other may catch the disease from members of the population. The representation of Mp can thus conveniently be called the field of influence of the epidemic in the population.

It follows that $\sim Mp$ is represented by those members of the neighbourhood, who for some reason or other cannot catch the disease from members of the population. The representation of $\sim Mp$ can thus conveniently be called the field of resistance ('immunity') of the neighbourhood.

If to the field of influence are added those members, if any, of the neighbourhood who, although they cannot catch the epidemic from members of the population, yet may for some reason or other catch it from such of their fellow members of the neighbourhood as may themselves catch it from members of the population, we get a representation of MMp.

If to the field of resistance are added those members, if any, of the field of influence who, for some reason or other, may catch the disease from a member of the field of resistance, we get a representation of $M \sim Mp$.

As to the relative magnitude of the population representing Mp and MMp, two different situations might occur:

1. The members of the field of resistance are totally immune from the disease and cannot, consequently, catch it from anybody. In this case, the populations representing Mp and MMp coincide.

2. The members of the field of resistance are secure from catching the disease from members of the population and yet not secure from catching it from infected fellow members of theirs of the neighbouring population. (This could be the case for biological reasons, but also because, say, the members of the field of resistance are segregated from contact with members of the population.) In this case, the population representing MMp would be larger than the population representing Mp.

If the fields of resistance of all populations concerned consist entirely of members, if any, which cannot catch the disease in question from non-members of those fields, we obtain a model of a modal logic, in which the First Identity holds.

As to the relative magnitude of the populations representing $\sim Mp$ and $M \sim Mp$, two different situations might also occur:

1. The members of the field of influence are secure from catching the disease from members of the field of resistance. (This would trivially be the case, if the members of the field of resistance are totally immune and, consequently, unable to acquire the disease. It would non-trivially be the case, e.g., if members of the field of resistance could acquire the disease, though only in a non-catching form.) Under this alternative the populations representing $\sim Mp$ and $M \sim Mp$ coincide.

2. The members of the field of influence are not secure from catching the disease from members of the field of resistance. (It may, for example, happen that a member of the field of resistance catches the disease from a fellow member of the neighbouring population, who has himself caught it from a member of the population, and that subsequently another member of the field of influence catches the disease from this infected member of the field of resistance.) Under this alternative, the

population representing $M \sim Mp$ would be larger than the population representing $\sim Mp$.

If the fields of influence of all populations concerned consist entirely of members, if any, who cannot catch the disease in question from non-members of those fields, we obtain a model of a modal logic, in which the Second Identity holds.

It is easy to see that a model in which the Second Identity holds (universally) is also a model in which the First Identity holds (universally). If the members of the population representing $\sim Mp$ cannot infect the members of the population representing Mp, then the second population equals its own field of resistance and the first its own field of influence. But if it is universally true of fields of influence that they consist entirely of members who cannot catch the disease from non-members, it follows that the population representing MMp must coincide with the population representing Mp.

VIII

We have seen that the 'logical behaviour' of natural processes which are, in a defined sense, *additive* with regard to their effects is governed by the same formal rules as the concept of possibility. These processes—or their fields of activity, influence, and resistance—can be said to afford models or illustrations of the possible. In the language which speaks about these processes there is a use for formal equivalents of higher order modalities and thus also for formal equivalents of the two identities with which we have been concerned in this paper. The criteria of truth at hand are such as to show that for some additive natural processes neither of the identities holds, for some both identities hold, and for some only the first identity holds.

It seems to me that the existence of such illustrations as these among natural processes shows that neither of the identities in question can claim universal validity for the concept of the possible (and the necessary) in modal logic, nor can either of them be rejected as contrary to the 'true' nature of modality.

It would be of some interest to investigate the 'logical behaviour' of non-additive natural processes with a view to the question whether this behaviour also illustrates some general notions of logic.

A NEW SYSTEM OF MODAL LOGIC

I. INTRODUCTION

As far as I know, modal logic from Aristotle to modern times has only dealt with modality (necessity, possibility, impossibility) as a *monadic* predicate or 'property' of propositions.

The system presented in this paper differs from the traditional systems of modal logic in that it studies the various modalities as *dyadic* predicates or 'relations' between propositions.[1] Such modalities may also be called *relative* modalities.

We introduce a symbol '$M(p/q)$'. It can be read: p is *possible* given q. Instead of 'given q', we may also read 'on conditions q' or 'relatively to q'. Accordingly, '$\sim M(p/q)$' can be read: it is not the case that p is possible, given q, or: p is *impossible*, given q, '$\sim M(\sim p/q)$' can be read: it is not the case that not-p is possible, given q, or: not-p is impossible, given q, or (by verbal convention): p is *necessary*, given q. (This, by the way, is not the only reasonable interpretation of necessity in terms of negation and possibility.)

The letters 'p' and 'q' stand for arbitrary propositions. The letter 't' will be used to represent an arbitrary tautology of propositional logic (PL).

Our notation must not mislead a reader into thinking that the letter 'M' and the stroke '/' represent *two* logical constants. Relative possibility is the *one* indefinable modal concept of our system. Instead of the stroke '/', we might have used the comma ','. This would have been in conformity with a usual notation in the logic of relations. There are, however, some practical reasons for preferring the stroke.

By the *absolute* possibility of a proposition we shall here understand its possibility on *tautologous* conditions. '$M(p/t)$' thus says that p is absolutely possible. In a similar manner,

---

[1] As an attempt in the same direction may be regarded E. J. Nelson's treatment of consistency (compatibility) and entailment in the paper 'Intensional Relations' in *Mind* **39**, 1930.

we define absolute impossibility [$\sim M(p/t)$] and absolute necessity [$\sim M(\sim p/t)$].

It will be shown later (p. 97) that absolute possibility means possibility on *some* (absolutely) possible conditions, that absolute impossibility means possibility on *no* (absolutely) possible conditions, and that absolute necessity means necessity on *all* (absolutely) possible conditions.

Absolute possibility (impossibility, necessity), as here defined, is thus a species (limiting case) of the generic notion of *relative* possibility (impossibility, necessity).

It would be rash to maintain that our notions of the absolute modalities were *the same* as the modal notions of the traditional systems. For, it is not clear what views the authors of those systems would have taken of the 'meaning' of their monadic concepts in relation to our dyadic modalities. (Some might have wished to regard the two kinds of modal concepts as being entirely different.)

By the 'classical' systems of modal logic I shall here understand the systems $S1$–$S5$ of C. I. Lewis, the system T of R. Feys, the systems M, M', and M'' of von Wright, and the system developed by O. Becker. The systems T and M may easily be shown to be equivalent. The systems M' and $S4$ are equivalent, and so also M'' and $S5$. The system of Becker is somewhat weaker than T and M.

It is an interesting fact that the laws (axioms and theorems) of the 'classical' systems of modal logic can be interpreted as laws of absolute modalities within our new system. In a sense, therefore, the 'classical' systems may be regarded as special or limiting cases of the logic of dyadic modalities. The precise meaning of this contention will be given later. (Section 8.)

Among the traditional systems of modal logic, a peculiar position is held by the system (or systems) developed by J. Łukasiewicz. Some comments on it will be found in an appendix to the present paper.

2. COMPOSSIBILITY, MODAL COMPATIBILITY, AND SELF-CONSISTENCY

It is important that our notion of relative possibility should not be confused with the notion of *compossibility* of the 'classical' systems. In other words: the meaning of '$M(p/q)$' ought to be distinguished from the meaning—using C. I. Lewis's symbolism for possibility—of '$\diamond(p \,\&\, q)$'. There is a significant difference between the two notions. $\diamond(p \,\&\, q)$ is false, i.e. p and q are *not* compossible, as soon as one of the two propositions, say q, is impossible. $\sim \diamond q \rightarrow \sim \diamond(p \,\&\, q)$ is a law of 'classical' modal logic. But $M(p/q)$ may be true, even though q is (absolutely) impossible. $\sim M(q/t) \rightarrow \sim M(p/q)$ is *not* a law of our system.

We shall distinguish between the *compossibility* of two (or more) propositions, and the *compatibility* or *consistency* of one proposition with another proposition. We shall say that '$M(p \,\&\, q/r)$' expresses the compossibility of p and q on conditions r, and '$M(p \,\&\, q/t)$' the absolute compossibility of p and q. And we shall say that '$M(p/q)$' expresses the compatibility or consistency of p with q. As will be seen presently (p. 100f.), the relation of compatibility is not unrestrictedly symmetrical.

Consider the three propositions 'there are exactly 23 primes between 0 and 100' and 'there are at least 21 primes between 0 and 100' and 'there are 25 primes between 0 and 100'. Shall we not say that the second is compatible with the first, and that the third is *in*compatible with the first? Namely, considering that the first entails the second and contradicts the third. But the first proposition is false. If we regard truths of arithmetic as necessary truths, we shall have to regard the first proposition as not merely false, but impossible. We shall, moreover, have to regard the second and third propositions as being necessary.

It seems to me that this is an example of an impossible proposition, with which one necessary proposition is compatible and another necessary proposition is incompatible—in a perfectly good sense of 'compatible'.[1] Yet neither one of the two necessary propositions is compossible with the impossible

[1] A logician, who holds the view that an impossible proposition *ipso facto*, i.e., by virtue of its impossibility alone, entails any proposition, may find the example unconvincing. For, he would say that our first proposition entails both the second *and* the third. And for this reason he may wish to say that the second and the third propositions are equally compatible with the first. But this view of entailment is, in my opinion, unsatisfactory. Anyone who denies that the first proposition entails the second but *not* the third, is either maintaining something which is not true or using the word 'entails' in some eccentric way. The concept of entailment and the view that impossible propositions entail anything and everything is discussed in the last essay of the present collection.

proposition. This would show that compatibility and compossibility ought to be distinguished. The fact, therefore, that the traditional modal systems are unable to make this distinction may be regarded as an insufficiency of those systems.

Compatibility, in our sense, is a 'typically relational' notion. Whether one proposition is compatible with another depends upon their mutual modal relation and cannot be established from the modal character (say impossibility) of *one* of them alone.

In our system, we can further distinguish between *absolute possibility* and *self-compatibility* or *self-consistency* of a proposition. The absolute possibility of p is expressed by '$M(p/t)$' and the self-compatibility (self-consistency) of p by '$M(p/p)$'. As will be seen presently (p. 97), the two notions are not formally equivalent. The former is stronger than the latter. All absolutely possible propositions are self-consistent, but not all self-consistent propositions are absolutely possible.

It may again be regarded as an insufficiency of the traditional systems that they are unable to distinguish between propositions which are 'simply' impossible and propositions which are self-inconsistent. The latter are a sub-class of the former.

3. M-EXPRESSIONS

M-expressions are defined recursively as follows:

By an M-expression of order $n(1 \leqq n)$ we understand an atomic M-expression of order n or a molecular complex of atomic M-expressions, at least one of which is of order n and none of which is of higher order than n.

By an atomic M-expression of order $n(1 \leqq n)$ we understand an expression of the form '$M(/)$', in which one of the blanks is filled by an M-expression of order n-1 and the other blank by an M-expression of order n-1 or of lower order.

By an M-expression of order zero we understand a propositional variable p, q, r, . . . or the tautology variable t or a molecular complex of propositional variables (or t).

It follows from the above definitions that atomic M-expressions of the first order are expressions of the form '$M(/)$', in which the blanks are filled by M-expressions of order zero.

It follows further that M-expressions of the first order are atomic M-expressions of the first order or molecular complexes consisting of atomic M-expressions of the first order and/or M-expressions of order zero.

An M-expression of the first order will be called *homogeneous*, if it is either an atomic M-expression of the first order or a molecular complex of atomic M-expressions of the first order.

M-expressions are the well-formed formulae of the various calculi of the new modal logic which we are going to present.

4. THE CALCULUS $M_d\mathrm{I}$

In this section we shall be studying, in some detail, a particularly simple modal calculus. We shall label it the system $M_d\mathrm{I}$. It constitutes the 'core' which is common to all the other modal calculi which we are going to mention. The system $M_d\mathrm{I}$ may be called the core of dyadic modal logic.

It is the distinguishing feature of $M_d\mathrm{I}$ that its well-formed formulae are the *homogeneous* M-expressions of the first order.

The axioms of the calculus are the following three formulae:

A1. $M(p/p) \rightarrow\, \sim M(\sim p/p)$

A2. $M(p/q) \vee M(\sim p/q)$

A3. $M(p\ \&\ q/r) \longleftrightarrow M(p/r)\ \&\ M(q/r\ \&\ p)$

The theorems of the calculus are all formulae which (recursively) satisfy one of the following four conditions:

i. The formula is obtainable from a tautology of propositional logic by substituting for all its propositional variables homogeneous M-expressions of the first order.

ii. The formula is obtainable from an axiom or theorem of our calculus by substituting for some propositional variables in it some M-expressions of order zero.

iii. The formula is the consequent in a material implication formula, which is itself an axiom or a theorem and whose antecedent is also an axiom or a theorem of our calculus.

iv. The formula is obtainable from an axiom or theorem of our calculus by substituting for some M-expression of order zero in it another M-expression of order zero, which is tautologously equivalent to the first.

The conditions which formulae have to satisfy in order to qualify as theorems could alternatively be described as rules of *inference* or *transformation*. Condition i. simply means that in our calculus, as indeed in most deductive theories, the laws of ('classical') propositional logic are taken for granted. Conditions ii. and iii., the Rules of Substitution and of Detachment (*modus ponens*) may be called basic rules of all formalized reasoning whatever. Condition iv. has a somewhat more special status. It may be called a rule of the Substitution of Identities or of Extensionality. 'Identity' is here defined as meaning tautologous equivalence in propositional logic.

There is a (well-known) difference between 'substitution' in the sense of i. and ii., and 'substitution' in the sense of iv., of which it may be well to remind the reader. If an expression is being substituted for a variable, it is necessary that the substitution should be carried out in *all* places where the variable occurs in the formula in question. But if an expression is being substituted for another expression, the two expressions being tautologously equivalent, then it is not necessary that the substitution be carried out in *all* places where the expression occurs in the formula in question.

For the sake of notational convenience we shall introduce a special symbol 'N' for (relative) necessity. '$N(p/q)$' can be read: p is necessary, given q. In view of the elucidation, given above (p. 89), of relative necessity in terms of relative possibility and negation, we shall regard '$N(p/q)$' as an *abbreviation* of '$\sim M(\sim p/q)$'.

The axioms call for some comments:

$A1$ says that if a proposition is self-consistent, then its negation is inconsistent with it. Using the symbol 'N', we can write $A1$ in the form $M(p/p) \rightarrow N(p/p)$. The axiom thus also says that a self-consistent proposition is self-necessary.

The notion of self-necessity is not without interest. Some comments on it are given in Appendix I of the present essay.

$A2$ says that either the 'positive' or the 'negative' of any other arbitrary proposition p is compatible with an arbitrary proposition q. The formula can also be written $\sim M(\sim p/q) \rightarrow M(p/q)$, or $N(p/q) \rightarrow M(p/q)$. The axiom in question thus also says that, if a proposition is necessary relative to another, then it is possible relative to it. ('Necessity entails possibility'.)

A3 strikes us as an analogue in the logic of the relative modalities to the so-called multiplication-principle in the theory of probability. This analogy will be explored in further detail later. (Section 10.)

We now proceed to the proof of some theorems.

The proofs will be presented in the form of a successive enumeration of formulae which are themselves theorems of $M_d 1$. It will be left to the reader to verify that the enumerated formulae satisfy the conditions i.–iv. above of theoremhood. The verification is usually quite simple; in order to facilitate it references to formulae are sometimes added within brackets.

*T*1. $M(p/q) \longleftrightarrow M(p \,\&\, r/q) \vee M(p \,\&\, \sim r/q)$

Proof:

(1) $M(p/q) \longleftrightarrow M(p/q)$

(2) $M(p/q) \longleftrightarrow M(p/q) \,\&\, [M(r/q \,\&\, p) \vee M(\sim r/q \,\&\, p)]$

(3) $M(p/q) \longleftrightarrow M(p/q \,\&\, M(r/q \,\&\, p) \vee M(p/q) \,\&\, M(\sim r/q \,\&\, p)$

(4) $M(p/q) \longleftrightarrow M(p \,\&\, r/q) \vee M(p \,\&\, \sim r/q)$ *Q.E.D.*

*T*2. $M(p \vee q/r) \longleftrightarrow M(p/r) \vee M(q/r)$

'The possibility of a disjunction is a disjunction of possibilities.'

Proof:

(1) $M(p \vee q/r) \longleftrightarrow M[(p \vee q) \,\&\, p/r] \vee M[(p \vee q) \,\&\, \sim p/r]$ (*T*1)

(2) $M(p \vee q/r) \longleftrightarrow M(p/r) \vee M(\sim p \,\&\, q/r)$ [Since $(p \vee q) \,\&\, p$ is equivalent to p alone, and $(p \vee q) \,\&\, \sim p$ to $\sim p \,\&\, q$.]

(3) $M(p \vee q/r) \longleftrightarrow M(p \,\&\, q/r) \vee M(p \,\&\, \sim q/r) \vee M(p \,\&\, q/r)$ $\vee M(\sim p \,\&\, q/r)$

(4) $M(p \vee q/r) \longleftrightarrow M(p/r) \vee M(q/r)$ *Q.E.D.*

*T*3. $N(p \,\&\, q/r) \longleftrightarrow N(p/r) \,\&\, N(q/r)$

'The necessity of a conjunction is a conjunction of necessities.'

This theorem is the 'dual' of *T*2. To prove it, replace N-expressions with that for which they are an abbreviation.

*T*4. $M(q/q) \to [M(p/q) \longleftrightarrow M(p \,\&\, q/q)]$

If q is self-consistent, then the possibility of p, given q, is equivalent to the possibility of p *and* q, given q.

Proof:

(1) $M(p \,\&\, q/q) \longleftrightarrow M(q/q) \,\&\, M(p/q)$ (*A*3)

(2) $M(q/q) \to [M(p/q) \longleftrightarrow M(p \,\&\, q/q)]$ *Q.E.D.*

*T*5. $M(q/q \vee r) \vee M(r/q \vee r) \to$
     $[M(p/q \vee r) \longleftrightarrow M(q/q \vee r) \,\&\, M(p/q) \vee M(r/q \vee r) \,\&\, M(p/r)]$

Proof:

(1) $M(q \vee r/q \vee r) \rightarrow [M(p/q \vee r) \longleftrightarrow M(p \,\&\, (q \vee r)/q \vee r]$ $(T4)$

(2) $M(q/q \vee r) \vee M(r/q \vee r) \rightarrow [M(p/q \vee r) \longleftrightarrow M(p \,\&\, q/q \vee r)$
$\quad \vee\, M(p \,\&\, r/q \vee r)]$

(3) $M(q/q \vee r) \vee M(r/q \vee r) \rightarrow$
$\quad [M(p/q \vee r) \longleftrightarrow M(q/q \vee r) \,\&\, M(p/q) \vee M(r/q \vee r) \,\&\,$
$\quad M(p/r)]$ [Since $(q \vee r) \,\&\, q$ is equivalent to q and $(q \vee r)$
$\quad \&\, r$ to r.] $Q.E.D.$

$T6.$ $M(p/t) \rightarrow M(p/p \vee q)$

Proof:

(1) $M[p \,\&\, (p \vee q)/t] \rightarrow M(p \vee q/t) \,\&\, M(p/p \vee q)$

(2) $M(p/t) \rightarrow M(p/p \vee q)$ $Q.E.D.$

$T7.$ $M(q/t) \,\&\, M(r/t) \rightarrow [M(p/q \vee r) \longleftrightarrow M(p/q) \vee M(p/r)]$

This theorem says that a proposition is possible relative to a disjunction of (absolutely) possible alternatives, if and only if it is possible relatively to *some* (at least one) of those alternatives individually.

Proof:

(1) $M(q/q \vee r) \,\&\, M(r/q \vee r) \rightarrow M(q/q \vee r) \vee M(r/q \vee r)$

(2) $M(q/q \vee r) \,\&\, M(r/q \vee r) \rightarrow$
$\quad [M(p/q \vee r) \longleftrightarrow M(q/q \vee r) \,\&\, M(p/q) \vee M(r/q \vee r) \,\&\,$
$\quad M(p/r)]$ [(1) and $T5$.]

(3) $M(q/q \vee r) \,\&\, M(r/q \vee r) \rightarrow [M(p/q \vee r) \longleftrightarrow M(p/q) \vee M(p/r)]$

(4) $M(q/t) \,\&\, M(r/t) \rightarrow M(q/q \vee r) \,\&\, M(r/q \vee r)$ $(T6)$

(5) $M(q/t) \,\&\, M(r/t) \rightarrow [M(p/q \vee r) \longleftrightarrow M(p/q) \vee M(p/r)]$
$\qquad\qquad\qquad\qquad\qquad\qquad\qquad\qquad Q.E.D.$

$T8.$ $M(q/t) \,\&\, M(r/t) \rightarrow [N(p/q \vee r) \longleftrightarrow (N(p/q) \,\&\, N(p/r)]$

This theorem says that a proposition is necessary relative to a disjunction of (absolutely) possible alternatives, if and only if it is necessary relatively to *all* those alternatives individually.

$T8$ is the 'dual' of $T7$. To prove that $T8$ is 'but another form of' $T7$, replace N-expressions with that for which they are an abbreviation.

This is a corollary of $T7$:

$T9.$ $M(q/t) \,\&\, M(\sim q/t) \rightarrow [M(p/t) \longleftrightarrow M(p/q) \vee M(p/\sim q)]$

And these are corollaries of $T8$:

$T10.$ $M(q/t) \,\&\, M(\sim q/t) \rightarrow [N(p/t) \longleftrightarrow N(p/q) \,\&\, N(p/\sim q)]$

$T11.$ $M(q/t) \,\&\, M(\sim q/t) \rightarrow [\sim M(p/t) \longleftrightarrow \sim M(p/q)$
$\&\, \sim M(p/\sim q)]$

$T9$–$T11$ may easily be generalized so as to become valid for the case in which, instead of the *two* alternatives q and $\sim q$, we have an arbitrary number n of mutually exclusive and jointly exhaustive alternatives $q_1, \ldots, q_n$. The theorems may then be rendered in words as follows:

The absolute possibility of a proposition is its possibility under *some* possible circumstances, i.e. on some (at least one) alternative in any arbitrary set of mutually exclusive and jointly exhaustive (absolutely) possible conditions. The absolute necessity of a proposition is its necessity under *all* possible circumstances, i.e. on all alternatives in any arbitrary set of mutually exclusive and jointly exhaustive (absolutely) possible conditions. The absolute impossibility, finally, of a proposition means that the proposition is possible under *no* possible circumstances, i.e. the proposition is not possible on any alternative in any set of mutually exclusive and jointly exhaustive (absolutely) possible conditions. (See above p. 90.)

From $A3$ we easily obtain:

$T12.$ $M(q/t) \rightarrow [N(p/t) \rightarrow N(p/q)]$

$T13.$ $M(q/t) \rightarrow [\sim M(p/t) \rightarrow \sim M(p/q)]$

In words: a (absolutely) necessary proposition is necessary relatively to any (absolutely) possible proposition. An (absolutely) impossible proposition is impossible relatively to any (absolutely) possible proposition.

$T14.$ $M(p/t) \rightarrow M(p/p)$

Proof:

(1) $M(p \,\&\, p/t) \longleftrightarrow M(p/t) \,\&\, M(p/p)$ (Since $t \,\&\, p$ is equivalent to p.)

(2) $M(p/t) \rightarrow M(p/p)$ $Q.E.D.$

The theorem says that, if a proposition is absolutely possible, then it is self-consistent. The theorem cannot be converted. Thus, according to the laws of our modal logic, a proposition may be self-consistent without being absolutely possible. The class of self-inconsistent propositions, in other words, is a subclass of the class of absolutely impossible propositions. (See above p. 92.)

To what extent the distinction between self-contradictory and impossible propositions is an important and useful one will in the last resort depend upon considerations which fall outside the scope of the present inquiry. What is noteworthy so far is only that the system *provides* for this distinction. Examples of self-inconsistent propositions would be 'this square is round' or 'he is a female brother'. On the face of things, it looks as though 'there are exactly 23 primes between 0 and 100' might be an example of an impossible but *not* self-contradictory proposition. Whether it really is an example cannot be decided before one has given criteria, *other* than those provided by the calculus itself, of absolute impossibility and self-inconsistency.

*T*15. $M(t/t)$

The tautology is self-consistent (and absolutely possible).

Proof:

(1) $M(p \vee \sim p/t) \longleftrightarrow M(p/t) \vee M(\sim p/t)$ (*T*2)

(2) $M(p/t) \vee M(\sim p/t)$ (*A*2)

(3) $M(p \vee \sim p/t)$

(4) $M(t/t)$ Q.E.D.

*T*16. $M(t/\sim t)$

Proof:

(1) $M(p \vee \sim p/\sim t) \longleftrightarrow M(p/\sim t) \vee M(\sim p/\sim t)$

(2) $M(p/\sim t) \vee M(\sim p/\sim t)$

(3) $M(p \vee \sim p/\sim t)$

(4) $M(t/\sim t)$ Q.E.D.

*T*17. $M(p/p) \longleftrightarrow N(p/p)$

'Self-consistency and self-necessity are one and the same.'

Proof:

(1) $M(p/p) \rightarrow N(p/p)$ (*A*1)

(2) $N(p/p) \rightarrow M(p/p)$ (*A*2)

(3) $M(p/p) \longleftrightarrow N(p/p)$ Q.E.D.

*T*18. $N(t/t)$

Proof:

(1) $M(t/t) \longleftrightarrow N(t/t)$

(2) $M(t/t)$

(3) $N(t/t)$ Q.E.D.

*T*18 can also be written $\sim M(\sim t/t)$. The tautology is thus absolutely necessary and the contradiction absolutely impossible.

*T*19. $\sim M(\sim t/\sim t)$

Proof:

(1) $\sim M(\sim t/\sim t) \longleftrightarrow \sim N(\sim t/\sim t)$ (From *T*17)

98

(2) $\sim N(\sim t/\sim t) \longleftrightarrow M(t/\sim t)$
(3) $M(t/\sim t)$ (T16)
(4) $\sim M(\sim t/\sim t)$ Q.E.D.

T19 can also be written $N(t/\sim t)$. The tautology is thus necessary (even) relative to the contradiction.

T20. $\sim M(p/p) \longleftrightarrow N(\sim p/p)$

'Self-inconsistency is the same as necessity of the negation relative to the proposition.'

Proof:

(1) $\sim M(p/p) \longleftrightarrow \sim M(\sim\sim p/p)$
(2) $\sim M(p/p) \longleftrightarrow N(\sim p/p)$ Q.E.D.

T21. $N(p/\sim p) \to N(p/t)$

Proof:

(1) $\sim M(\sim p/\sim p) \to \sim M(\sim p/t)$ (From T14 by contraposition.)
(2) $N(p/\sim p) \to N(p/t)$ Q.E.D.

This theorem says that if a proposition is necessary relatively to its own negation, then it is absolutely necessary. (Related to the so-called *consequentia mirabilis*.)

T22. $M(p/p) \vee M(\sim p/\sim p)$

Proof:

(1) $M(p/t) \to M(p/p)$ (T14)
(2) $M(\sim p/t) \to M(\sim p/\sim p)$
(3) $M(p/t) \vee M(\sim p/t) \to M(p/p) \vee M(\sim p/\sim p)$
(4) $M(p/t) \vee M(\sim p/t)$ (A2)
(5) $M(p/p) \vee M(\sim p/\sim p)$ Q.E.D.

Thus any given proposition either is itself self-consistent or has a negation that is self-consistent. Negatively speaking: it must not be the case that both a proposition and its negation are self-inconsistent.

By *antinomic* propositions one may understand propositions such that the truth of the propositions themselves and of their negations could be established by means of logic. Of such antinomic propositions it is usually characteristic that one could also establish the self-inconsistency both of the propositions themselves and of their negations. That is: one may show that the propositions and their negations entail their own contradictories. Thus propositions which give rise to antinomies break the laws of our modal logic in much the same way as they break the laws of 'classical' propositional logic and 'classical' modal logic.

It is important to observe that this is *not* a theorem of our modal logic: $M(p/q) \longleftrightarrow M(q/p)$. Compatibility is not (unrestrictedly) symmetrical. q may be compatible with p, and yet p not compatible with q.

But is not this in flagrant conflict with our 'logical intuitions'? That the conflict is apparent only, will, I think, be seen from the following considerations:

Let us consider *under what conditions* the notion of compatibility is, *in our modal logic*, symmetrical. We easily prove the following theorem:

$T23$. $M(p/t)$ & $M(q/t) \rightarrow [M(p/q) \longleftrightarrow M(q/p)]$

Proof:

(1) $M(p/t)$ & $M(q/p) \longleftrightarrow M(q/t)$ & $M(p/q)$ (From $A3$.)

(2) $M(p/t)$ & $M(q/t) \rightarrow [M(p/q) \longleftrightarrow M(q/p)]$ $Q.E.D.$

The relation of compatibility is thus symmetrical for (absolutely) possible propositions. In other words: if and only if (at least) one of two propositions is (absolutely) impossible, may it happen that the first is compatible with the second and yet not the second with the first. We can also prove the following theorem:

$T24$. $M(p/t)$ & $M(q/p) \rightarrow M(q/t)$

Proof:

(1) $M(p/t)$ & $M(q/p) \longleftrightarrow M(p$ & $q/t)$

(2) $M(p$ & $q/t) \rightarrow M(q/t)$

(3) $M(p/t)$ & $M(q/p) \rightarrow M(q/t)$ $Q.E.D.$

With an (absolutely) possible proposition there can thus be compatible only propositions which are themselves (absolutely) possible. But not any proposition which is compatible with an (absolutely) impossible proposition need itself be (absolutely) impossible. $\sim M(p/t)$ & $M(q/p) \rightarrow \sim M(q/t)$ is *not* a theorem of our modal logic.

Consider again (cf. *supra*, p. 91) the propositions 'there are exactly 23 prime numbers between o and 100' and 'there are at least 21 prime numbers between o and 100'. The first is an impossibility and the second a necessity. Thus the second proposition is also possible. The first proposition, moreover, entails the second. If we take the view, which is very natural indeed, that the logical consequences of a proposition are compatible with it,[1] then we shall have to say that the second proposition is compatible with the first. But is there any reason—apart from the presumed asymmetry of the relation of compatibility—*for* saying that the first proposition is compatible with the second? It may be doubted, whether there is one. But there certainly is a reason *against* saying thus, viz. the provability of a modal law to the effect that with possible propositions only other possible propositions can be compatible.

The theorems $T16$ and $T18$ offer another example of the occasional asymmetry of the relation of compatibility.

One may say that, in our system of modal logic, the relation of compatibility is 'normally' symmetrical, and only in 'extreme cases' not symmetrical. It may be suggested that the fact that the relation is not unrestrictedly symmetrical strikes us as being contrary to our 'logical intuitions' only because we forget about these extreme cases. Or could anyone maintain with perfect confidence that even in those cases he had an 'intuition' of the symmetry of the relation? And what would an appeal to 'intuition' be worth *here*?

A 'dual' of $M(p/q) \longleftrightarrow M(q/p)$ is $N(p/q) \longleftrightarrow N(\sim q/\sim p)$: p is necessary, given q, if and only if $\sim q$ is necessary given $\sim p$. This, of course, is *not* a theorem. From the fact that the relation of compatibility is not unrestrictedly symmetrical it follows that the operation of 'contraposition' (in the sense of the above formula) is not unrestrictedly valid in our modal logic. It is, however, 'normally' valid, i.e. valid under the conditions indicated by the following theorem which is a corollary of $T23$:

$T25$. $M(\sim p/t) \& M(q/t) \rightarrow [N(p/q) \longleftrightarrow N(\sim q/\sim p)]$

Thus if $\sim p$ and q are (absolutely) possible, the relation of necessity of p, given q, can be 'contraposed'.

Considering what was said above on the symmetry of the relation of compatibility, this restriction on contraposition can hardly be said to conflict with our 'logical intuitions'.

It is a further consequence of the restriction on the symmetry of the relation of compatibility that, although $M(p/q)$ v $M(\sim p/q)$ $(A2)$ is a truth of our modal logic, $M(q/p)$ v

---

[1]This view, of course, cannot be *proved* without further investigations into the way in which the concept of entailment is related to the dyadic modalities.

$M(q/\sim p)$ is *not unrestrictedly* true. This, however, is a theorem:

T26. $M(p/t)$ & $M(\sim p/t)$ & $M(q/t) \rightarrow M(q/p)$ v $M(q/\sim p)$

T26 is easily proved from A2 in combination with T23.

If a proposition and its negation are both (absolutely) possible, we call the proposition (absolutely) *contingent*. T26 thus says that any arbitrary (absolutely) possible proposition is compatible with either the 'positive' or the 'negative' of any (absolutely) contingent proposition.

T27. $M(p/t) \rightarrow [M(q/p)$ & $N(r/q) \rightarrow M(r/p)]$

Proof:

(1) $M(p/t)$ & $M(q/p) \longleftrightarrow M(p$ & $q/t)$

(2) $M(p$ & $q/t) \longleftrightarrow M(p$ & q & $r/t)$ v $M(p$ & q & $\sim r/t)$

(3) $M(p/t)$ & $M(q/p) \longleftrightarrow M(p$ & q & $r/t)$ v $M(p$ & q & $\sim r/t)$

(4) $M(q$ & $\sim r/t) \longleftrightarrow M(q/t)$ & $M(\sim r/q)$

(5) $\sim M(\sim r/q) \rightarrow \sim M(q$ & $\sim r/t)$

(6) $N(r/q) \rightarrow \sim [M(p$ & q & $\sim r/t)$ v $M(\sim p$ & q & $\sim r/t)]$

(7) $N(r/q) \rightarrow \sim M(p$ & q & $\sim r/t)$ & $\sim M(\sim p$ & q & $\sim r/t)$

(8) $[M(p$ & q & $r/t)$ v $M(p$ & q & $\sim r/t)]$ & $\sim M(p$ & q & $\sim r/t)$ & $\sim M(\sim p$ & q & $\sim r/t) \longleftrightarrow M(p$ & q & $r/t)$ & $\sim M(p$ & q & $\sim r/t)$ & $\sim M(\sim p$ & q & $\sim r/t)$

(9) $M(p/t)$ & $M(q/p)$ & $N(r/q) \rightarrow M(p$ & q & $r/t)$ & $\sim M(p$ & q & $\sim r/t)$ & $\sim M(\sim p$ & q & $\sim r/t)$

(10) $M(p$ & q & $r/t)$ & $\sim M(p$ & q & $\sim r/t)$ & $\sim M(\sim p$ & q & $\sim r/t) \rightarrow M(p$ & q & $r/t)$

(11) $M(p$ & q & $r/t) \longleftrightarrow M(p/t)$ & $M(q$ & $r/p)$

(12) $M(q$ & $r/p) \longleftrightarrow M(r/p)$ & $M(q/p$ & $r)$

(13) $M(p$ & q & $r/t) \rightarrow M(r/p)$

(14) $M(p/t)$ & $M(q/p)$ & $N(r/q) \rightarrow M(r/p)$

(15) $M(p/t) \rightarrow [M(q/p)$ & $N(r/q) \rightarrow M(r/p)]$ Q.E.D.

T27 says that if p is (absolutely) possible, q possible relatively to p, and r necessary relatively to q, then r is possible relatively to p, and, by virtue of T24, also absolutely possible.

A corollary of T27 is:

T28. $M(p/t)$ & $N(q/p) \rightarrow M(q/t)$

What is necessary relatively to an (absolutely) possible proposition is itself (absolutely) possible.

T29. $M(p/t) \rightarrow [N(q/p)$ & $N(r/q) \rightarrow N(r/p)]$

Proof:

(1) $M(p/t)$ & $M(\sim r/p) \longleftrightarrow M(p$ & $\sim r/t)$

(2) $M(p \& \sim r/t) \longleftrightarrow M(p \& q \& \sim r/t) \vee M(p \& \sim q \& \sim r/t)$

(3) $M(p \& q \& \sim r/t) \vee M(p \& \sim q \& \sim r/t) \to$
$\quad M(p \& \sim q \& r/t) \vee M(p \& \sim q \& \sim r/t) \vee$
$\quad M(p \& q \& \sim r/t) \vee M(\sim p \& q \& \sim r/t)$

(4) $M(p \& \sim q \& r/t) \vee M(p \& \sim q \& \sim r/t) \vee$
$\quad M(p \& q \& \sim r/t) \vee M(\sim p \& q \& \sim r/t) \longleftrightarrow$
$\quad M(p \& \sim q/t) \vee M(q \& \sim r/t)$

(5) $M(p \& \sim q/t) \to M(\sim q/p)$

(6) $M(q \& \sim r/t) \to M(\sim r/q)$

(7) $M(p \& \sim q/t) \vee M(q \& \sim r/t) \to M(\sim q/p) \vee M(\sim r/q)$

(8) $M(p/t) \& M(\sim r/q) \to M(\sim q/p) \vee M(\sim r/q)$

(9) $M(p/t) \to [M(\sim r/p) \to M(\sim q/p) \vee M(\sim r/q)]$

(10) $M(\sim r/p) \to M(\sim q/p) \vee M(\sim r/q) \longleftrightarrow N(q/p) \& N(r/q)$
$\quad \to N(r/p)$

(11) $M(p/t) \to [N(q/p) \& N(r/q) \to N(r/p)]$ *Q.E.D.*

*T*29 says that the relation of relative necessity among (absolutely) possible propositions is transitive.

A corollary of *T*29 is:

*T*30. $N(p/t) \& N(q/p) \to N(q/t)$

What is necessary relatively to an (absolutely) necessary proposition is itself (absolutely) necessary.

*T*31. $M(p \& q/p \& q) \to N(p/p \& q)$

Proof:

(1) $M(p \& q/p \& q) \longleftrightarrow N(p \& q/p \& q)$ (*T*17)

(2) $N(p \& q/p \& q) \longleftrightarrow \sim M(\sim p \vee \sim q/p \& q)$

(3) $\sim M(\sim p \vee \sim q/p \& q) \longleftrightarrow \sim[M(\sim p/p \& q)$
$\quad \vee M(\sim q/p \& q)]$

(4) $\sim[M(\sim p/p \& q) \vee M(\sim q/p \& q)] \longleftrightarrow \sim M(\sim p/p \& q)$
$\quad \& \sim M(\sim q/p \& q)$

(5) $M(p \& q/p \& q) \to N(p/p \& q)$ *Q.E.D.*

*T*31 says that any member of a self-consistent conjunction is necessary relatively to the conjunction.

*T*32. $M(p/p) \to N(p \vee q/p)$

Proof:

(1) $M(p/p) \to N(p/p)$

(2) $N(p/p) \to N(p/p) \vee N(q/p \& \sim p)$

(3) $N(p/p) \quad \vee \quad N(q/p \& \sim p) \quad \longleftrightarrow \quad \sim[\ M(\sim p/p \ \&$
$\quad M(\sim q/p \& \sim p)]$

(4) $\sim[M(\sim p/p) \& M(\sim q/p \& \sim p)] \longleftrightarrow \sim M(\sim p \& \sim q/p)$

(5) $\sim M(\sim p \& \sim q/p) \longleftrightarrow N(p \vee q/p)$
(6) $M(p/p) \to N(p \vee q/p)$ Q.E.D.

$T32$ says that the disjunction of a self-consistent proposition with any arbitrary proposition is necessary relatively to this self-consistent proposition.

In the monadic systems of modal logic the notion of a strict implication means a necessary material implication. If we accept the notion of an absolutely necessary material implication as that which 'corresponds' in dyadic modal logic to the notion of a strict implication in the monadic systems, we can prove that *relative necessity is stronger than strict implication*. For we have the theorem:

$T33$. $N(q/p) \to N(p \to q/t)$
Proof:

(1) $M(p \& \sim q/t) \longleftrightarrow M(p/t) \& M(\sim q/p)$
(2) $M(p \& \sim q/t) \to M(\sim q/p)$
(3) $\sim M(\sim q/p) \to \sim M(p \& \sim q/t)$
(4) $N(q/p) \to N(p \to q/t)$ Q.E.D.

$T33$ cannot be 'converted', i.e. $N(p \to q/t) \to N(q/p)$ is *not* a theorem of our modal logic.

As is well known, it has been claimed that the notion of a strict implication would be an adequate 'formalization' of the notion of entailment. In view of the so-called Paradoxes of Strict Implication, however, these claims must be regarded as futile. The paradoxes consist in the (dually related) facts that an impossible proposition strictly implies any proposition and that any proposition strictly implies a necessary proposition.

To the Paradoxes of Strict Implication correspond, in dyadic modal logic, the following two theorems:

$T34$. $\sim M(p/t) \to N(p \to q/t)$
$T35$. $N(q/t) \to N(p \to q/t)$

The theorems follow immediately from the equivalences $M(p \& \sim q/t) \longleftrightarrow M(p/t) \& M(\sim q/p)$ and $\sim (p \& \sim q) \longleftrightarrow (p \to q)$.

$T34$ says that if a proposition is absolutely impossible, then any material implication of which it is the antecedent, is absolutely necessary. And $T35$ says that if a proposition is absolutely necessary, then any material implication, of which it is the consequent, is absolutely necessary.

A NEW SYSTEM OF MODAL LOGIC

These theorems are, of course, 'paradoxical' only if it is claimed that absolutely necessary material implication and entailment are one and the same thing.

It is noteworthy, that there are no corresponding 'paradoxes' for the notion of relative necessity. For, neither is it the case that any proposition is necessary relatively to an absolutely impossible proposition, nor is it the case that any absolutely necessary proposition is necessary relatively to any proposition. Neither $\sim M(p/t) \rightarrow N(q/p)$ nor $N(q/t) \rightarrow N(q/p)$ are theorems of our modal logic.

5. THE CALCULUS $M_d0 + M_d1$

We shall next briefly consider a modal calculus, the distinguishing feature of which is that its well-formed formulae are *all* M-expressions of the first order. We may call it the calculus $M_d0 + M_d1$.

The axioms of this extended modal calculus are the axioms A1–A3 of M_d1 *and* one new axiom:

A4. $p \rightarrow M(p/t)$

A4 says that if a proposition is true, then it is also absolutely possible. This is what corresponds in the logic of relative or dyadic modalities to the well known '*ab esse ad posse*'-principle of traditional modal logic.

The theorems of $M_d0 + M_d1$ are all formulae which (recursively) satisfy one of the following *four* conditions:

i. The formula is obtainable from a tautology of propositional logic by substituting for its propositional variables M-expressions of the first order.

ii. As in M_d1 (*vide supra* p. 93, 'Our calculus' now means $M_d0 + M_d1$.)

iii. As in M_d1.

iv. As in M_d1.

All theorems of M_d1 are also theorems of $M_d0 + M_d1$. We shall prove a few theorems which are peculiar to the extended system.

T36. $p \rightarrow M(p/p)$

'A true proposition is self-consistent'.

Proof:

(1) $p \rightarrow M(p/t)$ (A4)

(2) $M(p/t) \to M(p/p)$ $(T14)$

(3) $p \to M(p/p)$ *Q.E.D.*

$T37.$ $p \to N(p/p)$

'A true proposition is self-necessary.'

Proof:

(1) $p \to M(p/p)$ $(T36)$

(2) $M(p/p) \longleftrightarrow N(p/p)$ $(T17)$

(3) $p \to N(p/p)$ *Q.E.D.*

This theorem may also be written $p \to \sim M(\sim p/p)$. 'A true proposition excludes its own negation.'

$T38.$ $N(p/t) \to p$

'An absolutely necessary proposition is true.'

Proof:

(1) $\sim p \to M(\sim p/t)$ (From $A4$).

(2) $\sim M(\sim p/t) \to p$

(3) $N(p/t) \to p$ *Q.E.D.*

$T39.$ $p \,\&\, q \to M(p/q)$

'All true propositions are compatible with each other.'

Proof:

(1) $p \,\&\, q \to M(p \,\&\, q/t)$

(2) $M(p \,\&\, q/t) \longleftrightarrow M(q/t) \,\&\, M(p/q)$

(3) $p \,\&\, q \to M(p/q)$ *Q.E.D.*

It would have been a more elegant solution to the problem of extending the calculus dealing with *homogeneous M*-expressions of the first order to a calculus dealing with *all M*-expressions of the first order, if we had been able simply to replace one of the original axioms $A1$–$A3$ by a new axiom 'linking truth with modality'. I have not, however, been able to find such a solution.

6. THE CALCULUS M_d

The well-formed formulae of M_d are all M-expressions of whatever order. M_d may be called a 'full' system of dyadic modal logic.

The axioms of M_d are the axioms $A1$–$A4$ of $M_d0 + M_d1$.

The theorems of M_d are all formulae which (recursively) satisfy one of the following *five* conditions:

i. The formula is obtainable from a tautology of propositional logic by substituting for its propositional variables M-expressions.

ii. The formula is obtainable from an axiom or theorem of M_d by substituting for some propositional variables in it some M-expressions.

iii. As in $M_d \text{I}$. (*Vide supra*, p. 93.)

iv. The formula is obtainable from an axiom or theorem of M_d by substituting for some M-expression in it another M-expression which is provably (in M_d) equivalent to the first.

v. The formula is of the form '$N(F/t)$' (or '$\sim M(\sim F/t)$') where F is an axiom or theorem of M_d.

All theorems of $M_d \text{I}$ and of $M_d \text{O} + M_d \text{I}$ are also theorems of M_d.

7. THE CALCULI M_d' AND M_d''

The well-formed formulae of M_d' and M_d'' are the same as those of M_d.

The axioms of M_d' are the axioms $A1$–$A4$ of M_d *and* a fifth axiom:

$R1$. $M[M(p/t)/t] \rightarrow M(p/t)$

'If it is absolutely possible that a proposition is absolutely possible, then the proposition in question is absolutely possible. The axiom may also be written in the form $N(p/t) \rightarrow N[N(p/t)/t]$. 'If a proposition is absolutely necessary, then it is absolutely necessary that the proposition is absolutely necessary.'

The axioms of M_d'' are the axioms $A1$–$A4$ of M_d *and* a fifth axiom:

$R2$. $M[\sim M(p/t)/t] \rightarrow \sim M(p/t)$

'If it is absolutely possible that a proposition is absolutely impossible, then the proposition in question is absolutely impossible.'

If in our formulation of the five conditions (i.–v., p. 106 f.) which formulae have to satisfy in order to qualify as theorems of M_d we replace 'M_d' by 'M_d'' and by 'M_d''' respectively, we obtain the five conditions which formulae have to satisfy in order to qualify as theorems of M_d' and M_d'' respectively.

In M_d'' we can prove $R1$ or the distinguishing axiom of M_d'. Proof:

(1) $\sim M(p/t) \rightarrow M[\sim M(p/t)/t]$ [From $A4$ by substituting $\sim M(p/t)$ for p.]

(2) $M(\sim M(p/t)/t) \rightarrow \sim M(p/t)$ ($R2$)

(3) $M(\sim M(p/t)/t) \longleftrightarrow \sim M(p/t)$

(4) $M(\sim M[\sim M(p/t)/t]/t \longleftrightarrow \sim M[\sim M(p/t)/t]$ [From (3) by substituting $\sim M(p/t)$ for p.]

(5) $M[\sim\sim M(p/t)/t] \longleftrightarrow \sim\sim M(p/t)$ [From (4) by substituting for $M(\sim M(p/t)/t)$ the provably equivalent formula $\sim M(p/t)$.]

(6) $M[M(p/t)/t] \longleftrightarrow M(p/t)$

(7) $M[M(p/t)/t] \to M(p/t)$ \qquad Q.E.D.

Thus all theorems of M_d are also theorems of M_d' and all theorems of M_d' are theorems of M_d''.

The systems $M_d\text{o} + M_d\text{I}$, M_d, M_d', and M_d'' are successive extensions of the system $M_d\text{I}$. They all contain $M_d\text{I}$ as their 'core'. One may, however, also evolve systems of dyadic modal logic which are not extensions of $M_d\text{I}$, but 'modifications' of $M_d\text{I}$. One such modification, which may be of some interest, is obtained by weakening the axioms $A2$ and $A3$ so as to take the form $M(q/t) \to M(p/q) \text{ v } M(\sim p/q)$ and $M(p \text{ \& } r/t) \to [M(p \text{ \& } q/r) \longleftrightarrow M(p/r) \text{ \& } M(q/r \text{ \& } p)]$ respectively. The modified system thus obtained is contained in $M_d\text{I}$, i.e. all theorems of the system in question are theorems of $M_d\text{I}$, but not conversely.

8. RELATIONS BETWEEN THE DYADIC AND THE ('CLASSICAL') MONADIC SYSTEMS OF MODAL LOGIC

$\diamondsuit$-expressions are defined recursively as follows:

By a $\diamondsuit$-expression of order n ($\text{I} \leqslant n$) we understand an atomic $\diamondsuit$-expression of order n or a molecular complex of atomic $\diamondsuit$-expressions, at least one of which is of order n and none of which is of higher order than n.

By an atomic $\diamondsuit$-expression of order n ($\text{I} \leqslant n$) we understand an expression of the form '$\diamondsuit e$', where e is a $\diamondsuit$-expression of order $n-\text{I}$.

By a $\diamondsuit$-expression of order zero we understand the same as by an M-expression of order zero. (*Vide supra*, p. 92.)

A $\diamondsuit$-expression of the first order will be called *homogeneous*, if it is either an atomic $\diamondsuit$-expression of the first order or a molecular complex of atomic $\diamondsuit$-expressions of the first order.

$\diamond$-expressions are the well-formed formulae of the 'classical' systems of monadic modal logic.

By the 'translation' of an arbitrary $\diamond$-expression into the symbolism of M-expressions we shall understand the M-expression which we get when we successively replace all parts of the form '$\diamond e$' in it by parts of the form '$M(e/t)$'.

For example: the 'translation' of $\diamond[p \vee \sim \diamond(q \to \diamond r)]$ is $M(p \vee \sim M[q \to M(r/t)/t]/t)$.

We shall first consider the system of monadic modal logic which in my *An Essay in Modal Logic* is called $M\textsc{i}$. Its well-formed formulae are homogeneous $\diamond$-expressions of the first order.[1]

The axioms of $M\textsc{i}$ are the following two:

$A\textsc{i}.$ $\diamond t$

$A2.$ $\diamond(p \vee q) \longleftrightarrow \diamond p \vee \diamond q$

The theorems of $M\textsc{i}$ are all formulae which (recursively) satisfy one of the following *four* conditions:

i. The formula is obtainable from a tautology of propositional logic by substituting for all its propositional variables homogeneous $\diamond$-expressions of the first order.

ii. As in $M_d\textsc{i}$. (*Vide supra*, p. 93. 'Our calculus' now means $M\textsc{i}$. M-expressions of order zero, it should be remembered, are the same as $\diamond$-expressions of order zero.)

iii. As in $M_d\textsc{i}$.

iv. As in $M_d\textsc{i}$.

As seen, the conditions i.–iv. of theoremhood in $M\textsc{i}$ are essentially the same as the conditions i.–iv. of theoremhood in $M_d\textsc{i}$. (The only difference being that, in formulating the conditions for $M\textsc{i}$ we speak of $\diamond$-expressions and of axioms and theorems of $M\textsc{i}$, and in formulating the conditions for $M_d\textsc{i}$ we speak of M-expressions and of axioms and theorems of $M_d\textsc{i}$.)

The axioms and theorems of $M\textsc{i}$ are axioms or theorems of all the 'classical' systems of monadic modal logic, with the exception of the very weak system $S\textsc{i}$ of C. I. Lewis. $M\textsc{i}$ may also be called the 'core' of classical modal logic.

If we now 'translate' the axioms of $M\textsc{i}$ we get the formulae $M(t/t)$ and $M(p \vee q/t) \longleftrightarrow M(p/t) \vee M(q/t)$ of $M_d\textsc{i}$. They are

[1] It may be noted that the 'Essay' uses the symbol 'M', and not '$\diamond$', for monadic possibility.

both theorems of M_d1. (The first is $T15$ above and the second an immediate corollary of $T2$.)

It follows from the sameness of the conditions of theoremhood in $M1$ and M_d1 that, since the 'translations' of the axioms of $M1$ are theorems of M_d1, the 'translation' of any theorem of $M1$ must be an axiom or theorem of M_d1.

Not any axiom or theorem of M_d1 is, of course, the 'translation' of some axiom or theorem of $M1$. M_d1 is an essentially richer system than $M1$.

In view of the above, $M1$ or the 'core' of classical modal logic may be regarded as a special or limiting case of M_d1 or the 'core' of the logic of relative modality. (Much in the same sense in which Euclidean geometry may be regarded as a limiting case of non-Euclidean geometry.)

We next consider the system of monadic modal logic which in my 'Essay' was called $Mo+M1$. Its well-formed formulae are $\diamondsuit$-expressions of the first order.

The axioms of $Mo + M1$ are the following two:

$A1$. $p \rightarrow \diamondsuit p$

$A2$. As in $M1$.

The theorems of $Mo + M1$ are all formulae which (recursively) satisfy one of the following *four* conditions:

i. The formula is obtainable from a tautology of propositional logic by substituting for its propositional variables $\diamondsuit$-expressions of the first order.

ii. As in $M1$.

iii. As in $M1$.

iv. As in $M1$.

As seen, the conditions i.–iv. of theoremhood in $Mo + M1$ are the same as the conditions i.–iv. of theoremhood in $M_do + M_d1$. (*Vide supra*, p. 105.)

If we 'translate' $A1$ of $Mo + M1$ we get $p \rightarrow M(p/t)$. But this is $A4$ of $M_do + M_d1$.

It is now clear that the 'translation' of any axiom or theorem of $Mo + M1$ will be an axiom or theorem of $M_do + M_d1$. But the latter system is essentially richer than the former.

The well-formed formulae of the system of monadic modal logic which in my 'Essay' was called M are all $\diamondsuit$-expressions of whatever order. M is thus a 'full' system of monadic modal logic.

The axioms of M are the axioms of $Mo + M\textsc{i}$.

The theorems of M are all formulae which (recursively) satisfy one of the following *five* conditions:

i. The formula is obtainable from a tautology of propositional logic by subsituting for its propositional variables $\Diamond$-expressions.

ii. The formula is obtainable from an axiom or theorem of M by substituting for some propositional variables in it some $\Diamond$-expressions.

iii. As in $M\textsc{i}$.

iv. The formula is obtainable from an axiom or theorem of M by substituting for some $\Diamond$-expression in it another $\Diamond$-expression which is provably (in M) equivalent with the first.

v. The formula is of the form ' $\sim \Diamond \sim F$' where F is an axiom or theorem of M.

As seen, the conditions i.–v. of theoremhood in M are 'essentially the same' as the conditions i.–v. of theoremhood in M_d.

It follows that the 'translation' of any axiom or theorem of M is an axiom or theorem of M_d. But the latter system is richer than the former.

The well-formed formulae of M' ($= S4$) and M'' ($= S5$) are the well-formed formulae of M.

The axioms of M' are the axioms of M *and* a third axiom:

$R\textsc{i}.\ \Diamond \Diamond p \rightarrow \Diamond p.$

'Possible possibility entails possibility.'

The axioms of M'' are the axioms of M *and* a third axiom:

$R2.\ \Diamond \sim \Diamond p \rightarrow \sim \Diamond p$

'Possible impossibility entails impossibility.'

If in our formulation above of the five conditions which formulae have to satisfy in order to qualify as theorems of M we replace 'M' by 'M'' and 'M''' respectively, we obtain the set of conditions which formulae have to satisfy in order to qualify as theorems of M' and M'' respectively.

As seen, the conditions of theoremhood in M' and M'' respectively are the same as the conditions of theoremhood in M'_d and M''_d respectively. (*Vide supra*, p. 107.)

It follows that the 'translation' of any axiom or theorem of M' is an axiom or theorem of M'_d and that the 'translation' of any axiom or theorem of M'' is an axiom or theorem of M''_d. But the dyadic systems are richer than the monadic ones.

Herewith has been shown, how the 'classical' monadic systems of modal logic are related to our dyadic systems, and in what sense the former may be regarded as limiting cases of the latter.

9. LOGICAL AND PHYSICAL MODALITIES

An interesting application of the logic of relative modalities is for the purpose of marking a *formal* distinction between *logical* and *physical* ('natural') modalities—between the logically necessary, possible, and impossible on the one hand, and the physically necessary, possible, and impossible on the other hand.

By the *logical* necessity, possibility, and impossibility of a proposition p we may understand that which we have called before its 'absolute' necessity, possibility, and impossibility. Thus we should have:

D1. 'p is logically necessary' $=$ '$N(p/t)$'
D2. 'p is logically impossible' $=$ ' $\sim M(p/t)$'
D3. 'p is logically possible' $=$ '$M(p/t)$'

In view of $T9$–$T11$ above, we may also say that the *logically* necessary is that which is *necessary* in *all possible* worlds, the *logically* impossible that which is *possible* in *no possible* world, and the *logically* possible that which is *possible* in *some possible* world. These definitions are not circular inasmuch as the notion of necessity, impossibility, and possibility in possible 'worlds' refer to the *generic* dyadic modalities, which are here regarded as fundamental.

The next task will be to say what it is for a proposition p to be *logically* necessary (impossible or possible) *relatively to* another proposition q. This task is accomplished as follows:

We say that p is logically necessary relatively to q, if p is necessary relative to q *and* this necessity is a necessity in all possible worlds. In symbols: $N(p/q)$ & $N[N(p/q)t]$. But, by virtue of $T38$, $N[N(p/q)/t]$ entails $N(p/q)$. Thus '$N(p/q)$' becomes redundant, and we have the definition:

D4. 'p is logically necessary relatively to q' $=$ '$N[N(p/q)/t]$'

That p is logically impossible relatively to q should mean that the impossibility of p relatively to q is a necessity in all possible worlds, or—since $N[\sim M(p/q)/t]$ entails $\sim M(p/q)$—:

D_5. 'p is logically impossible relatively to q' $=$ '$N[\sim M(p/q)/t]$'

That p is logically possible relatively to q is simply the negation of the proposition that p is logically *im*possible relatively to q. But $\sim N[\sim M(p/q)/t]$ is the same as $M[M(p/q)/t]$. Thus we have:

$D6$. 'p is logically possible relatively to q' $=$ '$M[M(p/q)/t]$'

That p is *logically* possible relatively to q thus means that in *some* possible world p is possible relatively to q.

One may distinguish between logical necessity (impossibility, possibility) in the *absolute* sense, meaning on no particular evidence or 'as such', and logical necessity (impossibility, possibility) in the *relative* sense, meaning on some evidence q.

It is noteworthy that logical necessity, impossibility and possibility in the relative sense are modal concepts of *the second order*.

We now proceed to the *physical* modalities.

The conditions, under which something can be physically necessary (impossible, possible), it would seem, must be logically *contingent*, i.e. they must be some conditions which (logically) can either be or not be. Otherwise we should get absurdities. (*Vide infra.*) Logical contingency is defined as follows:

$D7$. 'p is logically contingent' $=$ '$M(p/t)$ & $M(\sim p/t)$'

We introduce the abbreviation 'Cp' for 'p is logically contingent'.

We now suggest that the *physical* necessity of p on (contingent) conditions q means (*a*) that p is not logically necessary, (*b*) that p is necessary relatively to q but (*c*) that this necessity is *not* a necessity in all possible worlds, i.e., is not *logical* necessity relatively to q. Considering that '$\sim N(p/t)$' may also be written '$M(\sim p/t)$' and that '$\sim N[N(p/q)/t]$' may also be written '$M[M(\sim p/q)/t]$', we can say that the physical necessity of p relatively to q means that, although p is necessary relatively to q, yet *in some possible world* the denial of p is possible relatively to q. Thus we have the definition:

$D8$. 'p is physically necessary relatively to q' $=$ 'Cq & $M(\sim p/t)$ & $N(p/q)$ & $M[M(\sim p/q)/t]$'

The function of condition (*a*) is to rule out the absurdity of calling something, which is logically necessary 'as such', *physically* necessary relatively to *q*. If it should be thought that this is not an absurdity, one may drop condition (*a*).

That *p* is *physically* impossible relatively to *q* simply means that the denial of *p* is physically necessary relatively to *q*.

*D*9. '*p* is physically impossible relatively to *q*' = '*Cq* & *M*(*p*/*t*) & ~*M*(*p*/*q*) & *M*[*M*(*p*/*q*)/*t*]'

The physical impossibility of *p* relatively to *q* thus means that, although *p* (actually) is impossible relatively to *q*, yet *in some possible world p* is possible relatively to *q*. Or, in still other words: although *p* is impossible relatively to *q*, it is *not logically* impossible relatively to *q*.

There remains the physically possible. It is clear that it cannot be simply the negation of the physically impossible (as the logically possible is the negation of the logically impossible). For, the denial of physical impossibility covers four cases. If *p* is *not* physically impossible relatively to *q*, then it is the case *either* that *q* is not a contingent proposition (but logically necessary or logically impossible), *or* that *p* is possible (in the generic sense), *or*, finally, that *p* is logically impossible either 'as such' or relatively to *q*. Now, obviously, the physically possible cannot be logically impossible. Therefore the third and fourth alternatives ought to be excluded. It is equally plain that the physically possible ought to be possible in the generic sense (since it is a species of it). Thus the second alternative must be included. And since we have adopted the view that the physical modalities subsist relative to logically *contingent* conditions, the first alternative will have to be excluded. Thus physical possibility answers to the conjunction *Cq* & *M*(*p*/*t*) & *M*(*p*/*q*) & *M*[*M*(*p*/*q*)/*t*]. But *Cq* & *M*(*p*/*q*) entails *M*(*p*/*t*) (*T*24) and *M*(*p*/*q*) entails *M*[*M*(*p*/*q*)/*t*] (*A*4). Thus, omitting the redundant parts, we get the definition:

*D*10. '*p* is physically possible relatively to *q*' = '*Cq* & *M*(*p*/*q*)'

We are now in a position to see why the physical modalities should be taken relative to contingent conditions. For, if we omitted the condition '*Cq*' from the above definitions, physical possibility would become indistinguishable from possibility in the generic sense. Now it may happen that a proposition *p* is logically impossible 'as such'—$\sim M(p/t)$—and yet possible relatively to some impossible proposition q. If p's possibility relatively to q were enough to secure its physical possibility relatively to q, it would follow that a proposition could be at the same time physically possible relatively to another proposition *and* logically impossible. And this, I think, we should wish to reject as absurd.

The reader may easily satisfy himself that the following relations hold between the various logical and physical modalities under their above definitions D_1–D_{10}:

i. If p is logically *or* physically necessary relatively to q, then p is logically *and* physically possible relatively to q.

ii. Logical and physical necessity, relatively to one and the same proposition q, are exclusive.

iii. Logical and physical impossibility, relatively to one and the same proposition q, are exclusive.

iv. If p is physically possible relatively to q, then p is logically possible relatively to q and also logically possible 'as such'.

10. MODALITY AND PROBABILITY

Suppose that it were, somehow, possible to measure the *degree* to which a given proposition p is possible relative to another proposition q. (That is: suppose we could attach some meaning to such 'degrees of possibility'.)

In order to develop this idea, suppose further that, the degree to which a given proposition p is possible relative to another proposition is measured by a *unique* and *not-negative* real number. That the measure is 'unique' should mean that, for given p and q, there is one and one only numerical value of $M(p/q)$. That the measure is a not-negative real number means that is is o or greater than o. And suppose, finally, that if p is *not* possible given q, i.e. if $\sim M(p/q)$ is true, then the measure is o.

By an atomic P-expression we understand an expression of the form '$P(\ /\ )$', in which the blanks are filled by M-expressions of order zero. For example: '$P(p/q)$' is an atomic P-expression.

By a P-expression we understand an atomic P-expression or an expression formed of atomic P-expressions and the arithmetical connectives '$-$', '$+$', '$\times$', and '$:$'. (The full recursive definition may easily be supplied by the reader.) For example: '$P(p/q) - P(p \& q/r)$' is a P-expression.

By an atomic P-formula we understand a formula formed of P-expressions, numerical variables or constants, and the signs of equality or inequality ('$=$', '$>$', and '$<$'). For example: '$P(p/q) > 0$' is an atomic P-formula and so is also '$P(p/q) + P(p \& q/\sim r) = P(q/s)$'.

By a P-formula, finally, we understand an atomic P-formula or a molecular complex of atomic P-formulae, i.e. a formula formed of atomic P-formulae and the truth-connectives '$\sim$', '$\&$', 'v', '$\rightarrow$', and '$\longleftrightarrow$'. For example: '$\sim[P(p/q)>0] \rightarrow P(p/r) = P(q/r)$' is a P-formula.

A homogeneous M-expression of the first order may be regarded as a molecular complex of constituents of the form '$\sim M(/)$'. (By replacing unnegated atomic constituents in it by doubly negated ones.)

Let it now be that in a homogeneous M-expression of the first order we replace all constituents of the form '$\sim M(/)$' by atomic P-formulae '$P(/) = 0$', the M-expressions of order zero filling the blanks being left unchanged. On this 'principle of translation' the homogeneous M-expression is being turned into a P-formula.

If we apply this translation-rule to the axioms $A1$–$A3$ of M_d1 we get:

$A1$. $\sim[P(p/p) = 0] \rightarrow P(\sim p/p) = 0$

$A2$. $\sim[P(p/q) = 0]$ v $\sim[P(\sim p/q) = 0]$

$A3$. $\sim[P(p \& q/r) = 0] \longleftrightarrow \sim[P(p/r) = 0] \& \sim[P(q/r \& p) = 0]$

$A1$ can also be written $P(p/p) = 0$ v $P(\sim p/p) = 0$.

$A2$ can also be written $\sim[P(p/q) = 0 \& P(\sim p/q) = 0]$.

$A3$ can also be written $P(p \& q/r) = 0 \longleftrightarrow P(p/r) = 0$ v $P(q/r \& p) = 0$.

On the basis of these three axioms and after a slight modification of the rules of inference i.–iv. of M_d1 we could develop a calculus of P-expressions. *This* calculus, however, would hardly be of much interest, and we shall not stop to study it here.

Consider $A3$ in its above 'translation'. In it, three numerical quantities are involved. Let us call them, in order, x, y, and z.

$A3$ says that x is equal to zero, if and only if, at least one of the two other quantities, y or z, is equal to zero.

Now we may raise the following problem: supposing that we wanted x to be a *function* of y and z, such that for given values of y and z the value of x would be uniquely determined, which could this function be considering the condition imposed in $A3$? *One* answer is: x could be the arithmetical product of y and z. For, if $x = y \times z$, then x is zero, if and only if y or z is zero. This is, of course, not the only answer to the question. The function $x = 2yz$, for example, would also satisfy the requirement. But one is probably entitled to say that $x = yz$ is the *simplest* function which answers to the condition imposed in $A3$.

Consider next $A2$ in its above 'translation'. In it, two numerical quantities are involved. Let us call them x and y. $A2$ says that at least one of them is different from zero. In other words: if one of them is zero, the other is not zero.

We raise the following problem: Supposing that we wanted x to be a *function* of y (and y of x), which could this function be considering the condition imposed in $A2$? An answer is that x and y would be functionally related in a way answering to the requirement of $A2$, if the sum of x and y were a constant which is different from zero. *One* such possible constant is the value 1.

The constant, which is the sum of x and y, must also be the maximum value which the measure of a degree of possibility may attain. For, if x were greater than this constant, then y would be negative. And this, on our assumptions, cannot be the case.

Leaving $A1$ unchanged, we now replace $A2$ and $A3$ above by new axioms stating functional relationships between measures of degrees of possibility, conforming to the conditions which $A2$ and $A3$ impose on such relationships. We might then get the following set of axioms:

$A1$. $P(p/p) = 0 \text{ v } P(\sim p/p) = 0$

$A2$. $P(p/q) + P(\sim p/q) = 1$

$A3$. $P(p \ \& \ q/r) = P(p/r) \times P(q/r \ \& \ p)$

(We shall not here consider alternative axiom-systems which also satisfy the requirements.)

This axiom-system has a very interesting property: *It is an axiom-system of* (elementary[1]) *probability-theory.* (It is indeed the simplest axiom-system of this theory which I know of.) *This means that the notion of probability is a notion with exactly those structural properties required by the axioms of modal logic for a numerical measure of degrees of relative possibility.*

We shall call the calculus of elementary probability-theory the calculus *P*.

The theorems of *P* are all *P*-formulae which (recursively) satisfy one of the following *six* conditions:

i. The formula is obtainable from a tautology of propositional logic by substituting for all its propositional variables *P*-formulae.

ii. As in M_d1. (*Vide supra*, p. 93.) ('Our calculus' now means '*P*'.)

iii. As in M_d1.

iv. As in M_d1.

v. The formula is obtainable from a true formula of arithmetic by substituting for some number variables *P*-expressions.

vi. The formula is obtainable from an axiom or theorem of *P* by substituting for some *P*-expression in it another *P*-expression which is provably (in *P*) identical with it.

Condition v. may be regarded as an extension of condition i. This means that in probability-theory, beside propositional logic, arithmetic also is taken for granted.

Condition vi. may be regarded as an analogous extension of condition iv. This means that in probability-theory not only tautologically equivalent but also arithmetically identical expressions are interchangeable.

We shall only prove some few theorems as illustrations:

$T1.$ $P(p/q) = P(p \& r/q) + P(p \& \sim r/q)$

Proof:

(1) $P(p/q) = P(p/q)$
(2) $P(p/q) = P(p/q) \times [P(r/q \& p) + P(\sim r/q \& p)]$
(3) $P(p/q) = P(p/q) \times P(r/q \& p) + P(p/q) \times P(\sim r/q \& p)$
(4) $P(p/q) = P(p \& r/q) + P(p \& \sim r/q)$ *Q.E.D.*

$T2.$ $P(p \lor q/r) = P(p/r) + P(q/r) - P(p \& q/r)$

---

[1]For the meaning of 'elementary' here, see my *Treatise on Induction and Probability*, p. 175.

Proof:

(1) $P(p \vee q/r) = P[(p \vee q) \& p/r] + P[(p \vee q) \& \sim p/r]$
(2) $P(p \vee q/r) = P(p/r) + P(\sim p \& q/r)$
(3) $P(\sim p \& q/r) = P(q/r) - P(p \& q/r)$
(4) $P(p \vee q/r) = P(p/r) + P(q/r) - P(p \& q/r)$ *Q.E.D.*

T3. $P(\sim p/p) = 0 \rightarrow P(p/p) = 1$

Proof:

(1) $P(p/p) + P(\sim p/p) = 1$
(2) $P(\sim p/p) = 0 \& P(p/p) + P(\sim p/p) = 1 \rightarrow P(p/p) = 1$
(3) $P(\sim p/p) = 0 \rightarrow P(p/p) = 1$ *Q.E.D.*

T4. $P(p/p) = 1 \vee P(\sim p/p) = 1$

Proof:

(1) $P(\sim p/p) = 0 \rightarrow P(p/p) = 1$
(2) $P(p/p) = 0 \rightarrow P(\sim p/p) = 1$
(3) $P(\sim p/p) = 0 \vee P(p/p) = 0 \rightarrow P(p/p) = 1 \vee P(\sim p/p) = 1$
(4) $P(p/p) = 0 \vee P(\sim p/p) = 0$
(5) $P(p/p) = 1 \vee P(\sim p/p) = 1$ *Q.E.D.*

It should be observed that $P(p/p) = 1$, which states that p is probable to degree 1 relatively to itself, is *not* a theorem of P. (Just as $M(p/p)$ or that p is possible relatively to itself is not a theorem of M_d.)

If we accepted $P(p/p) = 1$ as an axiom of P we should get a contradiction in the system. This is easily shown. If *any* proposition is probable to degree 1 relatively to itself, then also the contradictory proposition $p \& \sim p$. Thus we should have $P(p \& \sim p/p \& \sim p) = 1$. But by virtue of A3, $P(p \& \sim p/ p \& \sim p) = P(p/p \& \sim p) \times P(\sim p/p \& \sim p)$. Thus $P(p/p \& \sim p) \times P(\sim p/p \& \sim p) = 1$, from which follow $P(p/p \& \sim p) = 1$ and $P(\sim p/p \& \sim p) = 1$. But from A2 and $P(p/p \& \sim p) = 1$ follows $P(\sim p/p \& \sim p) = 0$. Thus we have both $P (\sim p/ p \& \sim p) = 1$ and $P(\sim p/p \& \sim p) = 0$ and a contradiction is produced.

It may be suggested that one could accept $P(p/p) = 1$ as an axiom and avoid the contradiction by restricting substitutability so as to make $p \& \sim p$ an impermissible substitution for p. This way of proceeding would have certain technical advantages. A1 would become provable and could be dropped from its position as an axiom. It would now, moreover, be possible to prove 'unconditionally' a number of theorems which in the calculus, as its stands, can be proved only as consequents of implications, the antecedents of which contain conditions of the form $P(p/p) = 1$. For example: in the present calculus we can prove $P(q/q) = 1 \rightarrow P(p/q) = P(p \ \& \ q/q)$, whereas in the modified calculus we could prove $P(p/q) = P(p \ \& \ q/q)$.

Against the suggested modification one may, however, raise the objection that it is only a disguise for making certain assumptions, which the calculus in its present shape clearly displays whenever these assumptions are involved.

That $P(p/p) = 1$ is *not* an axiom or theorem of probability-theory is no 'intuitive absurdity'. When we think of $P(p/p) = 1$ [or of $M(p/p)$] as being, somehow, 'self-evident', it is only because we forget about such odd cases as those presented by self-contradictory propositions. Can anyone claim self-evidence for the proposition that the probability of the proposition 'this square is round' on itself as evidence is 1? The truth seems to be that an appeal to 'intuition' in such cases is useless.

It may finally be observed that one can embellish the calculus P with a new axiom.

$A4$. $\quad p \rightarrow \sim [P(p/t) = 0]$

corresponding to $A4$ of M_d. From this axiom and $A1$–$A3$ we can easily prove the theorem $p \rightarrow P(p/p) = 1$. This theorem says that, if a proposition is true, then it is also probable to degree 1 relative to itself. In other words: on its own *truth* as evidence any proposition is probable to degree 1. This would also hold good for the proposition $p \ \& \sim p$. Yet no contradiction would arise. [Since the deduction of $P(\sim p/p \ \& \sim p) = 0$ and $P(\sim p/p \ \& \sim p) = 1$ would now be *conditional* on the assumption $p \ \& \sim p$.]

It goes without saying that principles such as $A1$ or $A4$ play a very insignificant role for the further developments of probability-theory. For most purposes it would be quite sufficient to have a calculus with $A2$ and $A3$ as the *only* axioms.

The logic of probability could be called a numerical modal logic. Modal logic, one may say, is turned into probability-theory by the introduction of a metric for degrees of possibility. The relation between probability and modality which we have here been investigating is, it should be observed, purely 'formal'. It exists quite independently of any specific way of defining

A NEW SYSTEM OF MODAL LOGIC

probability and possibility. In particular, it is independent of the well-known 'modal' definition of probability as a ratio among a number of ('favourable' and 'unfavourable') possibilities.

APPENDIX I. THE NOTION OF SELF-NECESSITY IN ARISTOTLE'S LOGIC

It has occurred to me that the logic of relative modality may prove useful for the purpose of reinterpreting in modern terms some arguments, doctrines, and systems of ancient and medieval modal logic.

In *De interpretatione* 19ª23–24 Aristotle says: *Τὸ μὲν ὂυν εἶναι τὸ ὂν ὅταν ᾖ, καὶ τὸ μὴ ὂν μὴ εἶναι ὅταν μὴ ᾖ, ἀνάγκη.* As the schoolmen put it: *omne quod est, quando est, necesse est esse,* or: *unumquodque, quando est, oportet esse.* This has sometimes been taken to mean that, if a proposition is true, then it is necessary.[1] In symbols: $p \to \sim \diamondsuit \sim p$. This interpretation, however, is implicitly rejected by Aristotle in 19ª25–26, where he observes that: *ὁ γὰρ ταὐτόν ἐστι τὸ ὂν ἅπαν εἶναι ἐξ ἀνάγκης ὅτε ἔστι καὶ τὸ ἁπλῶς εἶναι ἐξ ἀνάγκης.*[2] Thus it is different for something to be necessary, when it is, (*ὅτε ἔστι*), and to be necessary simply (*ἁπλῶς*). Aristotle's observation has, in its turn, been interpreted as a distinction between 'it is necessary that, if *p*, then *p*' and 'if *p*, then it is necessary that *p*'.[3] In symbols: $\sim \diamondsuit \sim (p \to p)$ and $p \to \sim \diamondsuit \sim p$. The first formula is indeed a truth of 'classical' modal logic, whereas the second is not. But it may be doubted, whether the symbolic interpretation is altogether adequate to the distinction as intended by Aristotle.

It seems to me natural to relate the distinction which

---

[1] Thus by Łukasiewicz in 'Philosophische Bemerkungen zu mehrwertigen Systemen des Aussagenkalküls' (*Comptes Rendus des Séances de la Société des Sciences et des Lettres de Varsovie*, Cl. III, fasc. 1–3, 1930).

[2] The Oxford-translation (*The Works of Aristotle*, translated into English under the editorship of W. D. Ross, vol. I) reads: 'For there is a difference between saying that that which is, when it is, must needs be, and simply saying that all that is must needs be'. In view of the use which Aristotle elsewhere makes of *ἁπλῶς* in connexion with *ἀνάγκη* it seems to me certain that the translator has misplaced the word 'simply' here.

[3] Thus by Ph. Boehner in 'The Tractatus de Praedestinatione et de Praescientia Dei et de Futuris Contingentibus of William Ockham' (*Franciscan Institute Publications* 2, St. Bonaventure, N.Y., 1945), p. 70 ff.

Aristotle makes in the quoted passage to the distinction here made between absolute and relative modality. Aristotle in several places[1] distinguishes between that which is necessary absolutely or simply (ἁπλῶς) and hypothetically or relative to suppositions (ἐξ ὑποθέσεως).[2] Of the necessity which belongs to that which is, when it is, he says in the quoted passage from *De interpretatione* that it is not a necessity ἁπλῶς. One would therefore think that it must be a case of necessity ἐξ ὑπθέσεως. I would understand Aristotle's thought thus: relative to the hypothesis (supposition) that it is true, a proposition *cannot* be but true (is necessarily true). Thus *not*: if a proposition is true, then it is (absolutely) necessary. But: if a proposition is *true*, it is *self-necessary*.[3] In symbols: $p \rightarrow N(p/p)$. And this, as we have seen (p. 106), is a truth of the logic of relative modalities.

APPENDIX II. SOME REMARKS ON THE MODAL LOGIC OF
ŁUKASIEWICZ

A singular position in the family of modal logics is held by the systems developed by J. Łukasiewicz. A fair appreciation of their interest and value is made difficult by the fact that Łukasiewicz thinks of modal logic as a *many-valued logic*. But I think it can be shown and should be pointed out that his conception of the modal notions is *utterly different* from a conception of them which employs the ordinary, two-valued interpretation of the so-called truth-connectives and the terms 'true' and 'false'. The difference being what it is, Łukasiewicz's modal logic will, from the two-valued point of view, appear utterly absurd. Whether this is enough to 'condemn' it as a modal logic, I do not know—though I should feel inclined to think so. At any rate it is important that the absurdity should be clearly seen.

In its first version,[4] Łukasiewicz's system of modal logic

---

[1]See *Physica* 199ᵇ34–35; *De generatione et corruptione* 337ᵇ25–27; *De somno et vigilia* 455ᵇ26.

[2]Cf. *Analytica priora* 30ᵇ38–39 τούτων ὄντων.

[3]Cf. *De interpretatione* 18ᵇ9–11. I shall not here discuss the further question whether, on Aristotle's view, the necessity of that which is, when it is, can only belong to truths of the present and the past, and not to truths of the future.

[4]As presented in 'Philosophische Bemerkungen zu mehrwertigen Systemen des Aussagenkalküls'.

made use of a principle to the effect that any proposition implies its own necessity. (*Vide supra*, p. 121.) This, in combination with the principle that any proposition implies its own possibility and the usual definition of necessity in terms of possibility, which were also accepted, lead to the consequence that any proposition is provably equivalent, in this system of modal logic, to the proposition that the first proposition is necessary. If we were allowed to speak 'two-valuedly' of propositions and of implication and equivalence this consequence means that truth and necessity of a proposition coincide. Łukasiewicz later abandoned the view that this early system of his were a satisfactory modal logic.

In publications from towards the end of his life, Łukasiewicz developed a new modal logic.[1] This system, like ours, is based on ('classical') propositional logic. To this basis is being added a principle $\delta p \rightarrow (\delta \sim p \rightarrow \delta q)$, where δ is a variable proposition-forming functor of one propositional variable—such as ' $\sim$ ' in propositional logic or ' $\diamondsuit$ ' in modal logic. We shall refer to it as Leśniewski's Principle. A further axiom of the Łukasiewicz system is the familiar *ab esse ad posse*-principle $p \rightarrow \diamondsuit p$. Finally, there are two 'rejection-axioms' (*vide infra*).

Łukasiewicz says of his system that it 'fulfils, in my opinion, all our intuitions concerning modalities without having the defects of the known modal systems'. Of what we have here called 'classical' modal logic he says that 'the systems of Lewis are certainly very interesting and may have their own merits; I think, however, that they cannot be regarded as adequate systems of modal logic.'

Against this it must be pointed out, I think, that Łukasiewicz's system *could* be said to 'fulfil our intuitions concerning modalities' only within a logic which is contrary to our ordinary, 'two-valued', intuitions of truth and falsehood and the truth-connectives. And within the framework of such a logic,

---

[1] A System of Modal Logic' in *The Journal of Computing Systems*, **1**, 1953; 'Arithmetic and Modal Logic,' *ib.* 1954; 'On a Controversial Problem of Aristotle's Modal Syllogistic' in *Dominican Studies*, **7**, 1954. Łukasiewicz's views have been examined and compared with those of other modal logicians by A. N. Prior in 'On Propositions neither Necessary nor Impossible' in *The Journal of Symbolic Logic*, **18**, 1953 and 'The Interpretation of Two Systems of Modal Logic' in *The Journal of Computing Systems*, **1**, 1954.

I would contend, we *have* no 'intuitions concerning modalities' whatsoever.

The absurdities, from a two-valued point of view, come from the extension of Leśniewski's Principle from propositional logic to modal logic. The principle is certainly true for the one monadic proposition-forming operation of ordinary propositional logic, viz. negation. $\sim p \rightarrow (\sim \sim p \rightarrow \sim q)$ is a tautology of propositional logic. The principle, moreover, *sometimes* holds in modal logic too. The reader may easily verify that it holds both for necessity and impossibility. The status of possibility, however, with regard to Leśniewski's Principle would seem to be quite different. If the proposition-forming operation δ be 'possibilification', then the principle says that the contingent character of an arbitrary proposition p, i.e. the fact that both p and $\sim p$ are possible, implies the possibility of any other arbitrary proposition q. In symbols: $\diamondsuit p \rightarrow (\diamondsuit \sim p \rightarrow \diamondsuit q)$. Could anything more absurd be said about the logic of the concept of possibility—granting the ordinary two-valued interpretation of negation and material implication?

Another example to illustrate the absurdity of Leśniewski's Principle in modal logic will here be mentioned.

By means of this principle we can deduce $(p \longleftrightarrow q) \rightarrow (\diamondsuit p \rightarrow \diamondsuit q)$, which Łukasiewicz calls a Law of Extensionality. He expresses the law in words as follows: 'If p and q are equivalent to each other, then if p is possible, q is possible'. He says that the law is 'perfectly evident'. But it is perfectly evident that the law is false, if negation, implication, and equivalence are understood in the usual two-valued way. For, consider two propositions, p and q, which are both false: p because it just so happens that it is false and q because it is impossible. Here the material equivalence $p \longleftrightarrow q$ is true and the material implication $\diamondsuit p \rightarrow \diamondsuit q$ false, and therefore the Law of Extensionality false. The law, in other words, requires for its truth, that it must not be the case that of two arbitrary, false propositions the first is contingent and the second impossible!

Łukasiewicz shows that the Law of Extensionality is inconsistent with the acceptance of true propositions as being necessary. (As can in fact be easily deduced from the example just discussed.) Faced with the choice between the acceptance of the Law of Extensionality and necessary truths, he chooses the former. The Law of Extensionality, he says, 'should be taken as the corner-stone of any system of modal logic'. (The rejection of the alternative choice is laid down in a 'rejection-axiom'.)

Thus Łukasiewicz is forced to banish the notion of necessary truths as inconsistent with modal logic. This is a very awkward position. His defence for it is not very strong. 'It is certainly true', he says, 'that every *a* is an *a*, if *a* is not an empty form, but nothing is gained by saying that it is *necessarily* true.' In other words: nothing is gained by distinguishing, among true propositions, the contingent truths from the necessary truths. This seems to me to be a strange view as to what constitutes 'gains' in the development of logic.

With the above remarks I have not wished to exclude that the Łukasiewicz modal logic, *in its many-valued interpretation*, may not be of *some* importance to the study of modality. I do not think that one can monopolize this study for so-called two-valued logic. There may be *aspects* of the possible and the necessary which are, so to say, out of the reach of 'classical' modal logic—both in its monadic and in its dyadic form. But Łukasiewicz's formalism *by itself* does not establish that there are such aspects and therefore it is not clear whether it can appropriately be said to be a modal logic at all.

Note on Aristotle and the Law of Extensionality. Łukasiewicz seems to think that his Law of Extensionality can be found in Aristotle's modal logic.

In *Analytica priora* 34ᵃ5-7 Aristotle says: πρῶτον δὲ λεκτέον ὅτι εἰ τοῦ A ὄντος ἀνάγκη τὸ B εἶναι, καὶ δυνατοῦ ὄντος τοῦ A δυνατὸν ἔσται καὶ τὸ B ἐξ ἀνάγκης. This invites two interpretations in symbols: $\sim \diamondsuit \sim [\sim \diamondsuit \sim (p \to q) \to (\diamondsuit p \to \diamondsuit q)]$ and $\sim \diamondsuit \sim (p \to q) \to \sim \diamondsuit \sim (\diamondsuit p \to \diamondsuit q)$—depending upon how one understands the reference of the ἐξ ἀνάγκης at the end of the sentence[1]. (Łukasiewicz suggests the interpretation $\sim \diamondsuit \sim (p$

[1]The Oxford translation of the quoted passage runs: 'First we must state that if *B*'s being follows necessarily from *A*'s being, *B*'s possibility will follow necessarily from *A*'s possibility'. This supports the second symbolic interpretation. I do not think, however, that much weight can, on this point, be attached to the translation.

$\rightarrow q) \rightarrow (\Diamond p \rightarrow \Diamond q)$, from which, in 'classical' modal logic, the first of the above two formulae can immediately be derived.) The first formula and the one suggested by Łukasiewicz is indeed a truth of 'classical' modal logic. The second formula is a truth of the 'classical' systems M' and M'' (S_4 and S_5), but not of M. From Aristotle's argument in 34ᵃ7-24 it would seem that he has the first interpretation in mind. *This* point, however, is here of minor importance only.

In 34ᵃ29-31 Aristotle then refers to what has just been proved (ἐπεὶ γὰρ δέδεικται) as being that εἰ τοῦ A ὄντος τὸ B ἔστι, καὶ δυνατοῦ ὄντος τοῦ A ἔσται τὸ B δυνατόν. And this, obviously, suggests $(p \rightarrow q) \rightarrow (\Diamond p \rightarrow \Diamond q)$ or (a case of) Łukasiewicz's extensionality principle (at least if we accept the translation of 'if-then' by means of material implication[1]). There is, however, as far as I am able to see, nothing to support that Aristotle really believed *this* principle to be true. Aristotle uses the words, just quoted, to refer to the principle mentioned in 34ᵃ5-7. And, since 34ᵃ29-31 does not mean the same as 34ᵃ5-7, one would think that he is, in the later passage, simply guilty of inaccurate speech. In view of the clear-headedness and good common sense, characteristic of Aristotle's genius, it is difficult to believe that he would have been willing to commit himself to holding—as one ought to on Łukasiewicz's view—that of two arbitrary, false propositions, the first cannot truly be pronounced contingent and the second impossible.

---

[1]The Oxford translation of the quoted passage runs: 'if B's being is the conse-quence of A's being, then B's possibility will follow from A's possibility'. Here the translator has, in my opinion, at the expense of faithfulness to the text given a correct rendering of Aristotle's actual thought.

ON CONDITIONALS

For a number of years I had been planning to write some-thing on the problem of conditionals. My original plan was to give a survey of existing views of the subject from Frege and Russell onwards, and then add some thoughts of my own. One reason why I abandoned this plan was that the literature on the subject is at present growing at a rate which would make any attempted survey of the problem-situation obsolete within a short time. Another reason was that, as my own views of the subject developed, they seemed to me to become more and more unlike anything which I had encountered in my studies of the literature. As a consequence, the need of making my own thoughts clearer by trying to relate them to those of others became less urgent, and an attempt to satisfy this need for the reader's sake would, I believe, have been likely rather to promote misunderstanding.

In the following there will therefore be no references to literature. But I should like to mention that I have drawn much inspiration from two papers on the problem of so-called counter-factual conditionals—papers which may already be said to have acquired the status of 'classics' in the subject—viz. Chisholm's 'The Contrary-To-Fact Conditional', original-ly published in *Mind* 1946, and Goodman's 'The Problem of Counterfactual Conditionals' in *The Journal of Philosophy* for 1947.

I

1. Conditionals have usually been studied as a kind of pro-position, demanding analysis. Here I propose to deal with the conditional as a *mode of asserting*. This means that we shall be concerned, not primarily with the analysis of propositions but with the analysis of something which may, with due caution, be called 'acts' (or 'actions').

The notion of asserting has been comparatively little discussed among logicians. It presents many interesting problems. I shall here confine myself to a few general observations only:

We assert propositions. To assert a proposition entails that (some kind of) language (symbols) is being used. In this respect asserting seems to differ from knowing and believing. I may know p without saying anything 'about p', but I cannot assert p without saying something 'about p'. ('Saying' is here used in a broad sense, which includes writing and other uses of symbols.) (One cannot assert 'mentally' or 'in thought' only.) (On asserting 'by implication' *vide infra*.)

But to assert a proposition is not *the same* as to utter the words which express (mean) the proposition. In fiction, for example, sentences are used to express propositions but not to assert them.

A condition of the assertability of a proposition is that the proposition be either true or false. I shall not here inquire into the conditions for having a truth-value. It should be noted that I have not wished to say that *all* propositions are either true or false.

To deny p is to assert $\sim p$. Denying is a kind of asserting. (There are special aspects of the pair of opposites affirming-denying which will not be studied here.)

To assert p does not entail knowing or believing p. Indeed (deliberate) *lying* can be defined as asserting a proposition knowing that it is false.

The question may be raised: If I assert p, do I thereby assert also all (or some) logical consequences of p? If I assert p & q, do I assert p? This is an intriguing question. One could make a distinction between asserting *explicitly* or 'overtly' and *implicitly* or 'by implication'. Then one could say that in asserting a proposition explicitly we assert its consequences implicitly. I shall, however, not make use of this distinction here. One might also suggest that to assert p means to assert *it* and all propositions which we *know* to follow from p. But I shall not use 'asserting' in this restricted sense either. I shall understand it in a sense which covers both explicit and implicit asserting, as distinguished above. I shall therefore say that, if we have asserted a proposition p, we have therewith also asserted all p's consequences. This, of course, means that a person may in asserting (overtly) a certain proposition, often not be aware of everything which he asserts. In asserting, something must be *said*. That which is said is then also asserted, but not everything that is therewith asserted is also said.

Thus, in our terminology, if p is asserted and if p entails q then q is asserted too. The fact that q has been thus asserted as a consequence of asserting p does not, however, entail that the proposition that p entails q has been asserted. This observation has some bearing on the notion of *grounding*, which will be discussed presently.

To assert is to do something, to perform an *act*. It is convenient to say also that the not-performing (neglecting) of a certain act is an act. Performing and not-performing an act may be called contradictory or incompatible forms of behaviour. The contradictory of the act of asserting p is *not* the act of asserting $\sim p$ but is the act of not-asserting p. p and $\sim p$ are contradictories (contradictory propositions). But asserting p and asserting $\sim p$ are contraries (contrary forms of behaviour).

Asserting—like most forms of acting—is relative to an agent (person) and an occasion. A proposition is asserted by someone on a certain occasion. When, in the sequel, I speak of the asserting of a proposition I always mean, by implication, 'by some agent on some occasion.'

One and the same person *may* on one and the same occasion, so we shall say, assert both of two incompatible propositions. But one and the same person *cannot* on one and the same occasion, so we shall say, assert and not assert one and the same proposition. (This is part of our definition of 'one and the same occasion'.) He may, however, on one and the same occasion assert some or several propositions and not assert another or some other propositions.

A person who on one and the same occasion asserts both of two incompatible propositions may be accused of 'inconsistency'. An act of asserting p may be said to 'cancel' or to 'void' all assertions, if any, by the same person on previous occasions of propositions incompatible with p. One could give to the notion of asserting a secondary sense, according to which a person is said to assert p (in this secondary sense), if it is the case that (*a*) he has asserted *p* (in the primary sense) on some occasion, and (*b*) he has not cancelled this act on a later occasion. One can also make the (secondary) notion of asserting dependent upon willingness to assert under given circumstances. We need not consider these problems here. Some of them are important in ethics and the philosophy of law.

One can speak of relations of compatibility, incompatibility, entailment, etc., between acts, and thus also between acts of asserting. Two *acts* are said to be incompatible if the *proposition* that the one is performed by an agent on a certain occasion is incompatible with the *proposition* that the other is performed by the same agent on the same occasion. One act is said to entail another act, if the proposition that the first act is performed by an agent on a certain occasion entails the proposition that the second act is performed by the same agent on the same occasion.

The reader will have noted that I have talked above of 'asserting' and not of 'assertion'. The latter term is ambiguous. It sometimes means the *act* of asserting (assertion), sometimes the *proposition* asserted, and sometimes the *words* used in asserting a proposition.

In spite of these ambiguities, however, I shall in the sequel often use 'assertion' instead of the heavier and uncolloquial 'asserting'. But it must be carefully noted that by 'assertion' I always mean the *act* of asserting and never *what* is thereby asserted.

2. I shall distinguish two *modes of asserting*: the *categorical* and the *conditional*. When we assert the proposition *q* conditionally, we consider it conditional on or 'relative to' some other proposition *p*.

Asserting *q* conditionally, relative to *p* must, of course, not be confused with asserting *q* categorically, when the condition *p* is, in fact, fulfilled. One may say that when someone asserts *q* conditionally, relative to *p*, he *licenses* others to take him as having asserted *q*, *if* the condition *p* is found to be, in fact, fulfilled.

When, in the sequel, I speak of 'asserting *q* on the condition *p*' I always mean asserting *q* *conditionally*, relative to *p*.

In asserting q on the condition p, we often use a characteristic form of language. I shall call it the conditional *form*. In English, the standard conditional form is constructed by means of the pair of words 'if-then' and sentences expressing the propositions. (This description, as will be seen presently, stands in need of modification.)

It is not necessary, for the purpose of asserting a proposition conditionally, to use the conditional form of language. (The import of this statement will appear later.)

Does the form of language 'if p, then q', when used for asserting q on the condition p, itself express a proposition? This is a puzzling problem. If the form of language in question expresses a proposition, then this proposition may be asserted, either categorically or conditionally. It ought, moreover, to have a contradictory (negation). But what is the contradictory of that which is asserted, when q is asserted on the condition p? (What *could* 'not: if p, then q' mean?) Is the contradictory in question that which is asserted, when $\sim q$ is asserted on the condition p, i.e., is it that which—assuming that 'if p, then q' has propositional meaning, when used to assert q on the condition p—would be the propositional meaning of 'if p, then $\sim q$', when used to assert $\sim q$ on the condition p? *Or*, is the contradictory in question simply that q is *not* being asserted on the condition p? The last, one would have thought, is the contradictory of the proposition that q *is* being asserted on the condition p. This, however, is a proposition *about* an act of conditional asserting, and cannot very well be the negation of a proposition asserted by that act.

For reasons, which will be given later (p. 135), I shall take the view that the answer to the above question is in the negative. I shall never speak of the conditional as a proposition which is being asserted, but only of propositions being asserted conditionally, relative to other propositions. Therefore we must not say that 'if p, then q', when used to assert q on the condition p, expresses something which is either true or false. But we shall certainly have to agree to saying that a proposition may be truly or falsely asserted conditionally, relative to another proposition. The precise meaning of this will be explained later.

3. We shall have to make use of the important notion of a *ground* of a proposition. There are *deductive* and *inductive* grounds of propositions. *p* is a deductive ground of *q*, if and only if *p* entails *q*. To characterize the notion of an inductive ground is very difficult; we shall have to say something about this problem later.

It will be necessary to distinguish between grounds of a proposition and grounds for asserting a proposition. A ground of *p* is also a ground for asserting *p* categorically, and vice versa. But of what *proposition* a ground for *asserting p* on the condition *q* is a ground, will require careful consideration later.

Asserting *p and* that *p* is a ground of *q* will be called *giving p as a ground of q*. Thus, in particular, asserting *p* and that *p* entails *q*, is giving *p* as a deductive ground of *q*.

If *q* is asserted and *p* given as a ground of *q*, we shall say that asserting *q* is *grounded* on (asserting) *p*. (Asserting a proposition may be grounded on more than one ground.)

Grounding an assertion is thus itself a species of asserting. The act of grounding the assertion of *q* on *p* is the conjunction of *three* acts, viz. asserting *p* and asserting *q* and asserting that *p* is a ground of *q*. (If the ground is a deductive ground, then the first of these three acts entails the second act.)

If we have asserted *p* and if *p* entails *q*, then we have asserted *q* and asserted a (deductive) ground of *q*. But we have not therewith asserted that *p* is a ground of *q*—a fact of which we may not be aware.

A proposition may, of course, be either truly or falsely asserted. (Just as a proposition may be truly or falsely believed. Knowing, in what seems to be the usual sense, is different: if a proposition is known, it is true.) Therefore, asserting a proposition may also be either truly or falsely grounded on another proposition. Asserting *q* is falsely grounded on *p*, if either *p* is false *or p* is not a ground of *q*.

Grounds of a proposition must not be confused with *motives* for asserting a proposition. (Ground is an 'objective', motive a 'subjective' notion.) The term 'reason' is used ambiguously in ordinary language to refer to grounds of propositions and to motives for asserting them.

4. My problem can now be stated as follows: Is it possible to give an account (analysis) of conditional assertion in terms of categorical assertion?

Of the notion of categorical assertion nothing more will be said than is contained in 1. (and 3.) above.

It will here be necessary to distinguish two modes of conditional assertion. I shall call them the potential and the contrary-to-fact mode. The distinction is familiar. In asserting a proposition contrary to fact we consider it relative to a proposition which is asserted to be false.

This distinction necessitates a certain modification of our description of the conditional *form*. It will not do for all purposes to say, as we did, that the standard conditional form is 'if *p*, then *q*', where '*p*' and '*q*' are sentences expressing propositions. For, from this form we could never, by substitution, derive what might be called the standard contrary-to-fact conditional form. We may substitute for '*p*' 'there is lightning' and for '*q*' 'there is thunder'. But we may not substitute for '*p*' 'there had been lightning' and for '*q*' 'there would have been thunder'. For these phrases, the verb being understood in the subjunctive mood, are not sentences expressing propositions.

We might regard '*p*' and '*q*' as descriptive phrases, not containing a verb in the finite form, of something which might be called 'states of affairs'. 'Raining', 'thundering' would be examples of such phrases. Then we could distinguish between two standard conditional forms, viz. the form 'if *p* is, then *q* is' and the form 'if *p* had been, then *q* would have been'. The first is the standard form used in potential conditional asserting, the second the standard form used in contrary-to-fact conditional asserting. (See also below p. 145 f.)

I shall, however, not proceed in this manner, but continue to regard '*p*' and '*q*' as (variables for) sentences which express propositions. I shall henceforth reserve the phrase 'to assert *q*, on the condition *p*' for the *potential* case. And I shall introduce the phrase 'to assert *q* on the counterfactual condition *p*' the for *contrary-to-fact* case. I shall thus commit myself to saying that, in asserting that there would have been thunder yesterday, had there been lightning yesterday, I am asserting the proposition that there was thunder yesterday counter-conditionally, relative to the proposition that there was lightning yesterday. This is, admittedly, not a very 'natural' way of putting things, but it is convenient for present purposes.

It is important to emphasize that the distinction between potential and contrary-to-fact conditional asserting does not run parallel to a *linguistic* distinction. This is obscured, when one speaks of 'subjunctive conditionals', as if the use of the subjunctive verb-form corresponded to a characteristic mode of conditional asserting. But this is by no means the case.

Consider the form 'if *x* were, then *y* would be'. This form is used both in potential and in contrary-to-fact conditional asserting. I may say of an object of unknown material 'if it were of wood, it would burn'—and then make a test. This is a case of potential conditional asserting. Or I may, looking out of my window at the cloudy sky say 'if the sun were shining, he would come—but not now'. This is a conditional assertion contrary-to-fact.

The form 'if *x* had been, *y* would have been' is obviously *sometimes* used for potential and not for contrary-to-fact conditional asserting. I may say 'if there had been an accident on the way, news would have reached the town'—and then set out to investigate whether there is any news. This is a case of potential conditional asserting.

The typical use of the subjunctive 'had been' in conditional asserting contrary-to-fact appears to be in cases which are 'irrevocably' thus and thus and not otherwise. As for example past events. The typical use of 'were' appears to be in cases where either there is uncertainty or a *change* in characteristics is possible. ('If the house were red, it would look more friendly, therefore let us paint it red.')

II

5. I propose the following account of potential conditional asserting:

To assert *q* on the condition *p* is to assert that *p* materially implies *q* without asserting or denying the antecedent or the consequent of the material implication.

What a person *does* who asserts *q* on the condition *p* is thus the following: He, on one and the same occasion, asserts $p \rightarrow q$, and neither asserts nor denies p and neither asserts nor denies q.

If we assert $p \rightarrow q$, but neither assert nor deny p and neither assert nor deny q, we shall say that we assert the material implication in question independently of its antecedent and consequent. To assert a material implication independently of its antecedent and consequent will also be called asserting the material implication *intensionally*. Thus we can re-state our proposed analysis of the potential case as follows:

To assert q on the condition p is to assert p → q intensionally.

Thus when we assert q on the condition p, the only proposition which we assert (categorically) is $p \rightarrow q$. But it is essential to the situation that, beside *making* this one categorical assertion, we *refrain* from making some other assertions.

We are now in a position to see more clearly *in what sense* 'if p, then q', when used for asserting q on the condition p, can be said *not* to express a proposition. (Cf. above p. 131.) For, although *part* of what we do in thus using 'if p, then q' is that we assert a certain proposition, it is equally a *part* of what we do that we leave some propositions unasserted. Therefore the *whole* of what we do in asserting q on the condition p is not that we assert some proposition (or combination of propositions) categorically.

We are now also in a position to see in what sense q may be said to be *truly* or *falsely* asserted on the condition p. (Cf. above p. 131.) We propose the following definitions: If $p \rightarrow q$ is asserted intensionally and p and $p \rightarrow q$ are true, then q will be said to be truly asserted on the condition p. If again $p \rightarrow q$ is asserted intensionally and p is true but $p \rightarrow q$ false, then q will be said to be falsely asserted on the condition p. It follows that if q is truly asserted on the condition p, then q is true, and that if q is falsely asserted on the condition p, then q is false. It also follows that q is truly asserted on the condition p, if $p \rightarrow q$ is asserted intensionally and p and q are both true, and that q is falsely asserted on the condition p, if $p \rightarrow q$ is asserted intensionally and p is true but q false. This shows that to assert q on the condition p is not (necessarily) to assert the existence of a (logical or natural) 'connexion' between q and p. (The meaning of 'connexion' here will be discussed presently.)

It is a further consequence of the above definition that if $p \to q$ is asserted intensionally and p is false (in which case $p \to q$ is certainly true), then q is neither truly nor falsely asserted on the condition p. This must not be obscured by the possibility that, if q is asserted on the condition p and p subsequently found to be false, we may wish to 'strengthen' our previous conditional assertion into a counter-conditional assertion to the effect that, *had p* been true, q would have been true too. In doing so, we may be asserting truly q counter-conditionally, relative to p, although we can neither be said to have asserted q truly nor to have asserted it falsely conditionally, relative to p. (The conditions for asserting truly and falsely contrary to fact will be discussed later.)

To prevent confusion, I must stress again what the present analysis of potential conditional asserting is about. It is *not* about the normal (most common) meaning of the form of language 'if p, then q', but about something which is normally done by the use of that form, 'if p, then q'.

I believe that the normal use of 'if p, then q' also involves a *commitment* to a contrary-to-fact conditional assertion, in case the antecedent turns out to be false. This means that the words 'if p, then q' are normally used for a *double* assertion of (potential) conditionality, viz. for asserting (*a*) on the condition p: the proposition q, and (*b*) on the condition $\sim p$: the proposition that q would have been true, if p had been true. (As we shall see presently, there is no objection to speaking of counter-conditional *propositions*.)

This explains why the falsification of p, although it puts an end to the question whether we truly or falsely asserted the proposition q conditionally, relative to the proposition p, does *not* put an end to the question whether we asserted something truly or falsely in using the words 'if p, then q'. For, if p is falsified, the question of the truth or falsehood of the proposition that q would have been true, had p been true, becomes urgent.

The relation between asserting q on the condition p and using the form 'if p, then q' thus appears, in the normal case, to be as follows: by means of 'if p, then q' I assert q on the condition *p and do something more*. This 'more' is also an act of potential conditional asserting.

Although the use of 'if p, then q' does normally involve a commitment to a contrary-to-fact conditional assertion, it does not *always* do so. This will be shown later (p. 147 f.).

Some further consequences of the proposed analysis of potential conditional asserting will have to be mentioned:

I have said that the normal way of asserting q on the condition p is by means of the standard conditional form 'if p, then q'. But use of the conditional *form* is not necessary for the purpose. If we use 'it is not the case that p is true and q is false' to assert that p materially implies q and at the same time neither assert nor deny p or q, then what we have *done* is that we have asserted q conditionally, relative to p. This, however, by no means amounts to saying that material implication and the potential conditional were the same thing. The act of asserting q on the condition p entails the act of asserting that p materially implies q. And the second act, when supplemented with certain abstentions from asserting, is equivalent to the first act.

It follows from our analysis of potential conditional asserting that no person can, on one and the same occasion, both assert q on the condition p and deny p. For asserting q conditionally, relative to p *entails* not denying p. Similarly, no person can, on one and the same occasion, both assert q categorically and conditionally, relative to p. For if he asserts q on the condition p, then part of what he *does* is that he does *not* assert q categorically.

A person may, of course, *say* 'not-p and if p, then q'. And it may mean something. I am not disputing this. What I maintain is only that he cannot, saying 'not-p and if p, then q' be denying p and asserting q on the condition p. For, whatever he *says*, this is something which he *cannot do*.

(Asserting $\sim p$ *excludes* asserting q on the condition p. They are incompatible forms of behaviour. Cf. above p. 129.)

As is well known, $\sim p$ is a deductive ground of $p \to q$, and so also is q. Thus asserting a material implication may be grounded on denying its antecedent or on asserting its consequent. There is nothing 'odd' or 'paradoxical' in this. But it was rightly felt to be odd, if asserting q on the condition p could be grounded on denying p or on asserting q. On our analysis of conditional asserting, this cannot happen. This disposes of the so-called

Paradoxes of Implication in the context. (There are other aspects of the 'paradoxes' which are related to the notions of entailment and of confirmation. These aspects do not concern us here.)

To assert a material implication as a consequence of (cf. above p. 129) asserting its consequent or denying its antecedent will be called asserting the material implication *extensionally*.

It may be asked: May one not, contrary to what is entailed by our analysis, on one and the same occasion both assert p and assert q on the condition p? Is this not what we normally should be doing, if we were to say, e.g. '*if* this is iron, then it conducts electricity, and now that *is* iron, so therefore it conducts electricity'? The answer is that this is *not* what we should be doing. (Indeed it is something which we *cannot* do.) If we first assert q on the condition p, and later, for example upon investigation, come to assert p as well, then the two assertions, when combined into one, become the act of asserting p and $p \to q$ (and therewith also q). Conditionality, as it were, vanishes in the combination.

The same is to be said, *mutatis mutandis*, of the apparent possibility of asserting q on the condition p and denying q on one and the same occasion.

Finally, consider the following illustration of our analysis of potential conditional asserting and of the use of the conditional form:

Why is it that we do not *normally* say 'if ink is blue, then snow is white', although there is nothing logically odd about saying 'is it not the case that ink is blue and snow not white'? The answer is that asserting the material implication in question would normally be grounded on asserting that snow *is* white. But imagine a person, who does not know the colour of ink nor that of snow. He is being told that it is not the case that ink is blue and snow not white. It would make perfectly good sense, if this person were to say: 'I don't know what colour ink has nor what colour snow has, but I am informed that it is not the case that the former is blue and the second not white, so therefore: *if* ink is blue, *then* snow is white.'

6. I now pass to the question of *grounds* for potential conditional asserting.

A ground for asserting q on the condition p is a ground for asserting the material implication $p \to q$ intensionally, i.e. independently of its antecedent and consequent. I propose the following definition:

A ground for asserting q on the condition p is any proposition which is a ground of the material implication $p \to q$ but not a ground of the antecedent or its negation nor a ground of the consequent or its negation.

What could be an example of a proposition, thus providing a ground for a potential conditional assertion? We shall here only discuss one case, which I think may be called 'typical'.

Let p be the proposition Py attributing the property P to the individual y. Let q be the proposition Qy. We assume that Qy is being asserted on the condition Py.

Now consider the so-called general implication $(x)\,(Px \to Qx)$ which attributes the property Q to every (thing which is) P. This general implication entails, and is thus a deductive ground of, the singular (material) implication $Py \to Qy$. But it does not entail Py or Qy nor $\sim Py$ or $\sim Qy$.

It follows from our definition that $(x)(Px \to Qx)$ or that every P is Q is a ground for asserting Qy on the condition Py or for asserting that y is Q, if it is P.

But it must not be believed that any act of asserting $(x)(Px \to Qx)$ is giving a ground for asserting Qy on the condition Py. In order to see this quite clearly, let us proceed one step in the chain of possible grounds and ask, what could be a ground of $(x)(Px \to Qx)$.

It will then occur to us that the proposition $\sim(Ex)Px$ or that nothing whatever is P entails, and is thus a ground of, the proposition $(x)(Px \to Qx)$ or that every P is Q. And the same holds good of the proposition $(x)\,Qx$ or that everything whatever is Q—it too entails the universal implication in question.

It follows that asserting $\sim(Ex)Px$ or asserting $(x)\,Qx$ entails asserting $(x)(Px \to Qx)$.

But $\sim(Ex)Px$ also entails $\sim Py$ and $(x)Qx$ entails Qy.

It follows that if $(x)(Px \to Qx)$ is asserted as a consequence of asserting $\sim(Ex)Px$ or of asserting $(x)Qx$, then $(x)(Px \to Qx)$ *cannot* be given as a ground for asserting Qy on the condition Py. For, part of what we do when we give a ground for asserting

$Q\,y$ on the condition Py is that we assert a proposition which, although it is a ground of $Py \rightarrow Q\,y$ is at the same time *not* a ground of $\sim Py$ or of $Q\,y$.

We shall say that the general implication $(x)(Px \rightarrow Q\,x)$ is asserted *extensionally*, if it is asserted as a consequence of asserting that nothing whatever is P or of asserting that everything is Q. And we shall say that the general implication is asserted *intensionally*, if it is asserted without $\sim(Ex)Px$ or $(x)Q\,x$ being asserted.

It thus follows that a necessary condition for giving $(x)(Px \rightarrow Q\,x)$ as a ground for asserting $Q\,y$ on the condition Py is that $(x)(Px \rightarrow Q\,x)$ is asserted intensionally.

It is clear that this condition, though necessary, is not sufficient. To assert $(x)(Px \rightarrow Q\,x)$ intensionally is tantamount to giving a ground for asserting $Q\,y$ on the condition Py only when combined with asserting that $(x)(Px \rightarrow Q\,x)$ is a ground of (entails) $Py \rightarrow Q\,y$. (Cf. above p. 132.)

We shall not at present inquire into the possible grounds for asserting a general implication intensionally. They may be deductive grounds, e.g. some further general implication of which the first is a logical consequence. Or they may be inductive grounds.

It should be observed that the *truth* of $\sim(Ex)Px$ or $(x)Q\,x$ is no hindrance to asserting $(x)(Px \rightarrow Q\,x)$ intensionally or for giving $(x)(Px \rightarrow Q\,x)$ as a ground for asserting $Q\,y$ on the condition Py. But *asserting* $\sim(Ex)Px$ or $(x)Q\,x$ is such a hindrance.

Since $\sim(Ex)Px$ entails $\sim Py$ and $(x)Q\,x$ entails $Q\,y$, it follows that asserting $\sim(Ex)Px$ or $(x)Q\,x$ is incompatible with asserting $Q\,y$ on the condition Py. But it may be worth remarking already in this place that neither asserting $\sim(Ex)Px$ nor asserting $(x)Q\,x$ is incompatible with asserting $Q\,y$ on the counterfactual condition Py. ('If y were A, which neither it nor anything else is, then it would be B.')

Since $(x)(Px \rightarrow Q\,x)$ entails $Py \rightarrow Q\,y$, it follows that asserting the general implication entails asserting the singular implication. It should be observed, however, that asserting $(x)(Px \rightarrow Q\,x)$ intensionally does not entail asserting $Py \rightarrow Q\,y$ intensionally, i.e. asserting $Q\,y$ on the condition Py. For to assert $(x)(Px \rightarrow Q\,x)$ intensionally is compatible with asserting or denying both Py and Qy, whereas to assert $Py{\rightarrow}Qy$ intensionally is incompatible with asserting or denying Py or Qy. But asserting $(x)(Px{\rightarrow}Qx)$ intensionally without asserting or denying Py or Qy entails asserting $Py{\rightarrow}Qy$ intensionally and thus Qy on the condition Py.

We can distinguish between *singular* and *general* (potential) conditional asserting:

The propositions which we assert conditionally may be singular or general. We may assert the proposition that y is Q conditionally, relative to the proposition that y is P. We may also assert the proposition that everything is Q conditionally, relative to the proposition that everything is P. Both cases we shall call cases of *singular* conditional asserting.

But we may also assert *of everything* that it is Q, if it is P. That is: we may assert, *of every x*, the proposition that x is Q conditionally relative to the proposition that x is P. This we shall call a *general* conditional assertion.

General conditional asserting, it should be observed, is not the same as intensional asserting of a general implication. Asserting $(x)(Px{\rightarrow}Qx)$ intensionally is, in other words, not the same as asserting, of every x, the proposition Qx conditionally, relative to the proposition Px. But asserting $(x)(Px{\rightarrow}Qx)$ intensionally, without asserting or denying of any x either Px or Qx, is the same as asserting, of every x, Qx on the condition Px.

(It should be noted that to assert of every x that x is P is to assert (categorically) $(x)Px$. But not to assert of any x that x is P is an act of not-asserting, and not an act of asserting a negative proposition.)

It is thus important to distinguish, in the case of conditional asserting, between asserting *of everything that* . . . on the condition . . ., and asserting *that everything* . . . on the condition . . . Only the former I shall call general conditional asserting. Asserting a general proposition conditionally will count as singular conditional asserting.

7. In the last section we considered grounds for potential conditional asserting. It is clear that propositions are often asserted conditionally, no grounds being given for asserting

them. But it is of some importance to observe and perhaps not equally clear in itself, that it is in no way essential even to an act of asserting a singular proposition conditionally, relative to another that there should be some general proposition at hand, which may be given as a ground for asserting the singular proposition. (In certain attempts to deal with conditionals as a kind of proposition in need of analysis, this fact is overlooked or obscured.)

We say to a child: 'If you do not obey, I'll punish you'. That *could* be a straightforward case of potential conditional asserting. Without asserting that the child will obey or that it will not, and without asserting that we shall punish the child or that it will escape punishment, we assert (categorically) the material implication that either the child obeys or is going to be punished. And this may be *all* we assert. If asked for grounds (*not* motives), we may have no answer.

In this example, however, we encounter an ambiguity, of which it is important to be aware:

The conditional in question can be understood in at least two ways (has at least two 'meanings'). We may call them the 'objective' and the 'subjective' way. Objectively, the conditional is a *prediction* of what my behaviour will be, if certain things happen. This assertion *could* be grounded on asserting, from self-observation, the generalization that I always punish certain forms of disobedience in my child. But even if there is no such generalization at hand, even if I had never punished my child before, or only done so inconsistently, the conditional prediction of my behaviour in *this* case would nevertheless make perfectly good sense.

Subjectively, the conditional is a *declaration of intention*. It is difficult to see, how *it* could be grounded on asserting a generalization from experience. It seems that grounds for a declaration of intention must be something utterly different from grounds for predictions, or any other kind of 'objective' propositions. I am inclined to the view that in a declaration of intention no true or false proposition whatever is asserted. *A declaration of intention*, in other words, *is not an act of asserting.* If I am right, we shall have to recognize a characteristic use of the conditional form which is not for purposes of conditional *asserting*. This type of conditional is very important in ethics and law. It is not treated in the present paper.

8. It must have occurred to many a student of logic that although the conditional is not the same as material implication, the 'if-then'-*reading* of material implication formulae is often perfectly natural and obviously harmless. And similarly, it will have occurred to him that, in trying to 'formalize' deductive theories (branches of mathematics and physics) in which propositions are asserted conditionally, we are not guilty of an inaccuracy, if we 'formalize' the 'if-then' by means of material implication.

These observations can, I think, be satisfactorily explained on the basis of the account, given above, of potential conditional asserting. We shall consider two examples from the propositional calculus:

i. $p \rightarrow p \vee q$.

Why is it correct to *read* this as 'if p, then p or q'? Answer: Because the calculus *asserts* the material implication involved, but it neither asserts nor denies any arbitrary proposition p or the disjunction of any two arbitrary propositions p and q. The calculus, in other words, asserts the material implication $p \rightarrow p \vee q$ *intensionally*.

The fact that the calculus is here spoken of as the agent of asserting need not worry us. (I shall say that the propositional calculus asserts every tautology—and denies every contradiction.) But it may be relevantly objected that one cannot, strictly speaking, say of the calculus that it asserts the *singular* material implication $p \rightarrow p \vee q$. Rather one should say that what the calculus asserts is a *general* proposition, viz. the proposition that, for *all* propositions p and q, the material implication $p \rightarrow p \vee q$ holds true. The corresponding conditional assertion is a general conditional assertion. It is asserting, of all propositions p and q with unasserted truth-values, that p or q is true, if p is true.

Consider now the following slight transformation of i.:

ii. $p \& \sim p \rightarrow q$.

Why does it offend our 'logical ear' to read this as 'if p and $\sim p$, then q'? Obviously because the calculus, although it asserts the material implication in question, also denies its antecedent. $\sim (p \& \sim p)$ is a theorem of the calculus. The calculus, consequently, does not assert $p \& \sim p \to q$ intensionally and hence cannot be said to assert q on the condition $p \& \sim p$.

III

9. I now proceed to contrary-to-fact conditional asserting.

Two cases may be distinguished. I shall call them the deductive and the non-deductive case. The deductive case occurs, when a proposition q is asserted counter-conditionally, relative to another proposition p, and p *is a deductive ground of* q.

The deductive case appears to be perfectly easy to deal with. If p entails q, then to assert q on the counterfactual condition p is the same as to deny p *and* assert that p entails q. To assert that p (logically) entails q does not, as far as I can see (cf. below p. 190), entail the assertion of any proposition conditionally, either in the potential or in the counterfactual sense. Therefore the deductive case of contrary-to-fact conditional asserting may be analysed as a conjunction of two acts of categorical asserting.

In the sequel we shall be dealing only with the non-deductive case. Thus, whenever I speak of asserting q on the counterfactual condition p, I tacitly assume that p does not entail q. (But q may entail p.)

When we assert q on the counterfactual condition p, i.e. assert that q would have been true, had p been true, then *part* of what we do is that we deny p. In this respect, at least, asserting q on the counterfactual condition p differs from asserting q on the condition p. It would, however, be a serious mistake to think that asserting q on the counterfactual condition p differed from asserting q on the condition p *only* in that in the former, but not in the latter, case we deny p.

For, denying p entails asserting $p \to q$. If therefore denying p were the only respect in which the act of asserting q on the counterfactual condition p differed from the act of asserting q on the condition p, then asserting q on the counterfactual condition p would be *identical* with the act of denying p and neither asserting nor denying q. And this, clearly, is not what we wish.

We see from this, how different are the potential and the contrary-to-fact case of conditional asserting. To assert q on the condition p is to assert the material implication $p \rightarrow q$ *intensionally*. In asserting q on the counterfactual condition p, we deny p and therefore *a fortiori* assert the material implication in question *extensionally*. Our question now is: What *else* do we do in asserting q on the counterfactual condition p? And the answer which I am going to propose is that the 'else' which we do, in addition to denying p, is—that we assert q on the counterfactual condition p. This means that (not-deductive) contrary-to-fact conditional asserting, unlike potential conditional asserting, *cannot* be analysed in terms of categorical asserting (and not-asserting). This indeed is a profound difference between the two cases.

But the road to this insight will be a cumbersome one.

10. I shall first consider the status of q, when q is asserted on the counterfactual condition p.

It may be asked: Is part of what we do, when we assert q on the counterfactual condition p, that we deny q too? I shall take the view that denying q is *not* (necessarily) part of this act. Nor shall I regard it as part of this act that q is neither denied nor asserted. Nor even that q is not asserted.

In other words: asserting q on the counterfactual condition p is compatible with, but does not entail, denying q, and is compatible with, but does not entail, leaving q and its negation unasserted, and is compatible with, but does not entail, asserting q.

One may, accordingly, distinguish between three cases of asserting q on the counterfactual condition p: the case in which denying q happens to be part of the act, the case in which neither denying nor asserting q happens to be part of the act, and the case in which asserting q happens to be part of the act.

I shall in this paper be dealing only with the generic case. As far as I can see, the specific cases have no interesting logical peculiarities of their own. Before leaving them, however, a certain amplification of our previous description (p. 133) of the standard form of language used for purposes of contrary-to-fact conditional asserting may be called for.

One may say that to the three specific cases of asserting q on the counterfactual condition p answer the following three standard forms of language: to the case when q is denied, the form 'if p had been true, then q would have been true', to the case when q is neither denied nor asserted, the form 'if p had been true, then q would be true', and to the case, when q is asserted, the form 'even if p had been true, q would have been true'. It is not maintained that these three forms, in ordinary language, answer unambiguously to the three cases distinguished. On the contrary, there is in the case of the third form (the 'even if'-form) an important conceptual ambiguity to be noted:

The form 'even if p had been (or were) true, q would have been (or would be) true' is *sometimes* used for asserting q on the counterfactual condition p, but *sometimes*—perhaps even more often—used for an altogether different sort of assertion. I hope I can make this quite clear to the reader.

As we shall see presently, counter-conditional asserting is the assertion of a 'connexion'. The truth of one proposition (q) is asserted to be 'connected' or 'tied up' with the truth of another proposition (p). A given proposition q may have many such 'connexions' or 'ties', p, r, s, etc. Assume now that q is true and that we attribute its truth to its 'connexion' with r which is also true. And assume that p is false. In such a situation we might wish to assert that even if p, and not r, had been true, q would have been true. We are, in other words, anxious to assert that q is 'connected' with p too. And this is a case of asserting q on the counterfactual condition p.

Assume next that q is true but that we do not know to which proposition to 'attribute' its truth. We know or believe, however, that the truth of q is *not* to be attributed to $\sim p$ which is also true. This denial of a 'connexion' between the truth of q and the simultaneous falsehood of p we may then express by saying that *even if p* had been true, q would have been true. Here the *even if* denies something, viz. a 'connexion', the existence of which we assert when asserting conditionally contrary-to-fact. We may call this 'opposite' of a contrary-to-fact conditional assertion, an *assertion of non-conditionality*.

The 'even if'-form is thus sometimes used for conditional asserting contrary-to-fact and sometimes for the 'opposite' assertion of non-conditionality.

I shall not in this paper give a closer analysis of assertions of non-conditionality.

11. In this section I shall discuss the following proposed analysis of contrary-to-fact conditional asserting:

To assert q on the counterfactual condition p is to deny p and to assert a ground for asserting q on the condition p.

This suggestion has a certain *prima facie* plausibility. To deny p excludes asserting $p \to q$ intensionally, but is compatible with asserting some proposition which is a *ground* for asserting $p \to q$ intensionally. Such a ground is any proposition which is a ground of $p \to q$ but not a ground of p or $\sim p$ nor of q or $\sim q$. (See above p. 139.)

The suggestion, however, will have to be rejected. Rejecting it will help us to see more clearly what is the nature of contrary-to-fact conditional asserting.

It will suffice for our purposes to restrict the discussion to the case, when p is the proposition Py and q the proposition Qy.

As we know (see above p. 139), the general implication $(x)(Px \to Qx)$ is a ground for asserting $Py \to Qy$ intensionally. It is, of course, not the *only* ground for so doing. For example: $(x)(Px \text{ v } Rx \to Qx)$ is also a ground for asserting $Py \to Qy$ intensionally.

We could not say, therefore, that to assert Qy on the counterfactual condition Py is, under all circumstances, *identical* with denying Py and asserting $(x)(Px \to Qx)$ intensionally. But we could, if the above suggested analysis were correct, say, that denying Py and asserting $(x)(Px \to Qx)$ intensionally *entails* asserting Qy on the counterfactual condition Py.

That this, however, is not the case can be seen from the following example:

We are told that all persons who voted in the last general election wore red neck-ties on the election-day. We do not know who all those persons were. We may use the information to assert of a certain man y that, if he voted in the last election, then he wore a red tie on election day. From this we may go on to investigate, whether he voted or not, in order to find out whether he wore a red tie on election day. Suppose we find something which makes us *deny* that he voted. Have we now asserted that he would have had on a red tie on the day of election, *if* he had voted?

It is important that the question be quite clearly presented. It is this: Do denying that *y* voted and asserting intensionally that everyone who voted wore a red tie, i.e. asserting this without asserting that nobody voted or that everybody wore a red tie on the day in question, *entail* asserting that *y* would have had on a red tie, if he had voted?

Thus the question is *not*: Is asserting that *y* would have had on a red tie, if he had voted, *compatible* with denying that *y* voted and asserting intensionally that everyone who voted had on a red tie. I am not going to dispute that we *may* not, under the circumstances in question, make the counter-conditional assertion—and be right. (On the truth-conditions for assertions contrary to fact, see below p. 162). I am only saying that, *if* we make it, we are doing something 'over and above' merely denying that *y* voted and asserting intensionally that everyone who voted had on a red tie. And this I hope to be able to show by considering, briefly and schematically, the circumstances, under which we should regard ourselves as being *justified* in making the counter-conditional assertion in question.

Suppose we believe, or know, that voting in the election and wearing a red tie are somehow 'connected', so that no one *could* have voted *unless* he wore a red tie. On the strength of this belief, or knowledge, we should certainly consider ourselves entitled to assert that *y*, who abstained from voting, would have had a red tie on election day, had he not abstained. If, however, we regard the co-incidence of exercising one's right to vote and wearing a red tie as 'accidental' only, if, in other words, we think that 'it just so happened' that every voter wore a red tie, then we should not, on the strength of that 'accident' alone, consider ourselves justified in asserting the proposition that *y* wore a red tie counter-conditionally, relative to the proposition that he voted.

It is worth noticing that there are 'intermediates' between such 'connexions' as are thought to justify contrary-to-fact conditional assertions and 'pure accidents' which have no such power. If we hear that only communists voted, we may no longer regard it as 'accidental' that all voters wore red ties. And if we hear that only communists *could* have voted, we think ourselves justified in asserting of y that he would have been a *communist*, if he had voted. But unless we have reasons for believing that wearing a red tie was a necessary condition for voting, at least in y's case, we should not be justified in asserting that y would have had a *red tie*, if he had voted. Thus 'accident' is not the proper contradictory of the sort of 'connexion' which is relevant to conditional asserting contrary to fact.

Here it is interesting to compare with each other the assertion that, if y had voted—which he did not do—then he would have had on a red tie, and the assertion that, if y had been—which he is not—identical with some person, who voted, then he would have had on a red tie. The second conditional assertion contrary-to-fact unquestionably *is* entailed by denying that y voted and asserting intensionally that everybody who voted had a red tie. And this is so because, although there *may* be no 'connexion' between voting and wearing a red tie, there necessarily *is* a (logical) 'connexion' between being identical with a man and wearing that man's tie.

We can now answer our above question, whether to deny Py and assert $(x)(Px \rightarrow Qx)$ intensionally entails asserting Qy on the counterfactual condition Py. The answer is in the negative. It is not the intensional asserting of the general implication that 'matters'. What matters, beside denying Py, is that we should assert the existence of a certain 'connexion', *at least in y's case*, between the characteristics P and Q.

This assertion of a 'connexion' *may* entail asserting $(x)(Px \rightarrow Qx)$. But, as indicated by our phrase above 'at least in y's case', it is not necessary that it should do so.

The assertion of a 'connexion' we shall call *nomic asserting* or *asserting nomically*. If to assert a 'connexion' between P and Q entails asserting $(x)(Px \rightarrow Qx)$ we shall say that the general implication is asserted nomically.

As we have seen, to assert $(x)(Px \rightarrow Qx)$ intensionally does not entail asserting it nomically. But, it should be observed, the converse relation does not hold either. Asserting $(x)(Px \rightarrow Qx)$ intensionally is, by definition, incompatible with asserting either $\sim(Ex)Px$ or $(x)Qx$. But asserting $(x)(Px \rightarrow Qx)$ nomically is not. We may assert that, although nothing in the world actually is P, yet P and Q are so related that if anything were P, it would be Q too. Or we may assert that, although everything in the world actually is Q, if anything were not Q, it would not be P either. In such instances, the general implication $(x)(Px \rightarrow Qx)$ is being asserted *both* extensionally *and* nomically. (This combination, by the way, is no 'mere possibility'. Many of the most important laws in physics are asserted in precisely this manner. There are no ideal gasses, no absolutely elastic bodies, no unextended mass points. But many laws are nevertheless asserted to hold good for these admittedly non-existing entities.)

I hope it has now become quite clear, why we shall have to reject the idea, proposed at the beginning of the present section, that to assert q on the counterfactual condition p is the same as to deny p and assert a ground for asserting q on the condition p. The reason is, that one may assert a ground for asserting q on the condition p without asserting that p and q are 'connected'. Our next task will be to make this idea of 'connexion' clearer.

12. Throughout this section the discussion will be restricted to the case when p is the proposition Py and q the proposition Qy. I propose the following thesis which may also be called an auxiliary partial analysis of contrary-to-fact conditional asserting:

To deny Py and to assert $(x)(Px \rightarrow Qx)$ nomically entails asserting Qy on the counterfactual condition Py.

This proposal, unlike the proposed analysis at the beginning of the last section, will not be rejected. But it will be shown that the proposed partial analysis, though true 'by definition', does not help us to solve the problem of contrary-to-fact conditional asserting. For the problem of the counterfactual conditional will reappear in our attempt to clarify the nature of nomic asserting.

In this place we may introduce a distinction between *singular* and *general* contrary-to-fact conditional asserting. (See above p. 141.) We shall say that asserting $(x)(Px \rightarrow Qx)$ nomically entails asserting, *of every x which is not P*, the proposition Qx

counter-conditionally, relative to the proposition Px. The entailed act of asserting will be called a *general* contrary-to-fact conditional assertion. Asserting, of a particular y, the proposition Qy on the counterfactual condition Py is, accordingly, an act of singular contrary-to-fact conditional asserting. It should be observed that *general* contrary-to-fact conditional asserting does not entail the denying of any proposition. In this respect there is a significant difference between singular and general contrary-to-fact conditional asserting.

What is it to assert the general implication $(x)(Px \rightarrow Qx)$ nomically? What distinguishes a general implication, true by 'accident', from one true by virtue of a 'connexion'? (On the opposites 'connexion' and 'accident' see above p. 148 f.)

It may be thought that one characteristic of nomic asserting is that it is an asserting of *universality*. By this I mean the following:

The class of persons, who voted in a certain election, is a *closed* class. It is restricted both in number and in space and time. We can make a list of all its members. The class of persons, on the other hand, who ever voted, vote, or will vote in elections of a certain type ('general description') is an *open* class. It is unrestricted ('potentially infinite') in number. It may be that, from a certain date on, no new members will ever be added to the class, e.g. because elections of the type in question cease to be held. But the closed class of persons, who up to a certain date had exercised their right to vote in elections of the type concerned, is different from the open class. The latter has no 'logically last' member. It remains for ever 'in principle' open to new members.

These elucidations are unprecise—as indicated by the frequent use in them of quotation marks. But they will suffice for present purposes.

If possessing the property P is, by definition, a necessary and sufficient condition of membership in a class C, we shall call C 'the class determined by P'. We shall assume without further argument that, given a property P there is always a unique class C determined by P. If the classes determined by P, by $\sim P$, by Q, and by $\sim Q$ are all of them open classes, we shall call the general implication $(x)(Px \rightarrow Qx)$ a *universal* implication.

It may be suggested that membership in a closed class can

never be *nomically* connected with another characteristic and, vice versa, that no characteristic can be *nomically* connected with membership in a closed class. The suggestion, in other words, is that a general implication $(x)(Px \rightarrow Q\,x)$ cannot be true by virtue of a 'connexion', if it is not universal. This suggestion, I think, is true. But I shall not try to argue the point here.

It may also be suggested that a universal implication cannot be true, unless by virtue of a 'connexion'. The suggestion, to be more precise, is that the notion of the truth of a universal implication carries with it the notion of a 'connexion'. There could, on this view, be no 'universal accidents'. Therefore, to assert the universal implication $(x)(Px \rightarrow Q\,x)$ would entail asserting the general implication $(x)(Px \rightarrow Q\,x)$ nomically, and thus *a fortiori* asserting, of every x which is not P, the proposition $Q\,x$ on the counterfactual condition Px.

This second suggestion is, I think, *not* true. There *may* occur 'universal accidents'. In other words: to assert the universal implication $(x)(Px \rightarrow Q\,x)$ is compatible with not asserting, for every x which is not P, the proposition $Q\,x$ on the counterfactual condition Px.

If there is a tendency to think that 'universal accidents' are logically impossible, this is perhaps partly due to the fact that all such 'accidents' can be in principle, and a great many also in practice, averted at our own choice. If it really had so happened that every man, who up to the present day had voted in an election, had worn a red tie, although it is by no means the case that no one *could* have voted *unless* he had had a red tie, then we need only take care about a detail of our dress the next time we vote—and the impending 'universal accident' is for ever averted.

We would not wish to call a universal implication a 'law of nature' if we did not assert it nomically. And, as I shall try to argue presently, it is plausible to think that there cannot even be (inductive) *grounds* for asserting a universal implication in any other way but nomically. (See below p. 158.) But notwithstanding all this, there could exist true universal implications, the truth of which would be 'universal accidents' and the assertion of which would not entail a general conditional assertion contrary to fact.

Could it not be that everyone, who ever voted, votes, or will vote wore, or will wear a red tie, and at the same time *not* be that if *y*, who is dead and never voted, had voted, he too would have worn a red tie on that occasion? I think the answer is affirmative, but I find the question puzzling and I cannot claim to have proved my point, which thus remains open for further debate.

I shall anyhow provisionally conclude that the essential characteristic of nomic asserting of general implications is *not* that it is an assertion of universality.

Let us ask: *What* do we assert to be the case, when we assert $(x)(Px \to Qx)$?

Consider the division of the universe of discourse into four classes: things which are both P and Q, things which are P but not Q, things which are not P but Q, and things which are neither P nor Q. Then we may answer the above question by saying: In asserting the general implication we assert that the second of these four classes is empty. And this (and its logical consequences) is *all* that we assert.

Now ask: What *else* do we assert to be the case, when we assert $(x)(Px \to Qx)$ *nomically*?

This is a plausible answer: We assert that the second of the above four classes is, somehow, *necessarily* empty.

I shall accept the suggestion that the essential characteristic of nomic asserting is that it is an assertion of necessity. By this I wish in the first place to mark a contrast. Necessity, *not* universality, is the hallmark of 'nomic connexions'. ('Necessity' must not here be equated with *logical* necessity. The necessity about which we are now talking is that very thing which above we called a 'connexion'.)

But, once again, *what* do we assert to be the case, when asserting that this second class of things is *necessarily* empty, which we have not already asserted by asserting that it is (simply) *empty*? This much we can certainly say in answer to the question: We have asserted of everything which is a member of the third or fourth class that, if it *were* not a member of the third or fourth class, then it *would be* a member of the first class.

Is this all that we can say? In other words: Can we *distinguish* between asserting $(x)(Px \to Qx)$ nomically, i.e. asserting that the class of things which are P but not Q is necessarily empty, *and* asserting that everything which is P is Q and everything which is not P would, if it were, be Q ?

I think we shall have to give up the attempt to distinguish between these two assertings. But it is still worth asking: How does the necessity, which we assert in asserting $(x)(Px \rightarrow Qx)$ nomically, manifest itself? How do we come to assert it? And what can we do to test its existence? Perhaps a discussion of these questions will help us towards a final answer to our initial question concerning the nature of the contrary-to-fact conditional.

13. In the last section we set out from the question: What is it to assert a general implication $(x)(Px \rightarrow Qx)$ nomically? We reformulated the question as follows: What is it to assert that the class of things which are P but not Q is necessarily empty? And the only 'answer' which we have so far been able to give is this: It is the joint act of asserting that the class of things which is P but not Q is empty *and* asserting, of everything which is not P, that, if it were, it would be Q too.

Nomic asserting of a general implication may thus be analysed into two components: a categorical assertion of a general implication and a general conditional assertion contrary-to-fact. (Nomic assertion is thus a 'mixture' of categorical and (counter-) conditional assertion.) Considering that the notion of nomic assertion was introduced for the purpose of clarifying contrary-to-fact conditional assertion, the 'result' is not very satisfactory.

Can we explain the difference between asserting $(x)(Px \rightarrow Qx)$ categorically and asserting it nomically without falling back on that which we wish to explain by means of this difference, viz. what it is to assert conditionally contrary to fact?

It will be remembered that our discussion of the nature of nomic asserting of general implications originated from an attempt to illuminate contrary-to-fact conditional assertion by means of *grounds* for asserting. We found that to deny p and assert a ground for asserting q on the condition p is not sufficient to entail asserting q on the counterfactual condition p. Only if the ground for asserting q on the condition p is asserted *in a certain way*, viz. nomically, will asserting it, in conjunction with denying *p*, entail asserting *q* on the counterfactual condition *p*.

In order to proceed, we raise the question of grounds on a new level. What could be a *ground*, we ask, for asserting a general implication categorically and what for asserting it nomically? The hope is that the difference in grounds will illuminate the difference in modes of asserting.

Considerations pertaining to *deductive* grounds will not be of much help. To assert a deductive ground for asserting $(x)(Px \to Q\,x)$ nomically is to perform an act of asserting which *entails* the act of asserting $(x)(Px \to Q\,x)$ nomically. *Part* of this act will obviously be the asserting of some proposition which entails $(x)(Px \to Q\,x)$. But, for all I can see, it will necessarily also be part of this act that the proposition, which entails $(x)(Px \to Q\,x)$, is asserted *nomically*.

Thus the notion of a *deductive ground* for asserting nomically involves the notion of nomic assertion, and cannot be used to explain it without circularity.

Giving a deductive ground for asserting a general implication categorically cannot, *by itself*, entail asserting it nomically. This is in no way contradicted by the fact which has much impressed some students of inductive logic, that an important aspect of the justification of generalizations from experience ('inductive conclusions') is their subsequent *deduction* from a system of established laws. The discoveries of such deductive connexions are sometimes important steps in the advancement of the higher natural sciences. Thanks to them 'observed uniformities are raised to the higher rank of laws of nature'. This is one of the ways, in which the 'merely empirical' may be shown to be 'necessary'. But it should be observed that the incorporation of a generalization into a body of deductive grounds ('system') cannot do anything to 'nomify' the generalizations and thus to justify counterfactual conditional assertions, unless asserting *the grounds themselves* is nomic assertion. (Unless I am mistaken, there is a tendency on the part of supporters of 'deductivism' in scientific methodology to overlook this point. 'Systems' appear nomic by virtue of their coherence alone. But this is an illusion.)

We now proceed to *inductive* grounds.

Let us ask: What could—deductive grounds being ruled out for the moment—make us ('induce us to') assert that every P is Q ? It might be, for example, the repeated observation of P's which are Q in combination with the absence of any observation 'to the contrary', i.e. observations of P's which are not Q. We shall call this an observation of *regularity*.

We need not here commit ourselves to answering the question, whether a regularity of the above kind can rightly be called a *ground* for asserting that every P is Q. I have only wanted to indicate, roughly what sort of thing could, as I have said, 'make us' assert it. Whether something could, in the concrete case, make us assert this or that, is a question of psychology and cannot be decided by conceptual considerations. But a rough agreement about what would 'normally' belong to the causal background of the asserting-situation seems possible.

We next ask: What could—deductive grounds again being excluded—make us assert *nomically* that every P is Q. Since asserting that every P is Q is only one component or part of asserting it nomically, it follows that what makes us assert the general implication in question need not also automatically make us assert it nomically. That which makes us assert nomically that every P is Q must be something which makes us assert, *not only* of everything which is P that it is Q, *but also* of everything which is not P that, if it were P, it would be Q. We have already discussed what could make us assert the former, so the question really is what could induce us to assert the latter.

This seems to be a plausible answer: If we witness that things which, for some reason or other, *change* from not being P to being P, also change from not being Q to being Q, provided that they are not already Q, and/or that things which change from being Q to not being Q, also change from being P to not being P, provided that they are nor already not P, and if there are no observations to the contrary, then we may come to assert of everything which is not P that, if it were P, it would also be Q.

Supposing that, for some reason or other, we have made the general contrary-to-fact conditional assertion in question, and that we are asked to 'justify' it. The most expedient way to do so, in all probability, will be to *produce* some changes of the kind just mentioned. We might, for example, try to remove that characteristic Q from some things which are P and find either that we do not succeed unless we first remove P from them, or that P vanishes upon the removal of Q. Or we might try to produce the characteristic P in some things which are not Q and find either that we do not succeed unless we first produce Q in them, or Q comes into existence upon the production of P.

We need not commit ourselves to answering the question whether, or under what further circumstances, observations and experiments of the kind mentioned can rightly be said to constitute a *ground* for asserting of everything which is not P that, if it were P, it would also be Q. But I think we may agree about the truth of the following hypothetical proposition:

If there is something which can rightly be called a ground for asserting the general implication $(x)(Px \rightarrow Qx)$ categorically and also something which can rightly be called a ground for asserting the general implication $(x)(Px \rightarrow Qx)$ nomically, then it is the case that either the grounds for the first assertion simply are the grounds for the second assertion, and nothing else, or there is a specific difference between the grounds for the two kinds of assertion. In the latter case, moreover, the specific difference in the grounds is essentially related to the difference between an observation of a *regularity* of a certain kind and an observation of *changes* of a certain kind.

On the question of the existence of grounds, I think we may safely acknowledge that there are inductive grounds for asserting general implications *nomically*. To deny this would, as far as I can see, amount either to a refusal to acknowledge as 'grounds' for asserting general propositions anything but deductive grounds, or to maintaining that nothing which might in fact be proposed as such a ground would *really be* one. The former attitude is probably psychologically related to the insight that inductive grounds are utterly *different* from deductive grounds. And this is an important insight. The monopolization of the *term* 'ground' for deductive grounds, however, is sheer dogmatism. The latter attitude again presupposes that there *are* such things as inductive grounds for asserting general propositions. It therefore denies the existence of such grounds only 'empirically', and not 'conceptually'. But it is in their conceptual existence only that we are here interested. (This is not to say that the concept of an inductive ground may not somehow logically depend upon experiential matters.)

I do not think that one can, once and for all, describe the class of possible experiences which will constitute an inductive ground for asserting a general implication nomically. It seems to be of the essence of such grounds that one can only indicate in a *rough* way certain *typical* kinds of experience which, depending upon further circumstances of the individual case, will constitute an inductive ground. What they look like in the individual case can perhaps best be envisaged by imagining what kind of evidence a person would be asked or expected to produce, if he asserted a general implication nomically without giving any grounds at all for it. That one cannot lay down hard and fast criteria of inductive grounds, however, is in no way incompatible with there being such grounds, nor even with the obvious empirical fact that people on the whole agree about their presence or absence in the individual case.

Inductive grounds for asserting general implications nomically are *a fortiori* inductive grounds for asserting them categorically. Thus, if there exist inductive grounds for assertions of the first kind, there exist *a fortiori* inductive grounds for assertions of the second kind. On the question, whether there are inductive grounds for asserting general implications categorically which are not also grounds for asserting them nomically, I should, however, feel dubious. One may think that the notion of a 'ground' is somehow essentially linked with the notion of the 'nomic'. I shall not attempt to settle the question here. I shall only acknowledge my inclination to agree with those sceptics about induction who have said that no observation of a regularity in the past can ever be a ground for belief in its continuation in the future. But those sceptics tended to forget that 'the appeal to grounds' which we actually make in inductive thinking is seldom, if ever, an appeal to observed *regularities*. They overlooked the role played by the notion of *change* in the grounding of inductions. They overlooked, moreover, the role played by active *experimentation* (the production of changes in nature at will) as opposed to passive *observation*.

But since the things which they overlooked are precisely those which count from the point of view of nomic assertion, it becomes doubtful whether there are any inductive grounds for asserting general implications categorically as distinct from asserting them nomically.

We are now in a position to answer the question raised at the beginning of the present section. To the extent that we can characterize the difference in grounds for asserting a general implication categorically and asserting it nomically we can also characterize the difference between these two modes of assertion. If we think that there are no grounds for asserting a general implication categorically as distinct from asserting it nomically, we can nevertheless characterize the nomic assertion by way of *its* grounds. This way of characterizing nomic assertion, moreover, is not (at least not necessarily) circular.

But the fact that we can thus characterize the nomic assertion of general implications does *not* mean that we can analyse or define an act of nomic assertion and therewith of contrary-to-fact conditional assertion in terms of acts of categorical assertion. This is easily seen from the following considerations:

It is of the essence of inductive, as opposed to deductive, grounds that they never *entail* the proposition which they aim at supporting (establishing). Inductive grounds for asserting nomically (or categorically) that everything which is P is Q always *fall short of a proof* of the general implication $(x)(Px \to Qx)$. And from this it follows that an act of asserting a *ground* for asserting $(x)(Px \to Qx)$ nomically cannot entail, still less be logically equivalent to, the act of asserting $(x)(Px \to Qx)$ nomically. Therefore any attempt to analyse conditional assertion contrary-to-fact in terms of categorical assertions using the notion of grounds for nomic assertion of general implications must necessarily fail.

I contend that the only analysis of nomic assertions of general implications which we can give will have to be in terms of conditional assertion contrary to fact. 'To assert $(x)(Px \to Qx)$ nomically is to assert of every x which is P that it is Q *and* to assert of every x which is not P that, if it were P, it would be Q.' But we can ground such assertions inductively on other assertions which are not nomic.

14. We cannot 'get round' the concept of conditional assertion contrary-to-fact by the route of nomic assertion of general implications. Once this is clearly seen, we may also feel free to admit that the asserting of general implications is no part of the 'meaning' of contrary-to-fact conditional assertion.

Consider our previous example of saying to a child: 'If you do not obey, I'll punish you'. (See above p. 142.) Now suppose that the child obeys, and escapes punishment. Can we not say: 'If you had not obeyed, I would have punished you?' Obviously, we can, but the question is: What have we then asserted? One thing is clear: we have asserted that the child *did* obey. And this proposition alone entails the material implication that either the child obeyed or we punished it. Since making the contrary-to-fact conditional assertion cannot be equivalent to asserting that the child did obey, something *more* than the material implication in question must have been asserted.

I have heard it suggested that in asserting that we would have punished the child, had it not obeyed, we must be asserting, by implication, some general proposition about our behaviour towards either this particular child or children in general. 'I *always* punish disobedience in my children, so I would have done it in this case too.'

Now it may well be that, if asked for *grounds* for our conditional assertion contrary-to-fact, we should refer to something general concerning our behaviour. But to maintain that some such generality must be part of the 'meaning' of the conditional assertion contrary to fact, is to be victim to an illusion. This illusion, it would seem, exists by virtue of a belief that one can get round the counterfactual conditional via the notion of general 'connexions'. Once this belief is seen to be false, the motive force behind this particular 'myth of meaning' will cease to be active.

The adequate answer to the question what *else*, beside the proposition that the child did obey, we have asserted in asserting the proposition that we punished it counter-conditionally, relative to the proposition that it did not obey us, is that we have asserted that we *would have* punished the child, *had* it not obeyed. That is *all* we can say by the way of logical analysis of meaning.

That we would have punished the child, had it not obeyed us, may be called a 'prediction about the past'. In view of what was said above (p. 142) of the meaning of 'if you do not obey, I'll punish you', it may be asked whether we cannot understand 'if you had not obeyed, I would have punished you' too in two ways: 'subjectively' as a declaration of past intention and 'objectively' as a prediction about past events. I shall not discuss this problem here. I tend to think that there is *not* this ambiguity in the counter-conditional. One may declare ones intentions to do something now or in the future. But one cannot declare ones intentions to have done something. One can only speak 'objectively' about ones past intentions.

A typical use of contrary-to-fact conditional assertions which is, mainly at least, not associated with the asserting of general implications, occurs in speaking about past events in human history. 'If Hitler had not invaded Russia, he would still be ruling Germany.' Even if one admits that asserting nomically some general implication is no *part* of what we do when we make the conditional assertion contrary to fact, it may be thought that the only *ground* for this assertion which we could possibly produce must be some nomically asserted general implication. It must be some 'law' about the behaviour of such and such men under such and such circumstances. This, I believe, is to take a false view of the nature of 'historical explanations'. The general propositions, if any, which may be given as grounds for contrary-to-fact conditional assertions about history are not asserted nomically. They are propositions about what, things being thus and thus, *usually* happens. They always admit of a 'but perhaps not in this case'. It does not seem to me, moreover, at all obvious that grounds for contrary-to-fact conditional assertions about human affairs need be sought among general propositions. (See the previous discussion of the relation of the 'nomic' to universality and to necessity.) But I shall not here embark upon a discussion of this topic.

15. We found (p. 135) that there are strong, I believe conclusive, reasons for thinking that the form 'if p, then q', when used for asserting q on the condition p, does not express a proposition. For, part of what we do, when we assert q on the condition p is that we *refrain* from certain acts of categorical

asserting. But, although there are no 'conditional-propositions', we may distinguish between asserting truly and asserting falsely a proposition conditionally, relative to another.

The status of contrary-to-fact conditional assertions appears to be different.

It is not part of what we do, when we assert q on the counterfactual condition p that we leave certain propositions unasserted. I can see no conclusive reasons against saying that the form 'if p had been true, then q would have been true', when used for asserting q on the counterfactual condition p, expresses the *proposition* that, for example, there would have been thunder yesterday, had there been lightning yesterday. We may call such propositions *counter-conditional propositions*. We shall say that in asserting q counter-conditional on p we assert (categorically) two propositions, viz. the proposition that p is false and the counter-conditional proposition that q would have been true, if p had been true. The second proposition, moreover, entails the first.

We can now say that q is truly asserted counter-conditional on p, if the asserted counter-conditional proposition is true, and falsely asserted if it is false.

But what are the truth-conditions of the counter-conditional proposition that q would have been true if p had been true? A *partial* truth-condition is that p is false. If it is not fulfilled, we may safely conclude that the counter-conditional proposition is false. From what has been said, however, of the impossibility of analysing the act of contrary-to-fact conditional asserting in terms of acts of categorical asserting it follows that the *total* truth-conditions of the counter-conditional proposition can only be stated in terms of the truth of some counter-conditional proposition.

*

Summary. To the question: What do we do when we assert q on the condition p? we gave the answer: We assert $p \rightarrow q$ intensionally, and this means that we assert $p \rightarrow q$ but neither assert nor deny p and neither assert nor deny q. Conditional asserting is thus an act which is analysable into the performing and not-performing of acts of categorical asserting.

Of the act which we perform when we assert q on the counterfactual condition p, we cannot give an analysis in terms of categorical asserting. Part of what we do, when we assert q on the counterfactual condition p, is that we deny p, but for the rest we can only say that—we assert q on the counterfactual condition p. (This, of course, does not apply to the *deductive* case of asserting contrary to fact. See above p. 144.)

Potential conditional asserting may be grounded on intensional asserting of general implications (and in other ways). Intensional asserting of general implications is explicable in terms of categorical asserting.

Contrary-to-fact conditional asserting may be grounded on nomic asserting of general implications (and in other ways). Nomic asserting of general implications cannot be explained in terms of categorical asserting. It is defined as a way of asserting general implications which entails a certain general conditional assertion contrary to fact.

I ventured to suggest that inductive grounds for asserting a general implication are grounds for asserting it nomically. Thus the problem of contrary-to-fact conditional asserting is closely allied to the problem of the ground of induction.

It is not an essential characteristic of either potential or contrary-to-fact conditional asserting that it should entail an assertion of generality or universality.

APPENDIX. EPISTEMIC ATTITUDES AND CONDITIONALITY

In the essay I have treated conditionals as a kind, not of proposition, but of asserting. What has been said, however, must by no means be thought to imply that there can be no conditionality without some assertion. It is clear that, e.g., one may know or believe or think or judge that if . . . then . . ., without saying anything and therefore—since asserting entails using language (p. 128)—without asserting anything.

What is the proper account of these 'epistemic attitudes'?

If the conditional is contrary to fact, the *object* of the 'epistemic attitude' is that which I called (p. 162) the counterconditional proposition. To know, believe, think or judge that, if there had been lightning yesterday, there would have been thunder yesterday, is to know, believe, think or judge that a certain proposition is true. We shall not here consider the question, most interesting in itself, whether one can *properly* be said to *know* a counter-conditional (inductive) proposition, since it is of the essence of such propositions that they can be verified only on the basis of other counter-conditional propositions.

If the conditional is, not contrary to fact, but potential, the analysis of the epistemic attitude to it must take account of the fact which I have previously expressed by saying that there are no conditional *propositions*. To know, believe, think or judge that, if there is lightning tomorrow, there is also thunder tomorrow, entails but¦ is *not the same as* to know, believe, think or judge that a certain proposition is true. What is it then? The correct answer, so it seems to me, is this: It is to know, believe, think or judge that it will not be the case that there is lightning but no thunder tomorrow, *without* knowing, believing, thinking or judging either that there will or will not be lightning or that there will or will not be thunder. It is thus characteristic of the epistemic attitude in question that it should involve an *absence* or *lack* of attitude to certain propositions.

If we know, believe, think or judge that if p is true, then q is true, I shall say that we know, believe, think or judge q *conditionally*, relative to p. Knowing, believing, thinking or judging q conditionally, relative to p is thus incompatible with knowing, believing, thinking or judging that the truth-values of p or q are such and such—just as asserting q on the condition p is incompatible with asserting or denying either p or q. If we *first* know q conditionally, relative to p, and *later* come to know q, we *no longer* know q conditionally.

But—may one not believe (or even know) that *if* the sun rises tomorrow, there will be light, and *also* believe (or even know) *that* the sun will rise? The answer is, I think, that one may believe (know) this, only if what was suggested is supposed to mean that one believes (knows) that it will not be the case that the sun will rise but there be no light and *also* believes (knows) that the sun will rise—from which believed propositions one may then conclude that there will be light. The object of the epistemic attitude in question is 'thoroughly propositional'; it does not, in other words, contain a conditional as a part, although, through a careless description of the case, it may appear to do so. (Cf. above p. 138.)

I shall say that to know, believe, think, or judge q conditionally, relative to p is to know, believe, think or judge the material implication $p \to q$ *intensionally*.

THE CONCEPT OF ENTAILMENT

'ENTAILMENT' as a technical term in logic and philosophy was, as far as I know, first introduced by Moore in the paper on 'External and Internal Relations' (1919).[1] We require, Moore says[2], 'some term to express the *converse* of that relation which we assert to hold between a particular proposition *q* and a particular proposition *p*, when we assert that *q follows from* or *is deducible from p*. Let us use the term "entails" to express the converse of this relation'.

Russell and Lewis and others had used the term 'implication' to mean what Moore called 'entailment'. 'When a proposition *q* follows from a proposition *p*', Russell says,[3] 'so that if *p* is true, *q* must also be true, we say that *p implies q*'. Similarly, Lewis says[4] of the word 'implies' that it 'denotes that relation which is present when we "validly" pass from one assertion, or set of assertions, to another assertion'.

Implication is related to conditionality. W. E. Johnson made some interesting observations on this relationship. In 'if *p*, then *q*' the compound, i.e. the conditional proposition[5], is being treated as on a level with its components. But in '*p* implies *q*' the compound is an assertion *about* the way in which its components are related. The first compound proposition Johnson calls *primary*, the second he calls *secondary*.[6]

Implication is further related to inference. The theory of implication, Russell says,[7] is 'the theory of how one proposition

---

[1] *In Proceedings of the Aristotelian Society*, **20**, 1919–20. Reprinted, with some changes, in *Philosophical Studies*, London, 1922.
[2] *Philosophical Studies*, p. 291.
[3] *Principia Mathematica*, vol. i, p. 94. (Cambridge, 1910, quoted from the 2nd edn., Cambridge, 1925.)
[4] *A Survey of Symbolic Logic* (Berkeley, 1918), p. 324.
[5] Johnson treats the conditional as a proposition, viz. as a material implication. *Logic* (Cambridge, 1921), Pt. I, Ch. iii, §§5–6.
[6] This observation on 'if-then' and implication is made in *Logic* (Cambridge, 1922), Pt. II, Introduction, §6. On the distinction between primary and secondary propositions, see *Logic*, Pt. I, Ch. iv, § 1.
[7] 'The Theory of Implication', *American Journal of Mathematics*, **28**, 1906, p. 159.

can be inferred from another'. Yet the two notions ought to be carefully distinguished.[1] Inference, Russell says[2], 'is the dissolution of an implication'. Inference is a species of asserting.[3] That which in the relation of implication is put forward merely hypothetically, is in the act of inference asserted categorically.[4] In the preceding essay I have dealt in detail with the 'if-then'. Towards the end of the present paper I shall briefly indicate what I think is the proper place of entailment relatively to conditionality and to inference. (*Vide infra*, p. 190.)

2. It should be stressed that in this essay I only deal with entailment as a relation between (true or false) *propositions*.

It would seem that entailment relations can be properly said to hold also between other logical entities beside propositions.[5] For example, between commands and norms. (Whether norms may count as propositions or not is, of course, open to debate.) The 'possibility' of entailment relations between commands and norms constitutes a difficult and interesting problem. I shall call it the Problem of Practical Inference. I shall not deal with it here.[6] One reason for omitting it from discussion is that I believe the problem of entailment between true-false propositions to be more fundamental. Entailment between commands and norms may be accounted for in terms of entailment between true-false propositions.

3. Formulae (of formal systems) containing so-called free variables do not express propositions. Yet one speaks of

---

[1]Russell, *The Principles of Mathematics* (London, 1903), §§38–39; *Principia Mathematica*, vol. i, pp. 7–9; Johnson, *Logic*, Pt. II, Ch. i, §1.

[2]*Principia Mathematica*, vol. i, p. 9.

[3]On the relation between inference and assertion see Russell, *The Principles of Mathematics*, §38 and *Principia Mathematica*, vol. i, p. 8f., and Johnson, *Logic*, Pt. II, Ch. i.

[4]Johnson, *Logic*, Pt. II, Ch. i, p. 8.

[5]Trivially, one may say that entailment holds between sentences too, viz. if it holds between the propositions expressed by the sentences. This is to take the view that entailment between propositions is 'primary', entailment between sentences 'secondary'. Some logicians may wish to dispute this.

[6]The essay 'Deontic Logic' too ignores this problem. In it I assumed without discussion that norms can be treated as true-false propositions in logical reasoning. This assumption is, I believe, warranted. But it stands in need of justification. How this justification is to be given I have tried to show in some detail in my paper 'Om s.k.praktiska slutledningar' ('On so-called Practical Inferences') in *Tidsskrift for Retsvitenskap* (Oslo), 1955.

relations of deducibility or logical consequence between free variable formulae, and between free variable formulae and bound variable formulae (the latter being sentences expressing propositions). I prefer to classify such relations under the name *derivability* rather than under the name *deducibility* (which I shall take to mean the converse of entailment). I do not wish, however, to restrict derivability to formulae containing free variables. A general definition of the term will not be attempted here.

Relations of derivability between formulae may usually be said to 'reflect' relations of deducibility (entailment) between some propositions. The way in which this reflecting takes place may be quite complicated. Its clarification raises interesting problems. They will not be considered in the present paper. But it is of some importance to us to be aware of their existence. (*Vide infra*, p. 185.)

4. It is often said[1] that the notions of possibility, necessity, etc., which are studied in modal logic are the notions of *logical* possibility, necessity, etc. With the logical modalities are contrasted the notions of *physical* (or *natural*) possibility, necessity, etc.

This restriction to the scope of study of modal logic is in my opinion unwarranted. The laws of the 'classical' (*vide supra*, p. 90) systems of modal logic—with the possible exception of some disputed principles of iterated modalities—are, it would seem, valid indiscriminatingly for physical as well as for logical possibility, necessity, etc. It is therefore plausible to take the view that modal logic is, primarily, a study of *generic* modalities, of which the logical and the physical modal concepts are two *species*. The differentiation between the species is not primarily a matter of (formal) logic, but of epistemology and metaphysics. Yet *some* differences between the species may be expressed within modal logic also, viz. in a system of dyadic modalities. (*Vide supra*, p. 112 ff.)

The concept of entailment too may be understood in a generic sense, within the scope of which one may distinguish

---

[1]See Lewis-Langford, *Symbolic Logic* (New York, 1932), Ch. vi, sect. *4*, pp. 153–166. Also von Wright, *An Essay in Modal Logic* (Amsterdam, 1951), p. 28.

between a proposition entailing another *logically* and a proposition entailing another *physically*. 'Physical entailment' would then be the same as that which in the essay on conditionals I called 'nomic connexion'. (*Vide supra*, p. 149.) Nomic connexions may also be called 'necessary connexions in nature'.

Logicians and philosophers, who discuss the notion of entailment, usually understand by it the converse of *logical* consequence. Moore, for example, says that entailment is the converse of 'follows from' 'in the sense in which the conclusion of a syllogism in Barbara follows from the two premisses, taken as one conjunctive proposition; or in which the proposition "This is coloured" follows from "This is red".'[1]

It might therefore be suggested that, just as modal logic is best regarded as a general theory of the generic modal concepts, so a theory of entailment ought primarily to be a theory of the generic concept, which covers both logical consequence and nomic connexion. Such a comprehensive point of view *may* be helpful to an understanding of the concept.

Against this suggestion I shall only say that I have not become convinced of its usefulness. Therefore I shall not here attempt the creation of a theory of 'generic' entailment, but shall confine the treatment to 'logical' entailment. In doing this I, somewhat against my inclination, follow an established tradition in the field.

5. Historically, the modern study of modal logic originates from C. I. Lewis's criticism of Russell's theory of 'implication' (*vide supra*, p. viii).[2] Lewis, above all, wanted to show that Russell's concept of a material implication did not provide a proper account of the relation which is here called entailment. To give an account of entailment he introduced the notion of strict implication and a system of rules for this new notion. Of his system Lewis said[3] that 'its primary advantage over any

---

[1] *Philosophical Studies*, p. 291.

[2] The earliest relevant publication is his paper 'Implication and the Algebra of Logic' in *Mind*, **21**, 1912. Then followed 'A New Algebra of Implications and some Consequences' in *The Journal of Philosophy*, **10**, 1913; 'The Matrix Algebra for Implication', ibid. **11**, 1914; 'The Calculus of Strict Implication', *Mind* **23**, 1914; 'The Issues Concerning Material Implication', *The Journal of Philosophy* **14**, 1917; and the detailed expositions of the logic of strict implication in *A Survey of Symbolic Logic*, Berkeley, 1918 and in Lewis-Langford, *Symbolic Logic*, New York, 1932.

[3] 'Implication and the Algebra of Logic', p. 531.

present system lies in the fact that its meaning of implication is precisely that of ordinary inference and proof'.

A strict implication is a material implication which is necessary. Lewis's proposed account of entailment was thus in the combined terms of modal and truth-functional concepts. Lewis soon realized[1] that in his logic of strict implication, the other modalities too, beside necessity, make their appearance and that this logic 'is fundamentally a calculus of possibilities, impossibilities, and necessities'. And *this* indeed is Lewis's great achievement: to have been the first to explore with the tools of modern logic the long neglected province of modal logic. As a proposed account of entailment, however, his undertaking was not successful.

Before criticizing the theory of strict implication in this respect, let us consider why the notion of a material implication is inadequate as an account of entailment. The well-known objection is this: If material implication and entailment were the same, then any false proposition could truly be said to entail any proposition whatever, and any true proposition could truly be said to follow from any proposition whatever. These startling consequences of the proposed identification of the two notions are often referred to under the name The Paradoxes of Material Implication. It should be added that equally paradoxical are the consequences, which also follow, that any two true and any two false propositions would mutually entail one another. The 'paradox', I think, is best described by saying that, if entailment and material implication were the same, then relations of entailment between propositions could subsist by virtue of (or be established from considerations about) the truth-values, as such, of the propositions.

W. E. Johnson, who, as far as I know, also coined[2] the term 'Paradoxes of Implication', tried to show that the 'paradoxes' did not vitiate his account of implication (entailment). His idea was that the paradoxes were harmless, because they could not be legitimately utilized for purposes of inference. He argued[3] as follows:

[1]'The Calculus of Strict Implication', p. 247.
[2]*Logic*, Pt. I, Ch. iii, §7, p. 39.
[3]Ibid., Pt. I, Ch. iii, §§7 and 8.

From the denial of p we may validly infer that p materially implies q. And from the affirmation of p in combination with the material implication of q by p we may validly infer q. But if the material implication of q by p has been inferred from the denial of p, then we cannot use this material implication for drawing inferences in conjunction with the affirmation of p without committing a contradiction. Thus the denial of p cannot be legitimately used for inferring any arbitrary proposition from p.

From the affirmation of q again we may also validly infer that p materially implies q. But if the material implication of q by p has been inferred from the affirmation of q, then we cannot use this material implication in conjunction with the affirmation of p to infer q without circularity. Thus the affirmation of q cannot be legitimately used for inferring q from any arbitrary proposition.

'The solution of the paradox', Johnson says,[1] 'is therefore found in the consideration that though we may correctly infer an implicative from the denial of its implicans, or from the affirmation of its implicate . . ., yet the implicative . . . so reached cannot be applied for purposes of further inference without committing the logical fallacy either of contradiction or of circularity.'

Johnson's argument is ingeneous and, as far as it goes, quite correct. But it does not show that entailment is 'after all', the same as material implication. (Nor would it be fair to say that Johnson wanted to show *this*.) At most, it may be concluded from his argument that a material implication is an entailment relation when it can, without qualification, be used for inference. But when *can* a material implication be thus applied? Johnson's answer is[2] as follows: 'Such application is possible only when the composite has been reached irrespectively of any *assertion* of the truth or falsity of its components.''

This answer I would interpret as being in substantial agreement with the view of entailment which I am going to propose myself in this essay. For the time being I only conclude that the Paradoxes of Material Implication constitute an obstacle to an identification of entailment with material implication and that

[1]*Logic*, Pt. I, Ch. iii, § 7,
[2]Ibid., p. 47.

this obstacle cannot be removed by considerations about the 'inferential harmlessness' of those paradoxes.

We now proceed to strict implication. Lewis, who suggested that entailment and strict implication are the same, must also be credited with the discovery[1] of the so-called Paradoxes of Strict Implication. It is a law of his (and indeed of any reasonable) modal logic that an impossible proposition strictly implies any proposition whatever, and that a necessary proposition is strictly implied by any proposition whatever. The 'paradox' thus is that, if entailment and strict implication were the same, then relations of entailment between propositions could subsist by virtue of the modal status (impossibility or necessity) alone of the propositions.

This paradox, in my opinion, is just as disastrous to the theory that entailment is strict implication as the analogous paradox about material implication is disastrous to the view that entailment and material implication are the same.

Lewis, however, did not admit that his theory is refuted by the discovery of the paradoxes. His line of defence has been[2] to try to show that the paradoxes really *are true* for the notion of entailment. 'In the ordinary sense of "implies", an impossible proposition implies anything and everything', he says.[3] This he proposes to prove.[4] His argument, however, is a *non sequitur*.[5] Since his proposed proof[6] that necessary propositions are implied

[1]'The Calculus of Strict Implication', p. 245.
[2]See in particular the argument given in *A Survey of Symbolic Logic*, pp. 335–9. See also his article 'Emch's Calculus and Strict Implication', *The Journal of Symbolic Logic*, **1**, 1936.
[3]*A Survey of Symbolic Logic*, p. 336.
[4]Ibid., pp. 336–8.
[5]The proof starts from three principles about 'implication' (entailment) which seem unobjectionable. (Principles 1–3 on p. 336.) The error consists in passing (without argument) *from* the principle that if two premisses *p* and *q* entail a conclusion *r* and if one of the premisses is true whilst the conclusion is false, then the other premiss must be false, *to* the principle that if two premisses *p* and *q* entail a conclusion *r*, then the conjunction of one of the premisses with the negation of the conclusion *entails* (!)the negation of the other premiss. This last principle is then (p. 338) used for proving 'that every impossible proposition . . . implies anything and everything.'
[6]Ibid., p. 338. Lewis thinks that 'the "necessary" principles of logic and mathematics' are entailed by any proposition in the sense that they are 'presuppositions' of any proposition. By calling them 'presuppositions' Lewis means that the denial of those principles would entail anything and everything, and thus also any proposition together with its negation. But this is true only if we already take for granted that impossible propositions (i.e., negations of necessary propositions) entail anything and everything.

by anything and everything rests on his argument about impossible propositions, it too breaks down.

The fact that a *proof* that an impossible proposition entails any proposition and that a necessary proposition is entailed by any proposition breaks down is, of course, no hindrance to entertaining the *opinion* in question.

Another line of defence for the view that the 'paradoxes' do not vitiate the proposed identification of entailment and strict implication is to argue that the paradoxes are 'inferentially useless'. This line is, for example, taken by Arthur Pap in a recent paper.[1] Pap says:[2] 'If the antecedent of a strict implication is impossible, we cannot use the implication as a basis for proving the consequent, since the antecedent is not assertable; and if the consequent is necessary, the implication is useless as a rule of inference simply because no premiss is required for the assertion of the consequent (it is "unconditionally" assertable). But if it is only by reference to inferential utility that strict implication is distinguishable from entailment, then there is no basis for saying that these are distinct *logical relations*; for the concept of inference, and any concept defined in terms of it, is of course no logical concept at all.'

The first sentence in the quoted passage *might* be understood as a version, in less stringent terms, of Johnson's argument (*vide supra*, p. 171). about the inferential uselessness of paradoxical material implications on the ground that they 'cannot be applied for purposes of further inference without committing the logical fallacy either of contradiction or of circularity'. *This* observation on inferential uselessness is certainly relevant to the discussion of entailment.

It should be observed, however, that although the 'paradoxes' are inferentially useless, strict implications with impossible antecedents are *not*. Such implications, on the contrary, have a characteristic and important function for purposes of inference. This is in so-called *inverse proof* or proof by *reductio ad absurdum*. In such proof we demonstrate a proposition p by showing that its denial $\sim p$ entails (and thus also strictly implies) the denial of some proposition, the necessity of which is

[1]"Strict Implication, Entailment, and Modal Iteration'. *The Philosophical Review*, **64**, 1955.
[2]Ibid., p. 613.

already established or taken for granted, from which fact we then *modo tollendo tollens* conclude that *p* itself is necessary (and ~*p* impossible).

If one could not discriminate between propositions, which *are* entailed, and propositions, which are *not* entailed, by impossible propositions, inverse proof could not be validly conducted. For, it is essential to such proof that an impossible proposition should entail exactly such and such consequences, and not anything whatever.

Since, on the view that entailment is the same as strict implication, one has to say that impossible propositions entail anything and everything, one cannot discriminate between what is and what is not entailed by impossible propositions. Thus this view of entailment cannot account for inverse proof. And this, it would seem, is enough to wreck it.

One may try to defend the view by saying that the *sense*, in which impossible propositions can be said to entail certain consequences and not others, is a different sense of 'entail' from the one, in which impossible propositions can be said to entail anything and everything. But then our answer is that it is in this other sense of 'entail' that we are here interested (and which alone is interesting).

The second sentence in the quoted passage I find completely obscure. Why does Pap say that the concept of inference is, 'of course', not a logical concept?[1] For of course the concept of inference is eminently a logical concept. And even if it were *not*, I cannot see why the fact that some strict implications are, for logical reasons, useless for inference could not be a ground for saying that strict implication and entailment are *logically* distinct.[2]

6. If we are dissatisfied with the account of entailment in terms of strict implication, it is natural to look for an improved definition in terms of some other, perhaps more elaborated structure of modal concepts. For it may (rightly) be felt that

[1]Does this echo Russell's 'The process of inference cannot be reduced to symbols' (*Principia Mathematica*, vol. i, p. 9)?
[2]Pap speaks of 'distinct logical relations'. If 'inference' is not called a logical concept, then 'entailment', in so far as it is defined in terms of inferential utility, may presumably be said not to be a purely logical concept either. But relations, whether 'logical' or not, may yet be *logically* distinct. (The relation of brotherhood is logically distinct from the relation of fatherhood.)

Lewis's idea of relating entailment to modality was a step towards clarity in the discussion of the concept.

The failure of the attempt to give an account of entailment in terms of either material or strict implication consists, above all, in the fact that a relation of material or strict implication may subsist by virtue solely of the truth- or modal value of *one* of the two members of an entailment relation. Entailment, we feel, cannot exist on such grounds *alone*. Entailment is 'essentially relational.'

This observation may kindle a hope that a logic of dyadic or relative modality could supply an adequate 'formalization' of the concept of entailment.[1] In support of this hope may further be adduced the fact that the notion of relative necessity does not give rise to 'paradoxes' corresponding to those of material or strict implication. As was noted in the essay on the new modal logic, it is not a theorem of this logic that any proposition is necessary relatively to an (absolutely) impossible proposition, nor is it a theorem that any (absolutely) necessary proposition is necessary relatively to any proposition. (*Vide supra*, p. 104 f.)

Assuming for a moment that entailment could be successfully identified with relative necessity, we note that a number of obvious entailment theorems are provable in the new modal logic. We could prove, for example, that whatever is entailed by an (absolutely) necessary proposition is itself (absolutely) necessary (T30), or that a (absolutely) possible proposition can entail only (absolutely) possible consequences (T28), etc.

But, alas, this hope of 'formalizing' entailment is doomed to failure too. For, although we cannot prove analogues to the implication paradoxes, we can prove the following theorem:

T40. $M(q/t)$ & $N(p/t) \rightarrow N(p/q)$.

Thus any (absolutely) necessary proposition is necessary relatively to any (absolutely) possible proposition. (The theorem is proved from T12 by means of an easy transformation.)

The 'meaning' of this theorem of modal logic is something

[1]Attempts to cope with the problem of entailment with distinctions, which are reminiscent of the distinction between strict implication and relative necessity, have been made by E. J. Nelson ('Intensional Relations', *Mind*, **39**, 1930), A. F. Emch ('Implication and Deducibility', *The Journal of Symbolic Logic*, **1**, 1936 and 'Deducibility with respect to Necessary and Impossible Propositions', ibid., **2**, 1937), and P. G. J. Vredenduin ('A System of Strict Implication', *The Journal of Symbolic Logic*, **4**, 1939).

thoroughly acceptable. That a proposition is absolutely necessary means, in that logic, that it is necessary relatively to tautologous conditions. And it may be proved (T10) that a proposition which is necessary relatively to tautologous conditions is necessary 'in all possible worlds', i.e. necessary relatively to anything which can possibly be.

Only if we identify relative necessity with entailment is there a 'paradox'. (Just as the Paradoxes of Material and Strict Implication are no paradoxes in themselves, but become paradoxical if material or strict implication is equated with entailment.) For then we should have to say that any proposition which is (absolutely) necessary is entailed by any proposition which is (absolutely) possible.

One may think that this is at any rate a *lesser* paradox than the Paradoxes of Implication. For it would not follow that a relation of entailment could subsist by virtue of the modal status of *one* proposition alone. It would only follow that, under suitable conditions, the modal status of *two* propositions would by themselves establish a relation of entailment between the propositions.

But, whether this paradox is thought 'lesser' or not than the implication paradoxes, it is, in my opinion, quite enough to refute the suggestion that entailment and relative necessity are one and the same thing. The possibility of one proposition and the necessity of another cannot be sufficient to establish a bond of entailment between them.

At most, we might be justified in concluding that the notion of relative necessity comes 'nearer' to entailment than either material or strict implication. Such a conclusion could also be supported by the fact that it is a theorem of the new modal logic that if a proposition is necessary relative to another, then it is also strictly implied by it. (T33.) Relative necessity is stronger than strict implication.

I shall, however, not even maintain that relative necessity falls between entailment and strict implication—being weaker than the former but stronger than the latter notion. I shall leave the question of the precise nature of the relation between entailment and relative necessity open and content myself with a refusal to identify the two concepts.

Reviewing the situation and asking ourselves, why it is that entailment can be identified neither with material nor with strict implication nor with relative necessity, we may answer as follows:

It appears to be of the essence of entailment to be a relation between propositions which subsists quite independently of either the truth-values or the modal status of the propositions. No account of entailment is satisfactory, unless it can do justice to this idea of 'independence'. All the proposed analyses so far discussed fail in this respect—although the failure in the case of relative necessity may be said to be less drastic than in the case of material or strict implication.

7. We may take it for granted, I think, that if p entails q, then p also strictly implies q. Entailment is stronger than strict implication. In order that p shall entail q, it is a *necessary* condition that p shall strictly imply q.

It is, moreover, highly plausible to think that if p strictly implies q and neither p is impossible nor q necessary, then p entails q. It follows from laws of modal logic that if p strictly implies q and neither p is impossible nor q necessary, then p and q are contingent. (For, if p were necessary, q would have to be necessary too; and if q were impossible, p would have to be impossible too.) Thus strict implication between contingent propositions, it would seem, is a *sufficient* condition of entailment.

Can a condition of entailment be found (constructed) in modal logic which is both necessary *and* sufficient and which safeguards the 'independence' of the entailment relation of the modal status of its terms?

The suggestion that strict implication between *contingent* propositions is not only sufficient, but also necessary for entailment, would satisfy the requirement of 'independence'. This suggestion has in fact been made, by Mr. P. F. Strawson in an article called 'Necessary Propositions and Entailment-Statements' (in *Mind*, **57**, 1948).

Strawson's suggestion satisfies the requirement of 'independence' at the cost of excluding entailment relations from existing between propositions necessary or impossible. Strawson is, in the article under discussion, willing to pay this price.[1] No necessary proposition p can, on his view[2], be truly (significantly) said to entail another necessary proposition q. But the proposition that p is necessary may, on his view,[3] truly be said to entail the proposition that q is necessary. (He does, of course, not wish to maintain that the proposition that p is necessary always, for any p and q, entails the proposition that q is necessary.) But any proposition to the effect that a proposition is (logically) necessary or impossible is, on his view,[4] itself a *contingent* proposition. It is a contingent meta-statement about the use of expressions.[5] Whether something is necessary or not depends upon how words are used. Nothing can therefore be necessarily necessary, since expressions may always be so defined that what is necessary with one use of them is not necessary with another. And similar remarks hold for impossibility. Thus it follows that the entailment relations which 'apparently' hold between necessary or impossible propositions, are 'really' entailment relations between *contingent* propositions to the effect that something is necessary or impossible.

I think Strawson's theory imposes upon itself an *onus probandi*, under which it may be shown to break down. I do not find his account of the linguistic nature of modal propositions acceptable. One reason is that I do not think that propositions to the effect that something is (logically) necessary or impossible are

---

[1]In his later work *Introduction to Logical Theory* (London, 1952), Strawson does not repeat the account of entailment which he gives in the earlier paper. Here he says (op. cit., p. 24) that we are 'free to choose' between an identification of entailment with strict implication and a restriction of the entailment of q and p to such cases, in which the conjunction of p with $\sim q$ is impossible *on other grounds* than those of the impossibility of p or the necessity of q alone. But I do not think that there is any 'freedom of choice' here. The first alternative has to be rejected. With the second I substantially agree. But this alternative stands in need of further clarification. To account of its meaning *is* to account of the meaning of entailment. Yet no such account is attempted in Strawson's book.

[2]'Necessary Propositions and Entailment-Statements', p. 186.
[3]Ibid., p. 188.
[4]Ibid., p. 184.
[5]For this reason Strawson cannot (and does not) speak, as I do, of propositions 'to the effect that such-and-such a proposition is necessary', but he speaks (p. 187) of propositions 'to the effect that such-and-such expressions express necessary propositions'. Propositions to this effect he calls (p. 184) 'intensional contingent statements'. Such propositions (statements) *mention* expressions (p. 185). Strawson takes good care to indicate this meta-linguistic character of theirs by means of the use of quotation-marks.

propositions *about* language at all.[1] Another is that, even if some modal propositions were contingent meta-propositions about the use of expressions, the notion of their being *contingent*, i.e., not-(either necessary or self-contradictory),[2] seems to me to raise the problem of the meaning of the logical modalities on a new level. (What is the modal status of the proposition that modal propositions are contingent? Is it itself a contingent proposition? In that case it *may* be false, i.e. some modal propositions may, after all, be not contingent. Or is it a necessary proposition?—I should have thought that Strawson would have to say the latter. But I am not sure.) Further, I cannot accept the view that one could not truly say of necessary propositions themselves that they sometimes entail or are entailed by one another. I should, for example, have thought that the proposition that 7 is greater than 5 entailed the proposition that 5 is smaller than 7 quite independently of the fact that it may also be truly said that the proposition that it is necessary that 7 is greater than 5 entails the proposition that it is necessary that 5 is smaller than 7. (For, that 5 is smaller than 7, if 7 is greater than 5 is, so it seems to me, quite independent of the fact that propositions about relations of magnitude between numbers *are* necessarily true or false.)

I shall not criticize Strawson's views in detail, because I think that the difficulties confronting his theory can be either overcome or evaded by a different account of entailment.

But before proceeding to this different account, let us try the following 'modification' of the suggestion that strict implication between contingent propositions is the same as entailment: It is admitted that there is entailment between

---

[1] I agree, of course, with Strawson that 'statements descriptive of the use of expressions are contingent' (p. 184). It is also clear that the proposition that '*p*' is necessary, i.e. the proposition that the sentence (expression) '*p*' expresses a necessary proposition, does not entail *p*, or that the proposition that '*p*' entails '*q*' does not entail the material implication $p \rightarrow q$. (P. 193). But what I cannot agree to is the view that to say that *p* is necessary is to say that '*p*' expresses a necessary proposition. In other words, I cannot accept the view that any proposition to the effect that *p* is (logically) necessary or impossible or to the effect that *p* entails *q* is, in Strawson's sense, of *a different level* or of *a higher order* than the propositions *p* and *q* themselves (p. 189). But I would agree to saying, in something which I believe was the sense meant by W. E. Johnson (*vide supra*, p. 166) that the propositions that *p* is necessary or that *p* entails *q* are *secondary* and the propositions *p* and *q* themselves *primary*.

[2] Ibid., p. 184.

propositions which are not contingent, but it is required that if the antecedent proposition is impossible or the consequent proposition necessary, then they are contingently impossible or necessary. This suggestion *may* be thought to safeguard the condition of independence. For is it not of the nature of this 'independence' that, if p entails q and p is impossible or q necessary, then p would entail q even if p 'happened to be' possible or q 'happened to be' not necessary?

If all modal propositions are contingent, then the suggestion that p entails q if and only if p strictly implies q and p and q are either themselves contingent or p contingently impossible or q contingently necessary, reduces to the assertion that p entails q if and only if p strictly implies q. For, then the clause that p and q are either themselves contingent or p contingently impossible or q contingently necessary becomes redundant. And in that case the actual impossibility of a proposition would make it entail any proposition, and the actual necessity of a proposition would make it entailed by any proposition, and this does not become any the more plausible because of the fact that impossibility and necessity is contingent (upon our use of language or upon something else).

If, on the other hand, not all modal propositions are contingent, the suggestion that p entails q if and only if p strictly implies q and p and q are either themselves contingent or p contingently impossible or q contingently necessary, leads to another difficulty. For in this case it would follow that any impossible proposition which is possibly not impossible would entail any proposition whatever, and that any necessary proposition which is possibly not necessary would be entailed by any proposition whatever. And this is just as disastrous to a correct account of entailment as the original implication paradoxes.

Thus irrespective of whether modal propositions are contingent or not, the view that p entails q if and only if p strictly implies q and p and q are either themselves contingent or p possibly not impossible and q possibly not necessary, breaks down. It stumbles, moreover, on exactly the same obstacle as the suggestions previously examined, viz. its inability to give a satisfactory account of the 'independence' of the entailment relation of the modal status of its relata.

With this I conclude the discussion of attempts to define entailment in terms of truth-functional notions with the aid of the concept of possibility and other modal concepts definable in terms of possibility.[1]

8. I shall suggest the following definition (analysis) of entailment:

p entails q, if and only if, by means of logic, it is possible to come to know the truth of $p \to q$ without coming to know the falsehood of p or the truth of q.

It may be objected that the definition is *vague*, since we have not explained what 'means of logic' are. I believe that this vagueness is, so to say, of the nature of the case. I do not think that one can lay down hard and fast criteria for what is to count as *logical means* (any more than one can lay down hard and fast criteria for what are inductive grounds). But I do not think that *this* vagueness impairs a definition of entailment. On the 'openness' of logic a few words will have to be said later (p. 182 f.).

For the possibility of coming to know the truth of a proposition by means of logic there is a familiar technical term. Such a proposition is said to be *demonstrable* (provable). Thus, on my view, the concept of entailment is intimately related to the notion of demonstrability.

It is important to distinguish between a proposition's being *demonstrable* and its being *demonstrated*. If a proposition is demonstrated, it is certainly also demonstrable. But a proposition may be demonstrable without (ever) being actually demonstrated.

That a proposition is demonstrable means that it is *possible* to demonstrate it, or that it is possible for the proposition to be (become) demonstrated.

[1]Among the many papers from recent years, which discuss entailment and particularly the relation between entailment and strict implication, mention should be made of the following in addition to papers already mentioned: A. E. Duncan-Jones, 'Is Strict Implication the same as Entailment?', *Analysis*, 2, 1934–35; N. Malcolm, 'The Nature of Entailment', *Mind*, 49, 1940; S. Körner, 'On Entailment', *Proceedings of the Aristotelian Society* 47, 1946–47; S. N. Hampshire, 'Mr. Strawson on Necessary Propositions and Entailment Statements', *Mind*, 57, 1948; P. T. Geach, 'Necessary Propositions and Entailment-Statements', *Mind*, 57, 1948; A. N. Prior, 'Facts, Propositions and Entailment', *Mind*, 57, 1948; E. Toms, 'Facts and Entailment', *Mind*, 57, 1948; S. Körner, 'Entailment and the Meaning of Words', *Analysis*, 9, 1949; and C. Lewy, 'Entailment and Necessary Propositions' in *Philosophical Analysis*, ed. by M. Black, Ithaca, 1950.

We can now restate our definition of entailment in terms of demonstrability and demonstration as follows:

p entails q, if and only if, $p \to q$ is demonstrable independently of demonstrating the falsehood of p or the truth of q.

And this again I shall understand to mean:

p entails q, if and only if, it is possible that $p \to q$ is demonstrated but neither $\sim p$ nor q is demonstrated.

Using the symbols 'M' for 'possible' and 'D' for 'demonstrated', we can express the suggested definition of entailment in symbols as follows:

'p entails q' $=_{Df}$ '$M(D(p \to q)$ & $\sim D \sim p$ & $\sim D\ q)$'.

9. The notion of demonstration (of being demonstrated) is an *epistemic* notion. For a proposition to be demonstrated is for it to be *known* to be true in a certain way ('on grounds of logic').

The notion of demonstrability is not purely epistemic. But it may be said to contain an epistemic component or element.[1]

Since demonstrability is not (purely) epistemic, it cannot be objected to the suggested analysis of entailment that it would make entailment 'subjective', in the sense of making it dependent upon the *actual* knowledge of truth. p entails or does not entail q quite independently of whether anybody (ever) knows this.

But entailment, on the suggested analysis, presupposes demonstrability, and therefore *possible* knowledge of some truth. This may be thought objectionable, in view of the following:

As is well known, it is a characteristic of formal systems, which are rich enough to embody the arithmetic of natural numbers, that there should exist (logically) true propositions which are expressible in the language of those systems but which are not provable with their means of demonstration. Thus, in a certain sense, the category of logical truth can be said to transcend the category of demonstrability. And it may be asked, whether we ought not to say of a proposition $p \to q$ which is, in this sense, true but unprovable, that its antecedent entails its consequent.

Against this must be observed that the *sense*, in which it can

---

[1] In the terminology used in my *Essay in Modal Logic* I should say that the notion of demonstrability is a combination of alethic and epistemic modalities.

be proved (!) that there are true but unprovable propositions, is *relative* to a formal system. What the famous results of Goedel show, is that there can be no *system* of all logical truth. Mathematics is incomplete, open. This is perhaps the most important discovery ever made in logic.

But this discovery does not conflict with the view which is here taken of entailment. For, on this view, the entailment of *q* by *p* only presupposes the demonstrability of the material implication of *q* by *p* in *some* system (by *some* 'means of logic'). And this in no way conflicts with the fact that not all relations of entailment may become established within some *one* system.

Thus the incompleteness properties of formal systems cannot be invoked as an objection against the suggested analysis of entailment. They are quite consistent with this analysis.

10. The notion of *possibility* involved in the suggested analysis of entailment calls for special attention.

It seems that, in epistemic contexts, there are *two* senses of possibility which ought to be distinguished. Consider a proposition which is logically contingent and known to be false. Of this proposition it may be said that it is possible that it might have been true and, *a fortiori*, that it is possible that it might have become known to be true. Similarly, of any logically contingent proposition with unknown truth-value it may be said that it is possible to come to know that it is true and also possible to come to know that it is false. (Assuming, that is to say, that all logically contingent propositions are knowable.)

But possibility of coming to know can also be understood in a different way. When saying that it is possible to come to know the truth of a certain proposition, I may mean, by implication, that the proposition in question is true. In other words: only of true propositions may one—in this sense of 'may'—come to know the truth.[1] If a proposition is false, it is

---

[1] Cf. Keynes, *A Treatise on Probability* (London, 1921), p. 17: 'Only true propositions can be known'. Here it is appropriate to warn against a confusion. In the usual sense of 'know', if a proposition is known, it is true. Thus if a proposition *is* false, it *is not* known. This implication may itself be called necessary. Therefore it may also be said to be impossible that a proposition should be known *and* false. But this is not the same as to say that, if a proposition *is* false, then it is *impossible* to know it. What I maintain here is, however, that there is a sense of (im)possible, in which this last thing can be truly said.

impossible that it should be known to be true. Of course, it does not follow that every true proposition is known or even knowable (possible to come to know). Nor does it follow that every knowable proposition is known.

In ordinary language, 'possibility' is used in *both* these senses in connexion with knowing. Consider the proposition that London in 1955 had less than 1 million inhabitants. Can one not equally well argue that, since the proposition *is* false, no one *could* know that London in 1955 had less than 1 million inhabitants, and argue that, since the proposition *may* be (have been) true, some-one *might* know (have known) that London in 1955 had less than 1 million inhabitants? One may argue either way. But one must recognize that each way of arguing, if it is correct, uses a different notion of possibility of knowing.

Be it observed in passing that a characteristic use of 'possible' is for saying that *nothing is known to the contrary*. In such contexts 'possible' is another word for 'perhaps'.

The first sense, in which 'possibility' is used in connexion with knowing, conforms to the logical laws of 'classical' modal logic. The second sense, however, has at least one formal property which cannot be expressed in the traditional systems. It is the property, just mentioned, that possibility of knowing presupposes truth.

The formal logic of this second concept of possibility is worth a closer study (within a formalism combining alethic and epistemic modalities). Such a study, however, will not be undertaken in this essay.[1]

11. It is important to note that the suggested analysis of entailment, in speaking of possibility of coming to know, uses 'possibility' in the *second* of the two senses which we distinguished in the preceding section. It thus uses it in the sense, in which the possibility of coming to know a proposition entails the *truth* of that proposition. For, in calling a proposition demonstrable, we mean that the proposition in question *is* true—although its truth may not as yet have been established.

---

[1]The combined system of alethic and epistemic modalities which is sketched in my *Essay in Modal Logic* (the *MV*-calculus, pp. 42–56) is not adequate to *this* notion of possibility.

Truth, which has become established 'by means of logic', is, moreover (logically) *necessary* truth. This is a received opinion which I here accept without further discussion. One may say that it is of the essence of logical proof that it should establish the (logical) necessity of the proved proposition. ('Demonstration' ought, of course, to be distinguished from 'inference' and from 'derivation according to rules'. A proposition may be logically inferred from another without being itself logically true.)

From what has just been said about demonstration and necessity it follows that, instead of saying that if p entails q, then it is possible, by means of logic, to come to know the truth of $p \rightarrow q$,we could also say that if p entails q, then it is possible to come to know the logical necessity of $p \rightarrow q$.

Thus, on the suggested analysis of entailment, if p entails q, then p strictly implies q. The converse does not hold. p may strictly imply q without the other conditions of entailment which are embodied in our definition being satisfied. Entailment is stronger than strict implication.

About the relation, if any, between entailment and the concept of relative necessity it is not possible to prove anything on the basis of the suggested analysis. I shall not here inquire further into this relationship. It will suffice to have observed (above *p*. 175 f.) that the two concepts cannot be identified.

12. In this section some remarks will be made on the logic of the concepts of the necessary, the demonstrated, and the demonstrable.

All three concepts have this in common: If a proposition is necessary or demonstrated or demonstrable, then it is true.

All three concepts also have in common that they are distributive with regard to conjunctions. p & q is necessary or demonstrated or demonstrable, if and only if, both p and q are necessary or demonstrated or demonstrable.

Being demonstrable entails being necessary.

Being demonstrated entails being demonstrable and thus also being necessary.

Being demonstrated also entails being demonstratedly demonstrable. (If something *is* proved, then it is also proved that it *can be* proved.)

Since being demonstrated entails being demonstrable, it follows that being demonstrated entails being demonstrably demonstrable. (If something *is* proved, then it *can be* proved that it *can be* proved.)

Does being demonstrated entail being demonstratedly demonstrated? (If something *is* proved, is it then also *proved* that it is proved?)

I shall not attempt to answer this question here. I find it puzzling. But I shall make the following observation:

If the question can be answered in the affirmative, then the notion of the demonstrated has three properties which may be expressed in symbols as follows:

$$Dp \to p \quad Dp \to DDp \quad D(p \,\&\, q) \longleftrightarrow Dp \,\&\, Dq$$

Having these three properties would mean that the formal logic of the notion of being demonstrated is structurally the same as the system of modal logic, usually known as $S4$.

It should be observed that although being possibly demonstrated (meaning demonstrable) entails being (necessarily) true, being possibly not demonstrated does not entail being false. Similarly, being not possibly demonstrated (meaning undemonstrable), does not entail being false. But being *refutable*, i.e. being possible to demonstrate to be false entails being (necessarily) false.

13. Another notion involved in our analysis of entailment which calls for special attention is the notion of *independence* (the 'without' in the original formulation of the definition on p. 181). What does it mean for a proposition to be demonstrable independently of another proposition?

Our final definition of entailment, formulated in symbols on p. 182, suggests an answer. For a proposition to be demonstrable independently of another means that it is *possible* that the first proposition is demonstrated and the second undemonstrated. It follows from this that a means of showing (proving) that a proposition is demonstrable independently of another proposition is to produce a (full) proof of the first proposition without also producing a proof of the second proposition.

To see the meaning of this notion of independence more clearly, let us compare with one another the following two cases:

Why is it, apparently, quite in order to say that the self-contradictory proposition p & $\sim p$ entails the proposition p, but not in order to say that p & $\sim p$ entails any arbitrary proposition q?

p & $\sim p \rightarrow p$ and p & $\sim p \rightarrow q$ are both demonstrable truths of logic. We may use truth-tables to show that they are tautologies. By the same method we may also show that p & $q \rightarrow p$ is a tautology.

If p and q are regarded as proposition-variables, the three expressions just mentioned do not stand for propositions, but for proposition-schemas. To show, in a truth-table, that the three schemas are tautologies is to demonstrate the *general* proposition that, for any individual propositions p and q, such and such compound propositions are truths of logic.

Now, having in this way demonstrated that, for any propositions p and q, the proposition p & $q \rightarrow p$ is a truth of logic, we may use this insight to demonstrate that p & $\sim p \rightarrow p$ is a truth of logic too. For, if the first expression expresses a truth of logic for all values of 'q', then it also expresses a truth of logic for the particular value '$\sim p$'. The second expression, we may say, is a substitution instance of the first expression. Thus, without having demonstrated the falsehood of p & $\sim p$ or the truth of p, we may demonstrate the truth of the material implication p & $\sim p \rightarrow p$. This allows us to say that p & $\sim p \rightarrow p$ is demonstrable *independently* of demonstrating the falsehood of the antecedent or the truth of the consequent, and *a fortiori* to say that p & $\sim p$ entails p.

It is important to realize that the demonstrability and indeed even the actual demonstration of the falsehood of the antecedent is no hindrance to saying that it entails the consequent. It would be a hindrance only if the demonstration of the material implication *required* the demonstration of the falsehood of the antecedent. And this is precisely the reason, why we cannot say that p & $\sim p$ entails q.

For, consider how p & $\sim p \rightarrow q$ may be proved. It can be obtained neither by substitution nor by detachment from any formula which is provable in a truth-table without also disproving p & $\sim p$. And if a truth-table is used directly to prove the formula in question, this truth-table would also prove the falsehood of p & $\sim p$. The last step in the construction of the table would consist in making use of the fact that p & $\sim p$ is false under all the four truth-combinations of p and q for establishing that p & $\sim p \rightarrow q$ itself is true under all those combinations.

The problem of entailment may be said ultimately to lead to the problem of the conditions and meaning of demonstrability (logical proof). This problem, however, will not be discussed in the present essay. As already indicated (p. 181), I do not think that there is any final characterization, once and for all, of the means by which truths of logic become known.

14. In this section I shall say something about a distinction between two ways, in which a proposition may (logically) entail another proposition. I shall call the two ways *direct* and *indirect* entailment. A proposition entails another in the direct way, when it can be said to entail it 'by itself'. A proposition entails another in the indirect way, when it entails it 'with the aid of some other proposition.'

Be it observed at once that the phrases 'by itself' and 'with the aid of some other proposition' are ambiguous. To say that the proposition p entails the proposition r, not by itself, but with the aid of the proposition q, *may* mean that p does not entail r, but that p & q entails r. In this case, 'with the aid of q' means 'in conjunction (combination) with q'.

When the two phrases are used in this way, I shall *not* say that they are used to mark a distinction between direct and indirect entailment.

The following is a law of modal logic: Nq & $N(p$ & $q \rightarrow r)$ $\rightarrow N(p \rightarrow r)$. It is sometimes rendered in words, rather inaccurately, by saying that 'a necessary premiss may be omitted'.

Now suppose that we had established the necessity of the material implication p & $q \rightarrow r$ independently of its antecedent and consequent. This means that the conjunction p & q entails r, on my definition of entailment. Suppose further that we have also established the necessity of q. It then follows from the above law of modal logic that we have also established the necessity of the material implication $p \rightarrow r$. And since we have established it without either proving or disproving its antecedent and consequent, we shall also have to say that, on my definition, p entails r. All this is in good order. But, since a step in establishing the entailment of r by p was that we proved q, we may say that p has been shown to entail r 'with the aid of' q. Here 'with the aid of q' does not mean 'in conjunction with q', but it means 'by proving q'. This I shall call a case of indirect entailment.

Suppose that p could also be shown to entail r in some other way, not involving a proof of q. Then I shall say that, although p may be shown to entail r with the aid of q, p may also be shown to entail r without the aid of q.

The following definitions of direct and indirect entailment may now, tentatively, be suggested:

A proposition entails another *directly*, if and only if it may be shown to entail it with the aid of *no* further proposition.

A proposition entails another *indirectly*, if and only if it does not entail it directly, but may be shown to entail it with the aid of *some* further proposition.

It would seem always to make sense to ask, whether a given proposition p entails another given proposition r with or without the aid of the given proposition q. For this is to ask, whether it is necessary to prove q in order to show that p entails r.

But is it ever the case that a proposition entails another directly in the sense of the above definition? I shall not attempt to answer this question conclusively here.

It may be thought e.g. that p entails p v q directly, since the truth of $p \rightarrow p$ v q may be demonstrated in a truth-table. But proofs by means of truth-tables depend upon rules for the construction of truth-tables. Such rules are that every proposition, which enters into consideration, has a truth-value and that no proposition has more than one truth-value. (*Vide supra*, p. 8.) Must not these rules themselves be demonstrated, if a truth-table proof is to be a *proof*? So that it might, after all, be said that p entails p v q only *indirectly*, via these rules?

Yet to say that any entailment relation presupposes rules of proof is not the same thing as to say that any proposition may be shown to entail another proposition only with the aid of some further (proved) proposition.

15. How is entailment related to conditionality?

If p entails q, then one may come to know the material implication $p \to q$ without coming to know the truth-value of its antecedent or consequent. In other words: if p entails q, then one may come to know the material implication *intensionally*. (*Vide supra*, p. 163 ff.) And to know a material implication intensionally is to know the consequent *conditionally*, relatively to the antecedent. (*Vide supra*, p. 163 ff.)

Thus, if p entails q, it should be possible to come to know q conditionally, relatively to p.

But entailment, unlike conditionality, is *enduring*. If we have come to know q conditionally, relatively to p (for example, by showing that p entails q) and later come to know p, we no longer know q conditionally. Conditionality 'vanishes' in the new combination. (*Vide supra*, p. 164.) But if p entails q, it does this quite independently of whether p or q are proved or unproved or disproved, provable or unprovable or refutable. The status of entailment cannot be changed.

16. What, finally, has entailment to do with inference?

We here consider inference between propositions only.

If p entails q, then we are entitled to pass from the assertion of p to the assertion of q. The validity of the inference of q from p does not depend upon whether p is asserted truly or falsely. It depends only upon whether p entails or does not entail q. The inference is (deductively) valid, if p (logically) entails q, otherwise it is invalid. In this sense entailment between propositions can be said to be a 'prerequisite' of valid inference.

17. I have tried to show in this essay a way out of the difficulties, which logicians have had to face in view of the impossibility of identifying, without paradox, entailment and strict implication.

One thing which I have not done in this paper is that I have not investigated the *formal logic* of the concept of entailment. From what has been said, however, about the notions of entailment, possibility, and demonstration a number of entailment-laws can easily be extracted. For example, it may be shown that a possible proposition can entail only possible consequences, and a necessary proposition only necessary consequences. But it can also be shown that certain principles, which *may* be thought to be entailment-laws, are not unrestrictedly valid. It is, for example, not unrestrictedly true that a proposition entails a conjunction of propositions, if and only if it entails each conjunct individually. Entailment—unlike necessity and demonstrability—is not distributive with regard to conjunctions.

SUBJECT INDEX

SUBJECT INDEX

SUBJECT INDEX

INDEX OF NAMES

The
International Library
OF
PSYCHOLOGY, PHILOSOPHY
AND SCIENTIFIC METHOD

Edited by

C. K. OGDEN, M.A.
Magdalene College, Cambridge

The International Library, of which over one hundred and fifty volumes have now been published, is both in quality and quantity a unique achievement in this department of publishing. Its purpose is to give expression, in a convenient form and at a moderate price, to the remarkable developments which have recently occurred in Psychology and its allied sciences. The older philosophers were preoccupied by metaphysical interests which for the most part have ceased to attract the younger investigators, and their forbidding terminology too often acted as a deterrent for the general reader. The attempt to deal in clear language with current tendencies whether in England and America or on the Continent has met with a very encouraging reception, and not only have accepted authorities been invited to explain the newer theories, but it has been found possible to include a number of original contributions of high merit.

Published by

ROUTLEDGE & KEGAN PAUL LTD
BROADWAY HOUSE: 68-74 CARTER LANE, LONDON, E.C.4.

1957

INTERNATIONAL LIBRARY OF PSYCHOLOGY, PHILOSOPHY AND SCIENTIFIC METHOD

All prices are net

A. PSYCHOLOGY

GENERAL AND DESCRIPTIVE

The Mind and its Place in Nature. By C. D. Broad. £1 15s.

Thought and the Brain. By Henri Piéron. Translated by C. K. Ogden. £1.

The Nature of Laughter. By J. C. Gregory. 18s.

The Gestalt Theory and the Problem of Configuration. By Bruno Petermann. Illustrated. £1 5s.

Invention and the Unconscious. By J. M. Montmasson. Preface by H. Stafford Hatfield. £1 3s.

Principles of Gestalt Psychology. By K. Koffka. £2 2s.

Analysis of Perception. By J. R. Smythies. £1 1s.

EMOTION

Integrative Psychology: a Study of Unit Response. By William M. Marston, C. Daly King, and E. H. Marston. £1 10s.

Emotion and Insanity. By S. Thalbitzer. Preface by H. Höffding. 14s.

The Laws of Feeling. By F. Paulhan. Translated by C. K. Ogden. 18s.

The Psychology of Consciousness. By C. Daly King. Introduction by W. M. Marston. £1.

Pleasure and Instinct: a Study in the Psychology of Human Action. By A. H. B. Allen. 17s. 6d.

PERSONALITY

The Psychology of Character: with a Survey of Personality in General. By A. A. Roback. *Revised Edition.* £2 5s.

Problems of Personality: a Volume of Essays in honour of Morton Prince. Edited by A. A. Roback. £1 8s.

Personality. By R. G. Gordon. £1 3s.

Constitution-Types in Delinquency: Practical Applications and Biophysiological Foundations of Kretschmer's Types. By W. A. Willemse. With 32 plates and 19 diagrams. £1.

Conscious Orientation. Studies of Personality Types in Relation to Neurosis and Psychosis by J. H. Van der Hoop. £1 3s.

ANALYSIS

The Practice and Theory of Individual Psychology. By Alfred Adler £1 5s.

Psychological Types. By C. G. Jung. Translated with a Foreword by H. Godwin Baynes. £1 12s.

Character and the Unconscious: a Critical Exposition of the Psychology of Freud and Jung. By J. H. van der Hoop. £1.

The Development of the Sexual Impulses. By R. E. Money-Kyrle. £1.

SOUND AND COLOUR

The Psychology of a Musical Prodigy. By G. Revesz. With a portrait and many musical illustrations. 16s.

Colour-Blindness: with a Comparison of different Methods of Testing Colour-Blindness. By Mary Collins. Introduction by James Drever. 18s.

LANGUAGE AND SYMBOLISM

The Symbolic Process, and Its Integration in Children. By J. F. Markey. 14s.

The Meaning of Meaning: a Study of the Influence of Language upon Thought and of the Science of Symbolism. By C. K. Ogden and I. A. Richards. Supplementary Essays by B. Malinowski and F. G. Crookshank. £1 8s.

3

Principles of Literary Criticism. By I. A. Richards. £1 3s.

Speech Disorders. By S. M. Stinchfield. With eight plates. £1 5s.

The Spirit of Language in Civilization. By K. Vossler. £1.

CHILD PSYCHOLOGY, EDUCATION, ETC.

The Growth of the Mind: an Introduction to Child Psychology. By K. Koffka. Translated by R. M. Ogden. £1 12s.

The Language and Thought of the Child. By Jean Piaget. Preface by E. Claparéde. £1 1s.

The Child's Conception of Physical Causality. By Jean Piaget. £1 3s.

The Child's Conception of the World. By Jean Piaget. £1 5s.

The Child's Conception of Number. By Jean Piaget. £1 5s.

Judgment and Reasoning in the Child. By Jean Piaget. £1 1s.

The Moral Judgment of the Child. By Jean Piaget. £1 5s.

The Origin of Intelligence in the Child. By Jean Piaget. £1 8s.

The Child's Conception of Space. By Jean Piaget. £2 2s.

Educational Psychology: its Problems and Methods. By Charles Fox. *Revised Edition.* £1 5s.

The Mental Development of the Child. By Karl Bühler. 15s.

Eidetic Imagery, and Typological Methods of Investigation. By E. R. Jaensch. 14s.

The Psychology of Intelligence. By Jean Piaget. 18s.

The Psychology of Children's Drawings: From the First Stroke to the Coloured Drawing. By Helga Eng. With many line and coloured illustrations. *Second Edition.* £1 5s.

ANIMAL PSYCHOLOGY, BIOLOGY, ETC.

The Mentality of Apes, with an Appendix on the Psychology of Chimpanzees. By W. Koehler. With nine plates and nineteen figures. £1 5s.

The Social Life of Monkeys and Apes. By S. Zuckerman. With 24 plates. £1 5s.

The Psychology of Animals, in Relation to Human Psychology. By F. Alverdes. 15s.

The Social Insects: Their Origin and Evolution. By William Morton Wheeler. With 48 plates. £1 8s.

Theoretical Biology. By J. von Uexkuell. £1 4s.

Biological Principles. By J. H. Woodger. £1 10s.

Biological Memory. By Eugenio Rignano. Translated, with an Introduction, by E. W. MacBride, F.R.S. 18s.

ANTHROPOLOGY, SOCIOLOGY, RELIGION, ETC.

Psychology and Ethnology. By W. H. R. Rivers, F.R.S. Preface by Sir G. Elliot Smith, F.R.S. £1 5s.

Political Pluralism: A Study in Modern Political Theory. By Kung Chuan Hsiao. 18s.

The Individual and the Community: a Historical Analysis of the Motivating Factors of Social Conduct. By Wen Kwei Liao. £1 3s.

Crime and Custom in Savage Society. By B. Malinowski. With six plates. 16s.

Sex and Repression in Savage Society. By B. Malinowski. £1 1s.

Religious Conversion. By Sante de Sanctis. £1 5s.

The Theory of Legislation. By Jeremy Bentham. Edited, with an Introduction and Notes, by C. K. Ogden. £1 10s.

B. PHILOSOPHY

Philosophical Studies. By G. E. Moore. £1 8s.

The Philosophy of " As If ": a System of the Theoretical, Practical, and Religious Fictions of Mankind. By H. Vaihinger. Translated by C. K. Ogden. £1 10s.

Five Types of Ethical Theory. By C. D. Broad. £1 8s.

Speculations: Essays on Humanism and the Philosophy of Art. By T. E. Hulme. Edited by Herbert Read. With a frontispiece and Foreword by Jacob Epstein. 18s.

The Metaphysical Foundations of Modern Physical Science, with special reference to Man's Relation to Nature. By E. A. Burtt. £1 8s.

The Nature of Life. By E. Rignano. 14s.

Bentham's Theory of Fictions. Edited with an Introduction and Notes by C. K. Ogden. With three plates. £1 1s.

5

Ideology and Utopia: an Introduction to the Sociology of Knowledge. By Karl Mannheim. £1 8s.

Charles Peirce's Empiricism. By Justus Büchler. £1 1s.

The Philosophy of Peirce. Selected Writings. Edited by Justus Büchler. £1 15s.

Ethics and the History of Philosophy: Selected Essays. By C. D. Broad. £1 3s.

Sense-Perception and Matter : A Critical Analysis of C. D. Broad's Theory of Perception. By Martin E. Lean. £1 1s.

What is Value? An Essay in Philosophical Analysis. By Everett W. Hall. £1 5s.

Religion, Philosophy and Psychical Research: Selected Essays. By C. D. Broad. £1 5s.

The Structure of Metaphysics. By Morris Lazerowitz. £1 5s.

Methods and Criteria of Reasoning. An inquiry into the structure of controversy. By Rupert Crawshay-Williams. £1 12s.

LOGIC

Tractatus Logico-Philosophicus. By L. Wittgenstein. German text, with an English Translation en regard, and an Introduction by Bertrand Russell, F.R.S. £1.

Foundations of Geometry and Induction. By Jean Nicod. With an Introduction by Bertrand Russell, F.R.S. £1 3s.

The Foundations of Mathematics, and other Logical Essays. By F. P. Ramsey. Edited by R. B. Braithwaite. Preface by G. E. Moore. £1 3s.

The Nature of Mathematics: a Critical Survey. By Max Black. £1.

Logical Syntax of Language. By Rudolf Carnap. £1 10s.

An Examination of Logical Positivism. By Julius Weinberg. £1 5s.

The Conditions of Knowing: An Essay Towards a Theory of Knowledge. By Angus Sinclair, O.B.E., M.A., F.R.S.E. £1 3s.

A Treatise on Induction and Probability. By G. H. von Wright. £1 10s.

Bertrand Russell's Construction of the External World. By Charles A. Fritz, Junr. £1 3s.

C. SCIENTIFIC METHOD

METHODOLOGY

Scientific Thought: a Philosophical Analysis of some of its Fundamental Concepts in the light of Recent Physical Developments. By C. D. Broad. £1 12s.

Dynamic Social Research. By John T. Hader and Eduard C. Lindeman. 18s.

The Sciences of Man in the Making: an Orientation Book. By E. A. Kirkpatrick. £1 5s.

The Doctrine of Signatures. A Defence of Theory in Medicine. By Scott Buchanan. 16s.

The Limits of Science: Outline of Logic and of the Methodology of the Exact Sciences. By Leon Chwistek. Introduction and Appendix by H. C. Brodie. £1 12s.

HISTORY, ETC.

An Historical Introduction to Modern Psychology. By Gardner Murphy. With a Supplement by H. Kluver. £2.

The History of Materialism and Criticism of its Present Importance. By F. A. Lange. With an Introduction by Bertrand Russell. £1 15s.

Philosophy of the Unconscious. By E. von Hartmann. £1 15s.

Outlines of the History of Greek Philosophy. By E. Zeller. New edition, re-written by Wilhelm Nestle and translated by L. R. Palmer. £1 3s.

Psyche: the Cult of Souls and the Belief in Immortality among the Greeks. By Erwin Rohde. £1 15s.

Plato's Theory of Ethics: The Moral Criterion and the Highest Good. By R. C. Lodge. £1 12s.

Plato's Theory of Education. By R. C. Lodge, F.R.S. (Canada). £1 3s.

Plato's Theory of Art. By R. C. Lodge. £1 5s.

The Philosophy of Plato. By R. C. Lodge. £1 8s.

Plato's Phaedo. A translation with an Introduction, Notes and Appendices, by R. S. Bluck. £1 1s.

Plato's Theory of Knowledge. The Theaetetus and the Sophist of Plato. Translated, with a Running Commentary, by F. M. Cornford. £1 8s.

Plato's Cosmology: The Timaeus of Plato. Translated, with a Running Commentary, by F. M. Cornford. £1 12s.

Plato and Parmenides. Parmenides' " Way of Truth " and Plato's " Parmenides ". Translated with an Introduction and Running Commentary, by F. M. Cornford. £1 3s.

A LIST OF BOOKS PUBLISHED IN THE LIBRARY BUT AT PRESENT OUT OF PRINT

Analysis of Matter. By B. Russell.
Art of Interrogation. By E. R. Hamilton.
Chance Love and Logic. By C. S. Peirce.
Child's Discovery of Death. By Sylvia Anthony.
Colour and Colour Theories. By Christine Ladd-Franklin.

8.1.57.   PRINTED BY HEADLEY BROTHERS LTD 109 KINGSWAY LONDON WC2 AND ASHFORD KENT